PLAIN
TALK
ON
First and Second
Corinthians

PLAIN
TALK
ON
First and Second
Corinthians

MANFORD GEORGE GUTZKE
PH. D.

**Lamplighter
Books** Grand Rapids,
Michigan
Zondervan Publishing House

PLAIN TALK ON FIRST AND SECOND CORINTHIANS
© 1978 by The Zondervan Corporation
Grand Rapids, Michigan

Lamplighter Books are published by Zondervan
Publishing House, 1415 Lake Drive, S.E.,
Grand Rapids, Michigan 49506

Library of Congress Cataloging in Publication Data

Gutzke, Manford George.
   Plain talk on First and Second Corinthians.

   1. Bible.   N.T.   Corinthians—Commentaries.   I. Title.
BS2675.3.G87   227'.2'07   77-17113
ISBN 0-310-25641-0

Printed in the United States of America

85   86   87   88   89   90   91   92 / 15   14   13   12   11   10   9   8

CONTENTS

First Corinthians

Second Corinthians

First Corinthians

Chapter 1

INTRODUCTION TO 1 CORINTHIANS

As we begin our study of 1 Corinthians, let us keep in mind that this is a letter, an epistle, written by the apostle Paul to a group of Christian believers living in the city of Corinth. Someone might pose the question, "Why would an apostle write a letter of instruction to people who were already believers?" Consider what it takes to have a productive garden. If we acquire the land, prepare the soil, and plant the beans, is that not enough? Are we through for the summer? We know the answer: By no means. After we have prepared the soil and planted our vegetables, then we really go to work. When a baby is born, everyone rejoices and that is wonderful; but for the family, that is when their work begins. When a mother buys a shirt for her son, is that not enough? The shirt was clean when she gave it to him, but will it be clean from then on? Every mother knows better than that. Giving the shirt is an important thing, but that is when the laundry begins.

When a person becomes a believer, when he believes and accepts Christ as his Savior, can we say that all is finished? As far as becoming a Christian is concerned, that part is finished. Yes! But becoming a Christian is much like being born as an infant. Peter wrote:

> As newborn babes, desire the sincere milk of the word, that ye may grow thereby (1 Peter 2:2).

A Christian lives by faith. One does not become a Christian by what he does, nor by how much he does, nor how long he does it, but by believing. And in order to believe he needs to know that certain things are true. It helps to know how and why he should believe certain things. It is true that "whosoever

shall call upon the name of the Lord shall be saved" (Rom.
10:13), but Paul went on to say,

> How then shall they call on him in whom they have not be-
> lieved? and how shall they believe in him of whom they have not
> heard? and how shall they hear without a preacher? And how
> shall they preach, except they be sent? (Rom. 10:14-15).

Young Christians like those at Corinth, who want to grow and
become strong, need to learn from other Christians who know
the whole truth of the gospel. Someone must teach them and
show them what the truth is which they should believe. This is
exactly what the apostle Paul did when he wrote to the believers in Corinth. The promises of God need to be understood so
believers can know what to expect from God and how to
receive His blessing.

This matter of becoming a Christian is an intelligible process.
It is not magical experience. It is not as though I were to
suddenly change into a different kind of person. Rather, it is a
matter of finding out what God will do, according to His
promises. Then it is a matter of turning myself over to God and
believing those things which He has promised.

Even so, living the life of faith is not a matter of doing things
for God to earn His favor. It is a matter of receiving *from* God
what He is able and willing to give to all believers. It is only
then that we can respond to God's will.

The first important truth, as we consider our new relationship with God, is that God in Himself, in His own nature, is
holy. God is holy and He demands holiness on the part of His
people. The next truth is that I in myself as a human being am
unable to obey the will of God by being holy. The gospel truth
comes to my heart, which has already been disobedient.

The truth of the gospel can speak to the heart of a sinner and
bring him to God. This truth we preach to the world is that
Christ Jesus died for our sins, and by dying He reconciles us to
God. He took away our guilt and rose again for our justification.
He opened the way for us to be regenerated as sons of God. He
then enables us by His grace to respond to the will of God in
obedience. Christ Jesus has made all this available to me, but
I need to know this. I also need to know that all Christ Jesus
has done is for those who come in faith and put their trust in
Him.

Those who do not come will not be benefited by the death and resurrection of the Lord Jesus Christ. Only those who come in faith will receive that benefit. I am reminded of a prayer request by a man who desired to walk closer to God. Anyone who has such a desire will need to keep in mind that the way to walk closer to God is not by trying to be good or pious enough to qualify for this. No! It is only as I trust and believe in the Lord Jesus Christ and receive Him into my heart that I will be led by the indwelling Christ to a closer fellowship with God.

It is true that in every believer there is a constant warfare going on between the "old man" in the flesh and the "new man" in him, which is by the Holy Spirit. The victory of the Spirit over the flesh has been promised in Christ Jesus, but this promise needs to be heard. This promise must be believed to become operative in me. For this reason the apostle Paul, who was a preacher and a teacher, writes to the Corinthians to explain to them what the gospel really means, what Christ will do for them. Paul shows them that as the believer yields to God, he grows in grace and wisdom in the things of the Spirit. The wonderful truth about the promises of God is that I may reach out in faith and make them my own.

As a young believer, and then throughout my lifetime, I have often felt that my understanding of the gospel and of the life of faith is actually hindered by too much talk by people who themselves do not understand it. I am sure that all of us have at some time heard men and women talk as though they know the Bible, but their lives disprove it. They talk as if they know everything about evangelism and about praying, but they never win anyone to the Lord. There is no evidence of earnest prayer. It is like sitting in a restaurant and overhearing men talk about baseball as though they were big league managers or about military affairs as though they were brilliant military strategists. But listening to them helps us to know that they are just talkers. This kind of talking goes on with reference to gospel truth and the life of faith, and can result in frustration and discouragement.

The apostle Paul was a man who actually lived what he preached. As we begin our study in the First Epistle to the Corinthians, we will be able to appreciate this, as Paul discusses a number of important problems in the life of faith.

It is helpful to know specific facts about Paul. We learn something about him in the Book of Philippians. As a child he had been brought up in the things that had to do with the truth of God, and with the worship of Him. He says that he was "circumcised the eighth day," which means that his parents believed in God and committed him to God. He was ". . . of the stock of Israel, of the tribe of Benjamin, a Hebrew of the Hebrews; as touching the law, a Pharisee; concerning zeal, persecuting the church; touching the righteousness which is in the law, blameless" (Phil. 3:5-6). It is clear that Paul was an outstanding, sincere, and earnest religious man. He was a genuinely sincere person before he became a believer in Christ.

Paul wrote:

> Ye have heard of my conversation in time past in the Jews' religion, how that beyond measure I persecuted the church of God, and wasted it: and profited in the Jews' religion above many my equals in mine own nation, being more exceedingly zealous of the traditions of my fathers (Gal. 1:13-14).

As far as the apostle Paul was concerned, even when he was an unbeliever, he was conscientious in his zeal, in opposition to Christ. He had been trained in the Old Testament Scriptures by Gamaliel, one of the greatest and most renowned teachers of the Jewish people at that time. Paul is the man God chose to carry the gospel to the Gentiles.

As he journeyed to Damascus, Paul was personally confronted by the living Lord and was converted. He was endorsed by Barnabas, who brought him to Jerusalem. Barnabas declared to the apostles how Paul had seen the Lord on the Damascus road, how the Lord had spoken to him, and how he now boldly preached in the name of Jesus, whom before he had persecuted. After his remarkable conversion, Paul became a great teacher in the church of Antioch. Then he was called by the Holy Spirit to become a missionary and carry the gospel of the Lord Jesus Christ to many lands. As a called apostle of Jesus Christ, he became an outstanding leader of the church. He was the author of more New Testament epistles than any other apostle.

I am summarizing these things so we have them in mind

when we read and study Paul's First Epistle to the Corinthians. Surely he was qualified to preach and write and exhort. As we open the New Testament to 1 Corinthians, we read his own introduction in the first verse:

> Paul, called to be an apostle of Jesus Christ through the will of God, and Sosthenes our brother (1 Cor. 1:1).

Paul had evangelized Corinth as a city and had won these people to a living faith in the Lord Jesus Christ. He was addressing his own converts, whom he knew and who knew him. This gospel which the apostle Paul preached is as vital and transforming today as it was in his day. Christ died for us. When we come to Him in faith, He will receive us and bless us.

Chapter 2

THE IDENTITY OF THE BELIEVERS IN CORINTH

When Paul wrote to the Christian believers who lived in Corinth, he used at least four different words or phrases to refer to them. These are of interest to us because they could be used to identify Christians everywhere.

> Unto the church of God which is at Corinth, to them that are sanctified in Christ Jesus, called to be saints, with all that in every place call upon the name of Jesus Christ our Lord, both theirs and ours (1 Cor. 1:2).

Notice the first of these four terms, "the church of God which is at Corinth." This is a group term, one we would give to a company of people who were called out from all others. This company of people was called "the church of God" because of their relationship to God. Stephen in his address before the court used this same expression when referring to Israel in the Old Testament days. When Stephen made his defense, he spoke of the Israelites first as "the seed of Abraham." Then he used the words *kindred, brethren, the children of Israel, my people*, and *our fathers*. On another occasion he spoke of them as "the house of Israel." When speaking about Moses he said, "This is he that was in the church in the wilderness." These various titles and phrases in the Old Testament indicate that these people, this particular company, had been called out of all others in Egypt to belong to God. They are referred to as "the church in the wilderness."

These believers to whom Paul wrote were also a company of people called of God. The believers who made up "the church of God which is at Corinth" had each received the same call. This was the basis of their togetherness in Corinth. In another epistle we read, "the church which is in his house," meaning

16

the company of people who went into that man's house to worship God. Elsewhere we read of "the church of the Laodiceans," referring to the company of people in the city of Laodicea who believed in the Lord Jesus Christ. This phrase is used again, "the churches of Christ salute you." In all these instances it is obvious that the word *church* refers to a local assembly of people who profess faith in Christ.

The next phrase Paul applies to these believers in the city of Corinth is "to them that are sanctified in Christ Jesus." The word *sanctify* is not commonly used in ordinary speech, but it is not a difficult idea. To "sanctify" something means to set it apart and to reserve it for a special purpose. We know that at some public affairs, whether in an auditorium or a ball park, there are "reserved" seats. Paul is actually using *sanctified* as "set aside for a specific use," as opposed to "for common use."

Recently it was my privilege to visit a place in the Philippines called Nazalie, which is the field headquarters of the Wycliffe Bible Translators. I was with them almost a week. These people were housed in fifty or sixty buildings, which were made of bamboo slats and thatched roofs. These buildings could easily be destroyed by fire, but in this particular settlement there were no fire hydrants. Instead, in front of each house stood a red barrel filled with water; and on the side of the barrel in big white letters were the words "For fire only." These barrels contained "sanctified" water. This was water set aside for a specific purpose.

Someone might ask, "Shouldn't the word *sanctify* denote some degree of moral or spiritual excellence?" The moral and spiritual excellence that we associate with the word *sanctify* comes as a result of being sanctified. Any man or woman whose heart has been set apart, reserved for the purpose of living in the presence of God, will show forth virtue and devotion. The wonderful truth is that God can sanctify a worldly sinner. Such a sanctified person will not remain a sinner; he will not remain worldly. He will be committed to the Lord, and his conduct will manifest spiritual virtues.

In the Old Testament the word *sanctify* was often applied to a vessel, a room, or an entire house. Anything set aside for a special function had been sanctified. In all this the truth becomes apparent that believers are sanctified in Christ Jesus. It is much like when two persons get married: the woman gives herself to her husband with the understanding that she is for him and him alone. In that sense she is sanctified for him and to him.

We as believers are sanctified by Christ Jesus who lives in us. For Christ Himself lived in a sanctified life. "The Son can do nothing of himself, but what he seeth the Father do: for what things soever he doeth, these also doeth the Son likewise" (John 5:19). Only as His Spirit indwells and controls us can we do the will of God.

The next term that Paul uses when referring to the believers in Corinth is "called to be saints." The word *saint* is a noun that refers to persons who have been sanctified. In the course of time a specialized use of this phrase came to be applied to persons who had been sanctified and had achieved a high degree of virtue and devotion. We sometimes hear the expression "a saintly life" in regard to someone who is very good and pious. In our day it denotes an unusual degree of excellence and virtue. This is not what Paul had in mind when he wrote, "called to be saints." Let us keep in mind that a sinner cannot become a saint by himself. All of us have sinned. We are all sinners, and yet when we come to faith in the Lord Jesus Christ, we are actually "called to be saints."

Paul concludes this verse by saying that these people are united in spirit with all others who call upon the name of Jesus Christ our Lord. Becoming a believer begins in a moment of high dedication, but it goes on for life. About believers it can be said that they are the church of God, sanctified, set apart in Christ Jesus, and called to be saints. They are people who call upon the name of Jesus Christ.

Chapter 3

GRACE AND PEACE

In 1 Corinthians 1:3 Paul expresses his earnest desire for the spiritual well-being of these Christians in the words:

Grace be unto you, and peace, from God our Father, and from the Lord Jesus Christ.

Grace and *peace* are wonderful words. Many of us have an idea of what *peace* means, and yet we need to learn more about it. In the same way many of us might have trouble defining the word *grace*. Grace is something that God imparts to the hearts of believers. The phrase "grace be unto you" means a blessing from God that enables the believer to do God's will gladly and willingly.

The desire to do the will of God does not come naturally. Man's natural disposition is to do what he wants to do. How often we notice that small children do not want to be led. When a child and his parents are about to cross a busy street and the parent reaches down to take the child by the hand, almost without fail the child pulls away. He does not want to be led. That is natural human nature in action.

Many believe all that hinders men from walking in the way of the Lord is ignorance, but that is not true. It is not that men do not know enough. All too often they are unwilling in themselves. Sometimes they are weak. Sometimes they are spiritually ill. This is what the Bible calls "palsied," and it means paralyzed. The can see and hear, but they cannot move. Sometimes they are spiritually dead. They have no interest in the gospel. All this points to much more than ignorance.

Actually we lack the inward strength to do what we should, even when we understand what it is. At such times we need the grace of God in our hearts. Without it we would pray for health

19

and fortune and great opportunities. Have we never realized that people can be healthy and rich and yet be most unhappy? Have we never considered that people with great opportunities often do nothing about them? There is much more that is important in life. Jesus of Nazareth in the Sermon on the Mount tells us:

> Seek ye first the kingdom of God, and his righteousness; and all these things shall be added unto you (Matt. 6:33).

So when Paul writes, "Grace be unto you," he is actually praying that these believers be given grace, that inward capacity which enables believers to do the will of God. This grace is only possible when Christ dwells within one's heart. All who are saved by faith will be strengthened by the Holy Spirit in the inner man, so that they have everything they need for walking in the ways of God. This is carefully provided for each one of us in Christ Jesus, by His grace. When we read the words "Grace be unto you," we know the necessary conditions in which this grace will come.

To receive the grace of God, a person first must receive Jesus Christ as his Savior and trust Him with his sins. He must believe that Christ died for him and that He will deliver him. The next condition will be that when he has accepted Christ as his Savior, God becomes his Father. God is not just the Giver of gifts, not merely Santa Claus, but He is Father. When one receives the Holy Spirit into his heart, because he belongs to God, the Holy Spirit will be his Comforter and his Guide. The Holy Spirit will motivate him to yield himself into a willing obedience to the living Lord. The believer does not have to push; the Spirit pushes him. He does not need to pull; the Holy Spirit will pull him. He needs only to be willing to yield himself into the will of Christ.

The next step will be that the Holy Spirit will give him the inward strength and desire and enablement to do God's will. And that is the grace of God. It has been said that "Grace is unmerited favor," and surely we who have received it know that this is true. It is all the gift of God. People may praise the believer for his obedience to God; they may tell him what a fine person he is. But the believer knows deep down in his heart that if there is anything fine about him, it is not because he is good. Any good thing within him comes to him from the grace of God in his heart. It is the Holy Spirit who has given him the inward disposition to want to do God's will. Paul wanted the believers in Corinth to have the strength and the desire to do the will of God in everything. He knew that if they obeyed God in everything, all other things would be added unto them.

Peace is that blessed gift from God which enables the believer to have full and complete confidence in God. All through my lifetime as a believer, I have been greatly blessed by a certain hymn:

> Peace, perfect peace, with sorrows surging round?
> On Jesus' bosom naught but calm is found.
>
> Peace, perfect peace, with loved ones far away?
> In Jesus' keeping we are safe, and they.
>
> Peace, perfect peace, our future all unknown?
> Jesus we know, and He is on the throne.
>
> Peace, perfect peace, death shadowing us and ours?
> Jesus has vanquished death and all its powers.
>
> It is enough: earth's struggles soon shall cease,
> And Jesus call us to heav'n's perfect peace.

Yes, peace is something God gives to the believer when he yields himself into God's will.

Chapter 4

PROBLEMS IN THE CHURCH

In his first epistle to the believers in Corinth, Paul focused on a number of problems which troubled them.

The first problem that he discussed was the division in the congregation because of personal loyalty to individual preachers. Paul began by saying some things about preaching as a whole. He pointed out that one's preaching will not be acceptable to everyone, especially if it is based on the cross of Calvary. Not everyone is ready to find salvation in Christ Jesus. In 1 Corinthians 1:25-29 we read that not many wise or mighty persons are called to follow the Lord Jesus Christ. There are other passages of Scripture that have a definite bearing on this subject. Jesus of Nazareth taught that ". . . that which is highly esteemed among men is abomination in the sight of God" (Luke 16:15). The approval and praise of men has a great appeal to the individual. It is pleasing to the heart of a man to achieve success and to put this above all else. This attitude is an abomination in the sight of the Lord.

In the Book of Isaiah we read, "For my thoughts are not your thoughts, neither are your ways my ways, saith the LORD" (Isa. 55:8). Elsewhere in the Bible it says, "There is a way that seemeth right unto a man, but the end thereof are the ways of death" (Prov. 16:25). And again, "Every way of a man is right in his own eyes: but the LORD pondereth the hearts" (Prov. 21:2). These and other similar utterances in the Bible are warnings to us to seek the mind of the Lord. We certainly cannot trust our own minds, because we are so prone to become involved in constant changes.

> Because the foolishness of God is wiser than men; and the weakness of God is stronger than men (1 Cor. 1:25).

When Paul wrote "the foolishness of God," he was emphasizing that while human beings may count the preaching of the gospel just foolishness, this is God's way of saving people. The preaching of the gospel — that Jesus Christ died for our sins — is wiser than men, for no man can fully comprehend God's plan of salvation without illumination from the Lord. Paul wrote "the weakness of God," because he knew that many people in their blindness would say that Christ's dying on the cross of Calvary was a sign of weakness. But throughout the ages this "weakness," this dying for someone else, has become a symbol of strength for those who believe.

> For ye see your calling, brethren, how that not many wise men after the flesh, not many mighty, not many noble, are called (1 Cor. 1:26).

Perhaps we often overlook this verse, yet it has an important message for us. Isn't it true that many of us are inclined to be greatly impressed when a particularly influential and brilliant person comes to the Lord? When we hear that someone in high standing in the professional or educational world humbly accepts Christ as his Savior, we are greatly impressed. Yet we feel differently when a humble person comes to the Lord. Such an attitude on the part of believers is the very thing Paul pointed out to the Corinthians. He told them "not many wise men after the flesh" are called. Actually every believer is wise "in the Spirit." The mighty, the noble, and the wise men after the flesh are often too involved with their own achievements to heed the call of the gospel.

> But God hath chosen the foolish things of the world to confound the wise; and God hath chosen the weak things of the world to confound the things which are mighty; and base things of the world, and things which are despised, hath God chosen, yea, and things which are not, to bring to nought things that are: that no flesh should glory in his presence (1 Cor. 1:27-29).

The basic principle in this passage is "that no flesh should glory in his presence." This is why it is God's plan and purpose to call those who are considered weak and despised by this world. God calls them, and through them shows His own power and glory. Often when we come into a particular church, its various members tell us of the important or wealthy people they have in their membership. They seem to forget that as far as God is concerned, the fact that people are wealthy or prominent does not matter. It would be more honoring to God if no special attention were given to the position of men.

The fact that a man is considered important is not impressive in the sight of the Lord. God's way of doing things is not the human way. On the whole, men are impressed with human values. When someone prominent comes into the fellowship of believers, we are inclined to feel that he could be a great asset to the church. It is true the church may be helped by him, but why? Because he is intelligent? Because he is highly educated? Because he is wealthy? No. Such a man will be helpful to the church if the Holy Spirit controls his life. It is no handicap to a man to be well educated, if he does not let education obstruct his spiritual vision and if he is humbly obedient to God. Certainly there is nothing wrong with a person having a lot of money. The question is, What is he going to do with it? Will he use his money in the service of God, or will he let the money use him? Money and prestige count only when they are used to the glory of God.

God never considers a congregation to be poor because it is made up primarily of poor people. No church should feel humble for this reason. As a matter of fact, I remember Dr. R. A. Torrey saying that a church which has no poor people in its membership is a mighty poor church. This is the message Paul has for the Corinthians and for believers everywhere.

Chapter 5

THE BLESSING IN CHRIST JESUS

In 1 Corinthians 1:30-31 Paul restates and reemphasizes the truth we have just considered. He tells us again that God does not call men to Himself through philosophy or logic or reason. He does not call only those who are considered great. As a matter of fact, as far as God's dealing with men is concerned, one thing is characteristic all the way through: God does not do anything that will make it easy for men to become prominent. God calls men along the way of humility.

One way to keep man humble is to call those who are neither mighty, nor noble, nor great in the eyes of the world. God calls the poor, the unlearned, the simple-minded. God can call the wise and the powerful and mighty, and He does call some of them. But the great majority of people God calls are not considered prominent by other men. Paul points out the reason for this. God calls those who will not glory in themselves in His presence.

> But of him are ye in Christ Jesus, who of God is made unto us wisdom, and righteousness, and sanctification, and redemption: that, according as it is written, He that glorieth, let him glory in the Lord (1 Cor. 1:30-31).

"Of him are ye in Christ Jesus" means that all believers are in Christ Jesus. In this vital, dynamic relationship with Christ, being indwelt by Him, believers become partakers of His wisdom, His righteousness, His sanctification, and His redemption. Surely this is more than anyone could ever ask for or desire! Christ Jesus comes to believers not to show them how they can do something in themselves, in their human limitations. He brings to them the light and the life of God, by the grace of God.

When a person receives Christ Jesus as Savior and Lord, God works in his heart, and we say that that person is born again. It is then that the life of faith begins. This new life within the believer is there because God brought it to pass. After one has received Jesus Christ into his heart, he changes. His attitudes, his tolerance toward others, and the decisions he makes no longer originate in himself. All this comes to him from the Lord Jesus Christ. He finds this in his heart like a fountain of living water, springing up into everlasting life.

In these verses Paul drew the attention of the Corinthians to the fact that God works in all willing persons, that the mind of the Lord Jesus Christ may be in them. By the grace and work of God, Christ "is made unto us wisdom." In other words, the Lord Jesus Christ being in the heart gives wisdom in the believer's thinking, in his values, and in his plans for the future. Everything that he now has in heart and mind is there because God is working in him. God is causing the things of the Lord Jesus Christ to affect his thinking. "But of him are ye in Christ Jesus, who of God is made unto us wisdom, and righteousness." The believer's status before God has changed: rather than being a sinner, he is now righteous. The believer's standing before God is no longer one of guilt, because his guilt has been taken away, and God will now consider him guiltless.

Christ is made the believer's righteousness and sanctification. Sanctification refers to his belonging to God and to God alone, set aside for God's use and purpose in his life. As the believer yields himself to God, puts his trust in the Lord Jesus Christ, and receives His Holy Spirit, he will walk in fellowship with the Lord. As he turns himself over to God, God will work in him to do His will. God now becomes his refuge, his strength, and his ark of safety. He will be spared by the grace of God, as the Israelites were spared by the blood of the Passover lamb. Committing himself in this exclusive way to God, the believer will desire above all else to do God's will.

While here on earth the Lord Jesus Christ sought only to please His Father in all things. He came to do the will of God. It follows naturally that the believer will desire to be like Him, with the mind of Christ in him. This inclination does not come from himself. He has not suddenly become good in his own strength. It is Christ's faithfulness that becomes the believer's committal to God. Christ is made unto him "sanctification and redemption."

Redemption means the believer's deliverance from sin, from anything that keeps him from God. Such deliverance is found only in Christ Jesus. It can never be earned. Christ's wisdom, righteousness, sanctification, and redemption can never be attained through the believer's own effort or strength. All this is something that God will freely give us in Christ Jesus. "That, according as it is written, He that glorieth, let him glory in the Lord." I am sure that each of us who is a believer rejoices in these riches of grace which God bestows on us. If we want to glory and feel proud because we were forgiven and could walk into the presence of God easily and freely, then let us feel proud about the Lord Jesus and glory in Him. Every good desire and every good thing within us is a free gift of His grace.

Chapter 6

PAUL'S PROCEDURE

In the first chapter of Paul's letter to the Corinthians, he discussed certain divisions that existed among them, which in turn led to quarreling. This kind of conduct hindered their testimony and their spiritual growth.

Paul realized that much of this conflict was due to the fact that these were young and immature Christians to whom he was writing. Paul wrote to them in love, much as a father would to unruly children. We should notice that he does not condemn divisions as such, nor does he scold them for their divided loyalties. He does not criticize them because some liked Peter and Apollos better than they liked him. He does not criticize them because of their intense feeling toward any of their former pastors. Instead, Paul discusses the preachers themselves to show these young Christians that their loyalty and love should rather be directed to the Lord Jesus Christ Himself. If they had been putting the Lord first, they would not have been thinking so much about the individual preachers.

Paul writes of himself as a preacher and of his particular way of presenting the gospel. He explains the reasons for his manner of speaking and his way of approaching his listeners. Apollos, one of the men who had preached the Word of God in Corinth, was spoken of in the Book of Acts as an eloquent speaker. Paul himself had laid aside all eloquence. This emphasizes a very real truth about preaching.

> And I, brethren, when I came to you, came not with excellency of speech or of wisdom, declaring unto you the testimony of God (1 Cor. 2:1).

Here is frank acknowledgment of a total omission of oratory and philosophical style in his preaching. He did not come with excellency of speech, nor with great swelling words, nor with wisdom, to declare the testimony of God. It is not a preacher's function to tell what God will do and then to obscure his message with a display of oratory. Paul did not preach to give an exhibition of his pulpit skill or brilliant personality. Paul had one thing uppermost in his mind, namely, that God works according to His promises in response to faith. Paul deliberately set aside all else to make clear God's plan of salvation, what God would do for all who come to Him in faith.

> For I determined not to know any thing among you, save Jesus Christ, and him crucified (1 Cor. 2:2).

Paul chose to lift up the cross of Calvary as the very essence of Christian life and experience. He talked about it, emphasized it, and held it up for esteem above everything else. He gave to it a basic, essential, and primary significance. Paul could have talked of other matters. He must have talked about other things that the Corinthians needed for their life of faith; but whatever Paul talked about, he considered the cross of Calvary the focal point, basic to Christian understanding. It is important for us to know that when he says, "I determined not to know any thing among you," this meant that Paul was determined that nothing else was so worthy of his esteem. The first and only really important thing to have in mind is that Jesus Christ died for sinners and was raised from the dead for believers. This is the way souls will be brought into the blessing of God.

> And I was with you in weakness, and in fear, and in much trembling (1 Cor. 2:3).

This was a frank admission of the fact that Paul was aware that he could be criticized for this kind of preaching. In the same way, many people think that a kindergarten teacher does not know enough to teach higher grades and that she must be very naive. Actually, however, kindergarten teachers are often among the best-paid teachers, because of their great importance. They must have the facility to get down to the level of their pupils and to deal with them accordingly.

> And my speech and my preaching was not with enticing words of man's wisdom, but in demonstration of the Spirit and of power (1 Cor. 2:4).

This was open recognition that his delivery when preaching was not sophisticated in any intellectual way. The public would approve and praise brilliant preaching from a human point of view. Paul deliberately avoided such an appeal to human approval: "not with enticing words of man's wisdom." Paul's aim was to give a demonstration of spiritual thinking. Whenever the word *spirit* is used, it reflects an open awareness of the reality of God, of Jesus Christ, of heaven, of eternity. These are the vital essentials that Paul emphasized in all his preaching. "And of power" is a phrase that indicates the reality of the newness of life, which comes from and through the Resurrection.

> That your faith should not stand in the wisdom of men, but in the power of God (1 Cor. 2:5).

In other words, faith can never come from the wisdom of men. Faith must be founded and grounded by the power of God, who sent His Son to die and who raised Him from the dead. God sends His Holy Spirit into the hearts of all believers that they may grow in faith and be well-pleasing in His sight. This was Paul's reason for preaching.

Chapter 7

THE WISDOM OF GOD

> Howbeit we speak wisdom among them that are perfect: yet not
> the wisdom of this world, nor of the princes of this world, that
> come to nought: but we speak the wisdom of God in a mystery,
> even the hidden wisdom, which God ordained before the world
> unto our glory: which none of the princes of this world knew: for
> had they known it, they would not have crucified the Lord of
> glory (1 Cor. 2:6-8).

In these words the apostle indicated that his message was not
the result of natural reasoning but was a revelation from God.
Several words in this passage have special meanings. *Wisdom*
means "philosophy" or "explanation" in current talk. *Perfect*
means "full grown," "mature," "completed." *Princes* refers to
"leaders" or "prominent persons." *Mystery* is something "hidden," "unseen." *Ordained* means "intended" or "designed for
a purpose." With these specific meanings in mind, we can
grasp what Paul said.

Paul understood that the message he preached at Corinth
was hidden from the natural man. He preached it to those who
already believed in Christ. He knew that his message would
not be acceptable to the leaders, since they thought in natural
terms. The gospel is not seen in nature, and when anyone is
limited to the law of the harvest, "Whatsoever a man soweth,
that shall he also reap," he simply could not receive the gospel
as valid.

> But as it is written, Eye hath not seen, nor ear heard, neither
> have entered into the heart of man, the things which God hath
> prepared for them that love him. But God hath revealed them
> unto us by his Spirit: for the Spirit searcheth all things, yea, the
> deep things of God (1 Cor. 2:9-10).

What the natural man could never discover has been made
plain to the spiritual man by the Holy Spirit. This spiritual

revelation is made in the Scriptures, which structure the message so it can be grasped by the believer's mind. Just as the Son of God became incarnate in a human body so the disciples could see Him — "He that hath seen me hath seen the Father" (John 14:9) — so the Word of God became "literate" when "holy men of God spake as they were moved by the Holy Ghost" (2 Peter 1:21), in order that men could hear and understand.

Paul went on to discuss the basic principle involved.

> For what man knoweth the things of a man, save the spirit of man which is in him? even so the things of God knoweth no man, but the Spirit of God (1 Cor. 2:11).

Because a man can think only like a man, it is not possible for any man to think like God. No human being could possibly imagine what God had in mind or would do. But the Holy Spirit, being God in Himself, could think the thoughts of God, and so He could authoritatively reveal the will of God. By His operation in the hearts of "holy men of God," He could inspire the speaking and the writing of such men so that they would say and write the words that would be in human language what the message from God was. Peter indicates that there were times when such prophets did not even understand what they had written because the message in their writings was intended for a later generation (1 Peter 1:10-12).

Paul next pointed out that the purpose in sending the Holy Spirit into the believers was to enable them to know the things of God which had been freely given to them.

> Now we have received, not the spirit of the world, but the spirit which is of God; that we might know the things that are freely given to us of God (1 Cor. 2:12).

I note that Paul used the word *know* rather than the word *understand*. I can "know" by way of recognizing the thrust of any idea and realizing the importance of it, even though I may not understand its operation, how it works as it does. There are wonderful things given to believers in the gospel by the grace of God which may bless and enrich us greatly, and which can be known and appreciated, even though their manner of operation may be well beyond our grasp. Such things are given "freely," meaning "without charge," which means that anyone, "whosoever will," may have them.

Paul then stated that these "things" comprised the content of his own preaching. And immediately it is evident that his hearers and readers would need the indwelling Holy Spirit to be able to know what he was saying or writing.

> Which things also we speak, not in the words which man's wisdom teacheth, but which the Holy Ghost teacheth; comparing spiritual things with spiritual (1 Cor. 2:13).

In his preaching Paul did not use human arguments which another might refute or modify by reasoning or argument; he stated what had been revealed to him and compared that with revelation that had been given to other men. This was a matter of "comparing Scripture with Scripture" as a procedure to be used in getting to know what Paul had revealed. At no time did Paul seek to establish his truth by comparing it with human opinions.

This procedure was the only sound method to be used because of the very nature of human thinking.

> But the natural man receiveth not the things of the Spirit of God: for they are foolishness unto him: neither can he know them, because they are spiritually discerned (1 Cor. 2:14).

Times have not changed. Even today the ideas revealed in the Bible are treated commonly as foolish. In the vain effort to salvage the form of the ethics and the morals of the gospel, efforts are made to lift the teachings of Jesus of Nazareth out of their scriptural context and to promote them on the basis of their obvious human values. This procedure fails because there is never enough dynamic generated by human considerations. Confidence in the promise of the Resurrection is never based on human reason, but on the testimony of Scripture, which is inspired by the Holy Spirit. And it is that confidence which gives the believer the will and the strength to obey the Word of God.

Paul recognized that such thoughts implied that the believer knew things which remained unknown to natural minds. And he did not hesitate to make this claim.

> But he that is spiritual judgeth all things, yet he himself is judged of no man. For who hath known the mind of the Lord, that he may instruct him? But we have the mind of Christ (1 Cor. 2:15-16),

This could seem arrogant or conceited to some, but when it is remembered that Paul did not claim such superior understanding to be the result of his own wisdom or ability, but rather gave God all the glory because of His revelation of truth in Jesus Christ, one can see that Paul is not exalting himself. He is giving God in Christ by His Holy Spirit all the glory for anything he knows about the truth and the will of God.

Chapter 8

COMPARISON OF PREACHERS HAS NO BASIS

In 1 Corinthians 3 Paul again takes up the matter of the division in the congregation because of specific loyalties toward one or another of their former ministers. Apparently in this congregation Paul had been the original evangelist who had called these Corinthians out of idol worship to faith in the Lord Jesus Christ. Then Peter (Cephas) had come and preached at Corinth. Later Apollos also preached there. After these three great men had at different times ministered there, the Corinthian Christians differed in their feelings toward them. As a result there was division in the congregation even to the point of hostility between the various groups. Some said, "I am of Paul"; others said, "I am of Apollos"; and still others said they were of Cephas. In verses 3, 6, and 7 Paul tells them that it is superficial to make comparisons between the men who had ministered to them in the gospel of the Lord Jesus Christ.

The truth is that any blessing which follows the preaching of the gospel does not depend on the preacher. People often speak of "Rev. Smith's church." They may even say, "Rev. Smith is carrying on a program of evangelism." This is an unwise emphasis. To be sure, some preachers are more effective than others, but no man in himself can achieve results that are spiritual and permanent. All power and all increase come from God. It is God who performs, and ministers are simply His servants.

> Who then is Paul, and who is Apollos, but ministers by whom ye
> believed, even as the Lord gave to every man? (1 Cor. 3:5).

It is true that Paul's and Apollos' preaching had helped them to believe. No doubt Paul and Apollos had different ways of preaching, but God was in control of both men. "Even as the

Lord gave to every man" refers to their gifts. God had bestowed on Paul certain gifts of preaching and teaching, and He had given Apollos different gifts in teaching and preaching. Possibly Paul was a teacher who explained the Word of God, while Apollos was a preacher who emphasized it. In any case these two men, as different as they were, had something in common: neither one of them could add the blessing on their work.

"Who then is Paul, and who is Apollos?" The Lord gave something to Paul for him to use. Paul's only contribution would be his faithfulness in using his gift. And if the Lord gave a different gift to Apollos, the important thing would be how Apollos would use it. Not all preachers have the same capacity for preaching and teaching. If one man preaches better than another, it is because he was given a greater gift. We should understand that the important element of a minister is the inner capacity that enables him to go out and serve; and this also is a gift of God.

Verse 6 states the famous formula for comparing all preachers: "I have planted, Apollos watered; but God gave the increase." No doubt all can feel the intended emphasis. Certainly Paul worked when he planted the good seed of the Word. Certainly Apollos worked to have it grow by watering it. "But God gave the increase." Without God nothing would have followed the planting and the watering. All the preaching in the world could not have turned any man from idol worship and given him faith in Jesus Christ.

> So then neither is he that planteth any thing, neither he that watereth; but God that giveth the increase (1 Cor. 3:7).

Paul reduces all ministers to the same status. They are all the same in the sight of God as far as their work is concerned. They can make no contribution to it. It is a matter of emphasis when Paul says that he is not anything. He does not want anyone to think of him as exceptional as a human being, or as accomplishing the great things that followed his preaching. A man's preaching and praying is important, but it is God who blesses the preaching and the praying. In other words, Paul is saying that without the Lord neither he nor Apollos could accomplish anything. It is God who does it, and the glory belongs to Him.

Realizing this truth will keep us from overestimating any

preacher. Rather, we should give thanks to God because a certain preacher has been used in our life. We should pray for that preacher and thus encourage him. Praise God for what this man is doing, but don't ever give the glory to the preacher himself. Sometimes ministers are not as wise as they ought to be, and they can fall into a trap at this point. When certain results follow their preaching, they might think that this is their own doing. When someone comes to talk with them about it, they might strut around as though they alone had accomplished these things. Such an attitude is both unwise and childish.

Someone may remark, "Isn't that a wonderful church? Dr. Brown built that church." No! Dr. Brown did not build that church. As a matter of fact, the carpenters and masons built it with the money given by the people. But the great truth is that God built it, and God made it possible in the first place. When credit is given to certain people, it arouses envy. Paul points out to the Corinthians as well as to us that preachers should not be compared with one another. No divisions should occur because of this. It is Christ who died for them. It is Christ alone who rose from the dead for them and who is even now on the right hand of God making intercession for them.

Paul speaks of himself as a servant of the Lord. This is the proper attitude for all who labor together with God, who will build upon that sure Foundation which is Jesus Christ, to whom be all honor and glory.

Chapter 9

THE JUDGMENT OF WORKS

In the two preceding chapters we have considered at some length the way in which the apostle Paul lifts the thinking of the Corinthians to a higher plane than that of quarreling about the merits of former pastors. He has pointed out that since every minister is a servant of God, each one of them is responsible to God. He has emphasized the fact that Christ Jesus alone is entitled to a believer's foremost love and loyalty.

In 1 Corinthians 3:8-10 the apostle Paul presented himself as a man whose work was superior in its responsibility. He made it quite clear that God is no respecter of persons. But, Paul points out, there is a difference in the work which God has set before them.

> Now he that planteth and he that watereth are one: and every man shall receive his own reward according to his own labour (1 Cor. 3:8).

In the sight of God there is no difference between the one who plants and the one who waters. They are equal. Each man is responsible to God for his own work and his own record. It is also true that when men labor as unto the Lord, no one is really in a position to criticize another about the work he is doing. Only God is able to judge His servants.

> For we are labourers together with God: ye are God's husbandry, ye are God's building (1 Cor. 3:9).

This is an important verse and the key to this whole meditation. Here Paul writes of the ministers as "we" — that is, preachers who were laborers together with God — while "you" refers to the Corinthian Christians who were God's husbandry, His building. In this verse the important thing is that God calls men to be co-laborers with Him. God is the prime mover in this whole project. Paul says, "You are God's husbandry." The word *husbandry* refers to what a farmer or gardener does. It is a term that refers to nurturing growing things. There is a course in college that is called animal husbandry. It is a study of the care of cattle and horses. There is also plant husbandry, which deals with the raising of fruit trees, grain, and plants. As far as the believers in Corinth were concerned, God wanted them to grow more and more in faith and in grace. He worked through the ministers, and through the apostles, but He Himself guided, motivated, and accomplished.

"Ye are God's building." The word *building* is a term that refers to the structuring of joint actions. Suppose you make a building of brick. Each brick is just a brick; it is the way each is arranged and fitted together with other bricks that eventually results in a building. So when we say that we are God's building, we mean that God controls and structures the relationships of the believers in their joint actions. When Christians serve God, they may serve in different capacities, but what they are doing is related because each one seeks to do God's will.

"According to the grace of God which is given unto me, as a wise masterbuilder" (1 Cor. 3:10a). Paul here recognized his own supervisory gifts. He was an outstanding leader and he contributed this gift freely. "I have laid the foundation, and another buildeth thereon" (v. 10b). We notice a division of labor here. One man lays the foundation, the other raises the building. It is like saying that one man is an evangelist — God uses this man to call and to win men to Christ — while another minister may be used by God to help believers grow. "But let every man take heed how he buildeth thereupon" (v. 10c). No one can judge another, but God judges all men. Every individual is responsible to the Master Builder for the way he carries out his part of the work. In the sight of God, all faithful ministers are doing work which is important. None is better than another, even though the work one man is called to do may seem more important than the work of another.

In 1 Corinthians 3:11-15, Paul emphasizes that each preacher should be free to work in cooperation with other preachers. But this means that he should also be free to work alone if he feels so led. In other words, no one minister is responsible to any other minister, for each man is responsible to God alone. Paul had spoken of himself as a wise "master-builder." He made the plans and designs in much the same way as an architect does. Then he laid the foundation for other people to build on as they served the Lord.

Paul argues that the basic function of a master builder, or a minister or preacher, is found in these words, "For other foundation can no man lay than that is laid, which is Jesus Christ" (1 Cor. 3:11). While ministers may differ in their activities, and one may be different from another, no minister is free to bring in any kind of preaching that is not centered in the Lord Jesus Christ. No one has the right or the freedom to lay any other foundation "than that [which] is laid, which is Jesus Christ." We must reluctantly realize that there are preachers who do not conform to this basic formula for preaching.

Concerning the whole ministry today, a grave problem exists. There are people who preach contrary to the teachings of the Scriptures. Unfortunately we have men in pulpits who do not tell their people about God. They do not tell how to come closer to God through Christ Jesus. They simply give their opinion on various subjects. Paul made it clear that such preachers are not acceptable or obedient to God. There is no other foundation acceptable to God than the Lord Jesus Christ Himself. Although Paul, as the wise master builder, was superior in his function, he could not do as he pleased. All he could do was to set forth the truth as it is in Christ.

> Now if any man build upon this foundation gold, silver, precious stones, wood, hay, stubble; every man's work shall be made manifest (1 Cor. 3:12-13).

In other words, every man's work will be open before God for judgment. It will be accepted or rejected depending on whether gold, silver, and precious stones, or wood, hay, and stubble were used in the building. Everything a man says and does will be evaluated and judged on Judgment Day. "Every man's work shall be made manifest: for the day shall declare it, because it shall be revealed by fire; and the fire shall try every man's work of what sort it is (1 Cor. 3:13). This word *fire* in the Bible is often used to indicate judgment.

According to the Bible, it would appear that fire is a great testing of faith. Faith when it is tried by fire will come out pure and refined. The fact that a man works is not adequate. He must do what is acceptable to God.

> If any man's work abide which he hath built thereupon, he shall receive a reward (1 Cor. 3:14).

If the work is gold, silver, and precious stones, because the person worked as unto the Lord, "he shall receive a reward."

> If any man's work shall be burned, he shall suffer loss: but he himself shall be saved; yet so as by fire (1 Cor. 3:15).

All the activity, all the money, all a man has put into his work, if it was not to the glory of God, nor in the will of God, will be a total loss. All the time and effort spent will have come to nothing.

> But he himself shall be saved; yet so as by fire (1 Cor. 3:15b).

Here is one of the wonderful truths of the gospel. If a man really does believe in the Lord Jesus Christ, he will be saved. For instance, a man could allow himself to be tricked into doing things that are useless or even harmful. Because a man is a true believer, it does not follow that the things he does are always right. If in ignorance he does things that hinder his testimony for the Lord, if all he does amounts to wood, hay, and stubble, God will judge him by his faith in the Lord Jesus Christ. This applies not only to preachers and ministers, but to all believers.

All believers will be judged before God. He knows when we act in faith. He knows when we are truly conscious of His presence. When we seek to act according to His will, God will bless us. If it should be that the work we have done is self-centered, or if the activity we have carried on was a waste of our time, it can result in nothing of spiritual value. We may be foolish and have wasted our time and talents, but if we trust in the Lord Jesus Christ, we still belong to Him.

Often we have wondered whether believers will come into judgment. We are troubled by our own unprofitable lives, and we fear the day of judgment. Here we learn the wonderful truth that though our work will come into judgment and prove an utter loss, we ourselves will be safe because we believe and trust in the Lord Jesus Christ.

Chapter 10

TRUE WISDOM

No one who believes in Jesus Christ is ever alone in this world. When a person accepts Jesus Christ as Savior and Lord, he is never alone again, because the living Lord Jesus Christ is with him from then on. Through faith in Christ he is indwelt by the Holy Spirit of God. In other words, the consciousness of a believer includes an awareness of the presence of the living Lord Jesus Christ and the reality of the indwelling Holy Spirit. It is a tragedy that believers so often forget this. I believe one reason why this awareness is so easily pushed out of our consciousness is because so many people living around us are oblivious of it.

For example, let us consider Tom Smith who is a believer in Jesus Christ. This man goes down to the office and is treated like every other man there. It is true that in the sight of others he is Tom Smith, but inwardly he is actually not alone. He knows that the Lord is with him, that the Holy Spirit of God is indwelling him. This is something he must keep in mind at all times. Other people may not know it — they will continue to think, act, and judge him as if he were only Tom Smith. Unfortunately it is easy for him to adopt this idea of himself from other people. So the believer needs to be reminded, and this is what Paul did. A believer in Christ is not free to act as he pleases, or as other people desire, especially in the matter of his conduct.

In 1 Corinthians 3:16 Paul wrote, "Know ye not that ye are the temple of God, and that the Spirit of God dwelleth in you?" He was asking, "Are you keeping in mind that you are a believer in Christ?"

> If any man defile the temple of God, him shall God destroy; for the temple of God is holy, which temple ye are (1 Cor. 3:17).

This is also true of a church, a group of believing people, a congregation. No doubt about it! It is also true of the individual believer. Let us keep in mind that although it is true that the church is the temple of God, each individual believer is the temple of God. This applies to every believer who is indwelt by the Holy Spirit. If we miss this, we are in danger of making a grave error. "If any man defile the temple," if he does something that upsets or disturbs the congregation, if he lives in disobedience to the will of God, "him shall God destroy; for the temple of God is holy, which temple ye are."

Do we realize how something may be defiled? If a plate has a crack in it, is it defiled? No! The plate is defiled when something other than food is put on it. The plate is defiled when it needs to be cleaned, when there is dirt on it. When we apply this to a congregation, what are the things that defile it? The answer is, bringing into it something that is contrary to the worship of God. "For the temple of God is holy." The word *holy* here implies the idea of "discriminating." Worshipers should be very careful that only those things which are acceptable to God are brought into the sanctuary.

"Let no man deceive himself" (1 Cor. 3:18). Whenever I read these words, I realize that a man can fool himself, even if he does not fool anyone else. It is quite possible that a man may not deceive others, but he could fool himself about spiritual things. Paul warns, "Let no man get the wrong idea."

> If any man among you seemeth to be wise in this world, let him become a fool, that he may be wise (1 Cor. 3:18).

That is to say, if any believer is considered wise by the people of this world, if they approve of his conduct, let him beware. He should prefer to be considered a fool by them. May we never forget that "the preaching of the cross is to them that perish, foolishness." Paul is not saying that a believer ought to be foolish, but rather that he be willing to appear foolish in the eyes of unbelievers.

When we think about our loving Lord and express such thoughts in our daily conversation, some people will think of us as fools. Thus in the eyes of the world we may be considered fools. At such times we can remember that "the foolishness of God is wiser than the wisdom of man."

> For the wisdom of this world is foolishness with God. For it is
> written, He taketh the wise in their own craftiness (1 Cor. 3:19).

Here we can see that no matter how well educated or sophisticated we may be, when we act and do things according to
human values, we are actually being foolish in the sight of God.
"The wisdom of this world is foolishness with God."

There is a real danger that men become so intrigued and so
enamored with this world that they become foolish. Consider,
for example, parents of a son. As the boy grows up, what do
they want for him? In many cases they want him to have good
grades in school, to achieve distinction in his studies. Why? So
he can make money. Why? So that he can have things; so he
will have a great name and become wealthy. If these parents
are believers, I would like to ask them, "What difference does
all this make? If your boy becomes a millionaire, can he take it
with him? If your boy was to become a great engineer and
accomplish great things, can he take those things with him?"
Believing parents who scheme simply to get their children
ahead in this world are truly acting foolishly. They should know
that worldly values are temporal and that spiritual values are
eternal.

> The Lord knoweth the thoughts of the wise, that they are vain.
> Therefore let no man glory in men. For all things are yours;
> whether Paul, or Apollos, or Cephas, or the world, or life, or
> death, or things present, or things to come; all are yours; and ye
> are Christ's; and Christ is God's (1 Cor. 3:20-23).

Chapter 11

PAUL'S ESTIMATE OF HIMSELF

After Paul had explained that the ministers who had preached the gospel to the Corinthians were not to be compared with each other because each was serving the Lord and only He could know what the service really meant to the minister, Paul commented on his own ministry at Corinth.

> Let a man so account of us, as of the ministers of Christ, and stewards of the mysteries of God. Moreover it is required in stewards, that a man be found faithful (1 Cor. 4:1-2).

The only aspect of a man's stewardship that could be judged would be his faithfulness. Paul pointed out that such judgment by other men would be of no significance. In fact Paul did not attempt to judge himself and counted it "a very small thing" to be judged by the Corinthians. He was not conscious of anything wrong in his own conduct, but this did not mean he was all he should be. Paul realized that his true judgment would come from the Lord.

> Therefore judge nothing before the time, until the Lord come, who both will bring to light the hidden things of darkness, and will make manifest the counsels of the hearts: and then shall every man have praise of God (1 Cor. 4:5).

Having set forth this general truth about the nature of man, Paul wanted the Corinthians to look at him and Apollos in that light. Since they could not adequately judge man's conduct, they should avoid comparing their judgments of their preachers. The believers were not able to judge which minister had been most faithful, and so they should avoid rating them according to their personal preferences. These comparisons could easily lead to a feeling of superiority on the part of some, and this would hinder their joy in fellowship in the Lord.

Paul then emphasized the actual situation of men.

> For who maketh thee to differ from another? and what hast thou
> that thou didst not receive? now if thou didst receive it, why dost
> thou glory, as if thou hadst not received it? (1 Cor. 4:7).

Since no one has any ability but that which God has given him
as a gift, it is foolish for one man to be proud of himself in
comparison to anyone else.

The Corinthian believers had been richly blessed to where
they "reigned as kings" without any special help from the
apostle. Paul did not begrudge this evidence of their ability to
control their circumstances. In fact he wished them victory so
that he could share in it, because his own experience was by no
means so fortunate.

> For I think that God hath set forth us the apostles last, as it were
> appointed to death: for we are made a spectacle unto the world,
> and to angels, and to men (1 Cor. 4:9).

Apparently Paul is making reference to a custom in which the
victory parade of military heroes would bring captives sen-
tenced to death at the end of the procession. He felt that the
apostles generally seemed to be so despised and dishonorable
that they seemed like condemned captives. In the next verse
Paul writes in a style that suggests sarcasm, though I do not
think he was being petty about this. Undoubtedly, he was
describing the situation as it would appear to others:

> We are fools for Christ's sake, but ye are wise in Christ; we are
> weak, but ye are strong; ye are honourable, but we are despised
> (1 Cor. 4:10).

Paul then describes in more detail the treatment given to the
apostles of Christ. It is the most complete picture to be found in
the New Testament, and it is sobering to realize that such is the
lot of men and women who are "bearing His reproach."

> Even unto this present hour we both hunger, and thirst, and are
> naked, and are buffeted, and have no certain dwelling-place;
> and labour, working with our own hands: being reviled, we
> bless; being persecuted, we suffer it: being defamed, we en-
> treat: we are made as the filth of the world, and are the offscour-
> ing of all things unto this day (1 Cor. 4:11-13).

It is more than a figure of speech when a servant of Christ is
made to feel that he is being treated like dirt.

Paul then hastened to explain why he wrote in this way. He did not want to make the Corinthians feel bad; he wanted to warn them. They should know that this could and probably would happen to them as they witnessed to Him.

> I write not these things to shame you, but as my beloved sons I warn you (1 Cor. 4:14).

Realizing that he had written very directly to them about their attitude toward former ministers, Paul then explained more carefully why he felt free to write in this fashion. He had been the evangelist who won them to the Lord, and so he felt toward them as a father to his children.

> For though ye have ten thousand instructors in Christ, yet have ye not many fathers: for in Christ Jesus I have begotten you through the gospel. Wherefore I beseech you, be ye followers of me (1 Cor. 4:15-16).

Chapter 12

A CONTENTIOUS SPIRIT IN A BELIEVER IS CHILDISH

In the fourth chapter of his First Epistle to the Corinthians, Paul concluded his discussion of the first big problem that troubled the Corinthian believers. We have studied Paul's dealing with the divisions which existed among them. These were actually a sign of immaturity and childishness. Paul climaxed his observations by pointing out to the Corinthian believers that Christ Jesus alone should be uppermost in their minds and hearts and lives, since He had died for them and had risen from the dead for them.

Today we often hear of people who put one church over another. They will not go to hear a Bible teacher if he happens to be speaking in a church other than their own denomination. They feel that no other denomination but their own presents the truth. This is acting like children, who compare and quarrel over their toys. Yet this sort of thing often goes on among grown people.

In the days when I was in the Canadian army, there was a strong feeling among those who were in the infantry, as over those who were in the cavalry. There was a strong feeling among those who were in the artillery, over those who were in the navy. Today there is scrambling for first place among the men of the army, the air corps, and the navy. One could almost think that these units were actually against each other. This is immature since all these military men belong to the same country. They all serve the same national interest.

It is this common relationship among believers that Paul is emphasizing throughout his writings. Toward the close of chapter 4, Paul's concern for the Corinthians is quite evident. In our day it has often been pointed out that a pastor leaving his pastorate should not cling to former pastoral relationships. I would agree with this as far as church organization is concerned; but I do not feel this means that a pastor should try to forget the people whom he, at one time, led to the Lord Jesus Christ. When an evangelist comes into a community and is used by God to call men to a saving faith in the Lord Jesus Christ, should he feel that he has done his work? Or should he seek to help them become established as mature believers? Would he not have some concern for their future spiritual welfare, since he had been privileged to turn them to the Lord?

First Corinthians 4:18-21 contains some pertinent ideas on this subject. As we look at these, we should keep in mind that Paul was writing to people who were still babes in Christ, and who were acting like children. Whenever we find people who disagree because they favor different pastors, we also find divisions in the church. We know from observation and experience how far-reaching such divisions can become.

> Now some are puffed up, as though I would not come to you (1 Cor. 4:18).

The expression "puffed up" is familiar to most. It spells arrogance and conceit. I have nothing against teen-agers, but it is commonly known that there comes a time for most of them when no one can tell them anything. They are so full of themselves that they think their parents are ignorant and that their teachers do not know anything. I would say that such teen-agers are "puffed up." They are arrogant and conceited in their childish pride in themselves.

"As though I would not come to you." Some of these Corinthians had the feeling that now that Paul was gone, they could go ahead and do as they pleased.

> But I will come to you shortly, if the Lord will, and will know, not the speech of them which are puffed up, but the power (1 Cor. 4:19).

The Phillips' translation of this passage reads, "Some of you have apparently grown conceited enough to think that I should not visit you. But please God it will not be long before I do come to you in person. Then I shall be able to see what power, apart from their word, these pretentious ones among you really possess." In another translation we read, "Some of you have become conceited and arrogant and pretentious, counting on my not coming to you. But I will come to you [and] shortly, if the Lord is willing, and then I will perceive and understand not what the talk these puffed up and arrogant spirits amount to, but their force — that is, the moral power and excellence of soul they really possess" (Amplified). This is the meaning of these verses:

> For the kingdom of God is not in word, but in power (1 Cor.
> 4:20).

In other words, your personal relationship with the Lord is not in what you say, but in what you do. It is not how you talk, it is how you walk. This is what Paul wrote to the Corinthian believers. He would come and find out how these big talkers actually act and live. Paul concluded this whole discussion with these words:

> What will ye? shall I come unto you with a rod, or in love, and in
> the spirit of meekness? (1 Cor. 4:21).

He asked these people, as one would ask children, "Would you like me to come lovingly and gently, or must I come with a rod to correct you? I would like to come in love, but if I must I will come and correct you." In Phillips' translation of this passage we read, "For the kingdom of God is not a matter of words but of the power of Christian living. Now it's up to you to choose! Shall I come to you ready to chastise you, or in love and gentleness?" How true this is even today. The same Scripture that is for our correction if we do wrong can comfort us when we do what is right in the sight of God.

Chapter 13

JUDGMENT UPON SIN

In chapter 5 of his First Epistle to the Corinthians, Paul takes up a second grave problem, which in a real sense concerned the whole congregation at Corinth.

> It is reported commonly that there is fornication among you, and such fornication as is not so much as named among the Gentiles, that one should have his father's wife. And ye are puffed up, and have not rather mourned, that he that hath done this deed might be taken away from among you. For I verily, as absent in body, but present in spirit, have judged already, as though I were present, concerning him that hath so done this deed, in the name of our Lord Jesus Christ, when ye are gathered together, and my spirit, with the power of our Lord Jesus Christ, to deliver such a one unto Satan for the destruction of the flesh, that the spirit may be saved in the day of the Lord Jesus (1 Cor. 5:1-5).

In these verses Paul urges the church to take public action against those whose lives bring disgrace upon the church of God. Personally I have the feeling the truth in this portion of Scripture can be best recognized when one is careful not to limit the application of principles here too narrowly.

The word *fornication* need not be limited to one specific act. I would take this word to refer to irregular immoral conduct between men and women in various acts. Paul applies this to a situation in which one "[had] his father's wife." I do not think this means that this man married his mother. In those days among the people of Corinth a man might have several wives. It is possible that one of these wives was much younger than the man's own mother. In other words, this man may have taken to himself his stepmother, violating the seventh commandment. In any case, this act was an offense to the sen-

51

sibilities of all people, both in the congregation and in the community. All illicit relations between men and women are wrong, but this case was so scandalous that even people who were not Christians were shocked by it. Everyone in the community was scandalized by this shameful conduct.

When Paul wrote, "You are puffed up," he was referring to the fact that the congregation had not acted immediately in this matter. They apparently felt superior, "and hath not rather mourned." This attitude was a blemish on the congregation.

> For I verily, as absent in body, but present in spirit, have judged already, as though I were present, concerning him that hath so done this deed (1 Cor. 5:3).

Paul would not have hesitated to judge the shameful conduct of this person, and he felt this was what the congregation should have done.

> In the name of our Lord Jesus Christ, when ye are gathered together, and my spirit, with the power of our Lord Jesus Christ (1 Cor. 5:4).

The judging of the man's conduct should be done with the authority and approval of the Lord and as led by His Spirit.

Verse 5 records the sentence passed on this man who had brought shame and disgrace on the church of God:

> To deliver such a one unto Satan for the destruction of the flesh, that the spirit may be saved in the day of the Lord Jesus (1 Cor. 5:5).

"To deliver such a one unto Satan" is a phrase taken from the Jewish culture. It has to do with a certain attitude concerning willful sinners. Such a one, when "delivered over to Satan," will go on in his sinfulness and wickedness. In fact all Satan can do is to influence and lead him "for the destruction of the flesh." In other words, Satan is here spoken of as the agent of physical suffering.

Christians must not stand by and overlook or condone flagrant disobedience to the commandments of God. Paul said that if anyone by his conduct brings dishonor upon the Lord and His church, he should be put out of the company of believers. In Paul's Second Epistle to the Corinthians, apparently referring to this case, he wrote, "Sufficient to such a man is this punishment, which was inflicted of many" (2 Cor. 2:6). If however such punishment resulted in true repentance and sorrow and a changed way of life, then such a man should be forgiven, "that his soul may not be lost." People of the world might think that punishing and then forgiving is not consistent. In reality, this is a matter of discipline and correction.

If a child does something wrong, faithful and wise parents will take action against their child. I have seen parents who have brought their child to school to be disciplined, because the child had violated some rules of the school. They wanted their son to learn from this experience that punishment must follow the offense and that a change of attitude must be evident before forgiveness can be granted.

Whenever well-meaning parents and friends try to protect someone from the judgment of God, they are actually hindering God's dealings with that person. Based on the passage of Scripture we have read here, I would like to point out several things. First, church members should be concerned about flagrant conduct of other church members. If after exhorting the wrongdoer, he does not repent, they should show their condemnation and disapproval by withdrawing from the wrongdoer (Matt. 18:15-17). Also, believers should not interfere with chastening when God sends it. Suppose we know of someone who is worldly and does not obey the will of God. If he gets into real trouble, believers should be careful not to rush in and deliver him if he has not learned from it. It may be that trouble is what he needs to turn him to the Lord in true repentance. Such is the mercy of God — that all who come to him in repentance will be forgiven and restored.

Chapter 14

BAD EFFECTS OF SIN IN A CONGREGATION

In our previous chapter, I reached into the Second Epistle to the Corinthians to show that after judgment can come restoration. Now let us continue in our study of Paul's First Epistle to the Corinthians, where he points out the effects on a congregation which withholds judgment and punishment. "Your glorying is not good" (1 Cor. 5:6). In what sense was this church glorying? Apparently they were glorying in the fact that they were strong in their faith. They had many gifts and had been blessed in their experience together. They gloried in the blessings which God had bestowed on their congregation. Yet at the same time, one of their members was living in a shameful way. Paul told these Corinthian believers that their smug self-assurance was dangerous. Feeling that everything was all right would make them reluctant to see, admit, and discipline the shameful conduct on the part of a member. One of their members was dishonoring the church of God, yet they had done nothing about it.

Once while I was pursuing my studies in seminary, I had occasion to approach a pastor and the session of his church with this question, "What is there in your congregation that could be improved?" The pastor said, "I can't think of a thing. Everything is perfect." And the elder said, "I don't know of anything that is wrong with us." I wondered whether statements like that indicated that some persons were just blind. That particular church had practically no local mission work at all. They were doing nothing to reach out to others in the city. The people who belonged to the church were attending services. They had money enough to support their church and to do some of the things they wanted to do. Yet none of their wealth was used for helping the poor or supporting missions. In spite of this, these officers felt there was nothing wrong with their congregation. To such a church Paul would have said, "Your glorying is not good."

> Know ye not that a little leaven leaveneth the whole lump? (1 Cor. 5:6).

The word *leaven* is not common in our conversation, but most people know the meaning of the word is "yeast." We know enough about the baking of bread to know that when yeast is put into batter it increases and spreads. Little plants, as it were, grow in the dough, causing the dough to rise. Anyone who has baked bread knows that yeast put into a batter of dough does not require any great amount of mixing. One can just put it in and leave it alone. It will grow and spread through the whole lump.

We have a common saying along this line — "One rotten apple can spoil the whole barrel." Sin spreads. In the same way, we could say something like this, "One child with measles can spread measles through the whole school." Things that are wrong spread from one to another. The influence of personal conduct upon others is very important. Then what should be done?

> Purge out therefore the old leaven [remove the yeast before the whole lump becomes affected], that ye may be a new lump, as ye are unleavened (1 Cor. 5:7).

If we have a sickness in our body such as gangrene, it means that some part of our body is actually beginning to decay. I remember a close friend of mine whose toe started to decay with gangrene. The doctor immediately removed the toe, but he had not taken it off soon enough. Soon the rest of the foot showed evidence of the infection, that the gangrene had spread. The doctor now took off the foot at the ankle, but even that was not enough. In this particular case the man's leg was amputated to the knee and finally to the hips. Only in this way could he be saved from the gangrene spreading through his whole body. What Paul meant in verse 7 was, "Amputate the diseased member and save the body." At whatever cost, they were to get rid of the bad example in the church.

Chapter 15

THE RESPONSIBILITY TO JUDGE SIN
IN FELLOW BELIEVERS

In 1 Corinthians 5:9-13 Paul pointed out several things that would be helpful to the believers. He made it clear why they should not have fellowship with someone whose conduct is scandalous. Paul did not urge believers to cast judgment on unbelievers. Rather he urged upon church members their responsibility toward a fellow believer who is dishonoring the Lord and His church by his conduct. Such a sinful man not only dishonors the Lord, but he gives unbelievers an opportunity to deride the church and its teachings.

There are not many ways a congregation can discipline a member who sins openly and refuses to repent. They cannot sentence him to prison, nor arrange to have him beaten. However, they can do something in their attitude toward him. They can withdraw their fellowship from him. The public will judge believers by their attitude. If they show no disapproval, it can only mean that they tolerate and are actually indifferent to evil conduct in their midst. Paul pointed out their responsibility in such a case.

> Therefore put away from among yourselves that wicked person (1 Cor. 5:13).

Apparently in the city of Corinth social life was marked by many irregularities of conduct. The matter of men and women living together under circumstances which we would consider wrong was quite common. To Paul this was an added reason why the church should sit in judgment on a man who was a church member but who lived an evil life. Breaking off fellowship with such a man would prove to the community at large that believers feel a responsibility for the conduct of their members. At times we see people whose own lives are above reproach socialize with persons who lead evil lives. In this way they show their indifference to evil. They take a chance that their attitude might even denote approval of such conduct to those who are outside the church.

This very situation is dealt with in other Scriptures. For example,

> If there come any unto you, and bring not this doctrine, receive him not into your house, neither bid him God speed: for he that biddeth him God speed is partaker of his evil deeds (2 John 10-11).

In other words, when we bid a person Godspeed, we are showing the world that we are sympathetically involved in what that person is doing, and we are approving of him. This actually makes us partakers with him in his evil deeds.

Someone might ask, "How can we help a person unless we are in touch with him? How can we deal with a man of whose conduct we disapprove, if we do not have fellowship with him?" This may seem like a difficult problem, but it is not nearly as difficult as it may seem. We do such things every day. For example, suppose a child comes to school with smallpox. Would a good teacher tolerate the child with smallpox in her classroom? We know what would be done. The teacher would immediately separate that child from the other children and take him to the hospital. Surely no one would say, "Oh, how cruel, to take the child away from his classes and interfere with his life." In reality the teacher interferred with his life to save it and the lives of the other children. If such a child came to school, we would not whip him; we would treat him as if he had smallpox. We would separate him from the others. We certainly would not help any child by letting him come to school with the measles or smallpox.

In a sense such actions are included in the issues Paul set before the Corinthians. Those who serve the Lord must abstain from even the slightest approval of those who do not honor the Lord or His gospel. A shallow feeling of sympathy when correction is needed will not help any wrongdoer. It is only as he is disciplined that he may come to repentance. This is the way in which Paul presented this whole matter of judgment and punishment of those whose shameful conduct has brought disgrace and dishonor upon the Lord Jesus Christ and His church.

Yet, although this chastening is necessary, Paul indicated clearly that this did not mean that the congregation should act in anger or with a feeling of self-righteousness. Rather, they should put such a one out of their midst with a sense of deep compassion. They should mourn that one who has believed in the Lord Jesus Christ could grieve the Lord who redeemed him by living in willful sin. May we who love the Lord walk in humility lest we fall. May we be ready and willing at all times to be guided and directed by the Holy Spirit of God who alone can keep us from falling.

Chapter 16

CONTENTIOUSNESS TO BE AVOIDED

Paul had come as a missionary to Corinth and had preached there as an evangelist. Therefore, he had a special interest in the members of the congregation in Corinth. In this first epistle he discusses a number of problems that threatened to hinder the fellowship and the testimony of the Corinthian believers. In chapter 6 he discusses their disposition to quarrel among themselves. Apparently they had fallen into the practice of bringing their quarrels before the public courts of law for settlement. Paul felt that in doing so they were acting unwisely.

> Dare any of you, having a matter against another, go to law before the unjust, and not before the saints? Do ye not know that the saints shall judge the world? and if the world shall be judged by you, are ye unworthy to judge the smallest matters? Know ye not that we shall judge angels? how much more things that pertain to this life? (1 Cor. 6:1-3).

In going to the public courts of law the believers would be bringing their problems to pagan magistrates for judgment, and Paul felt they should have known better. Since believers pass judgment on the world, it would not be reasonable to ask the world to pass judgment on the affairs of believers. Paul went on to say that believers "shall judge angels," and so why would they not be competent to judge "things that pertain to this life"?

> If then ye have judgments of things pertaining to this life, set them to judge who are least esteemed in the church (1 Cor. 6:4).

Paul advised the Corinthian believers that if they had any problem in worldly matters which called for judgment, they should designate some members of the congregation to act as judges. He felt that he was actually shaming them by his advice. They could have done this themselves. Surely they would have known some brother who was competent to judge their problem.

> But brother goeth to law with brother, and that before the unbelievers (1 Cor. 6:6).

Apparently the practice of taking their problems before the public court was common among the Corinthians. Paul felt this was definitely a fault in this congregation. He then went on to intimate it would have been better to be wronged, even to the point of being defrauded by one another, than to hurt their testimony in the community by publicly advertising their differences.

> Now therefore there is utterly a fault among you , because ye go to law one with another. Why do ye not rather take wrong? why do ye not rather suffer yourselves to be defrauded? (1 Cor. 6:7).

Apparently Paul realized that there could be situations in which one believer could do wrong in dealing with a fellow believer. In such cases Paul would have had the injured party meekly endure the wrong without making any public attempt to secure his rights. But Paul then went on to warn them that God would not overlook unrighteousness in anyone.

> Nay, ye do wrong, and defraud, and that your brethren. Know ye not that the unrighteous shall not inherit the kingdom of God? Be not deceived: neither fornicators, nor idolators, nor adulterers, nor effeminate, nor abusers of themselves with mankind, nor thieves, nor covetous, nor drunkards, nor revilers, nor extortioners, shall inherit the kingdom of God (1 Cor. 6:8-10).

Several questions come to mind as we read this passage. Was Paul warning the Corinthian believers that such evildoers might be among them? Was he saying that if there were such, these should not be counted as fellow believers? Or was he simply warning all to avoid such conduct? Throughout his discussion of this matter Paul had counseled the injured party to meekly accept his situation, suffering the wrong without recourse to any public court for the sake of his testimony as a believer in Christ. Did he now address the wrongdoer with a sober warning that his wrong would be seen and judged by God? Despite any possible final answer to such questions, the implication of Paul's comment seems plainly to emphasize that believers are expected to be led of the Holy Spirit to deal righteously with each other for Christ's sake.

Paul concluded his discussion with two general comments. He reminded the Corinthians that sinfulness had been their condition before they came to Christ; and then he assured them that they had been delivered from such conditions by the grace of God in Christ.

> And such were some of you: but ye are washed, but ye are sanctified, but ye are justified in the name of the Lord Jesus, and by the Spirit of our God (1 Cor. 6:11).

He then made a general statement as to how a believer deals with the affairs of this life. Using himself as a case in point, Paul said plainly:

> All things are lawful unto me, but all things are not expedient: all things are lawful for me, but I will not be brought under the power of any (1 Cor. 6:12).

This statement seems to imply that there is always the possibility that a believer could come into bondage to worldly, selfish interests, and Paul recommends that every believer guard carefully against such a lapse in his obedience to the indwelling Christ.

Chapter 17

DELIVERANCE THROUGH RESURRECTION

In the latter part of the sixth chapter of Paul's first letter to the Corinthians, the apostle stresses the fact that when men and women believe the gospel and accept Jesus Christ as their Savior, they are no longer their own, but they belong to the Lord Jesus Christ. In verses 13, 14, and 15 Paul uses this important truth in trying to help deliver the Corinthian believers from their sinful practices, which were a part of their lives before they came to believe in Christ Jesus.

> Now the body is not for fornication, but for the Lord; and the Lord for the body. And God hath both raised up the Lord, and will also raise up us by his own power. Know ye not that your bodies are the members of Christ? shall I then take the members of Christ, and make them the members of a harlot? God forbid (1 Cor. 6:13-15).

It is natural for a person to think that his body is his own and that it is his right to use it any way he wants to.

No believer would deliberately want to use his body for wrong, because then God would judge him. For example, what a person eats and how much he eats is his own responsibility. And if he does not eat, that is his business too. When he uses his body for noble purposes, he is called noble. When he uses his body for evil purposes, he is called evil. Everything depends on how he handles himself, because he is in charge of his body.

But this is not true for a believer. A believer does not have the right to use his body for good or evil, as he may feel inclined. In this matter Paul says that the believer's body is not his own. It is a purchased possession. The body belongs to the Lord. As our Lord died in His body on Calvary's cross, so should we as believers reckon our bodies dead to sin. In that way we will be set free from every carnal sin. Paul argues that no believer who has been redeemed should be guilty of fornication.

Paul does not spend time pointing out that carnal acts are sinful. Everyone knows that. He does not argue that stealing is wrong. Everyone knows it is wrong to steal. But Paul does argue that no believer should be guilty of evil conduct that involves the body. Paul did not have to come preaching that fornication is evil. They knew this, though this knowledge did not stop them from such carnal sin. But Paul wrote to them about a principle that would deliver them from such sinning. This principle, this new truth which would set them free, was the realization that their bodies were no longer their own.

Paul left no doubt in their minds that Christ died for the sins of all men committed in the body. Then he went on to point out that Christ Jesus arose from the dead into the newness of life. Christ did this in order that all who believe on Him might partake of the new birth, be dead to trespasses and sins, and be alive to good works.

In his Epistle to the Romans Paul wrote on this subject:

> Know ye not, that so many of us as were baptized into Jesus Christ were baptized into his death? Therefore we are buried with him by baptism into death: that like as Christ was raised up from the dead by the glory of the Father, even so we also should walk in newness of life (Rom. 6:3-4).

Walking in newness of life means living our lives in a new way, with new thoughts and desires.

> For if we have been planted together in the likeness of his death, we shall be also in the likeness of his resurrection: knowing this, that our old man is crucified with him, that the body of sin might be destroyed, that henceforth we should not serve sin. For he that is dead is freed from sin (Rom. 6:5-7).

This is the hope of all believers, that they who have been buried with Christ, in the likeness of His death, shall also be raised in the likeness of His resurrection.

When believers reckon their bodies to be dead, the things that are sinful, the temptation to self-indulgence, self-pleasure, vanity, and pride will no longer trouble them. These temptations to sin would not occur to a dead man. In other words, "he that is dead is freed from sin."

Paul concludes this portion of his letter to the Romans by saying:

> Now if we be dead with Christ, we believe that we shall also live with him: knowing that Christ being raised from the dead dieth no more; death hath no more dominion over him. For in that he died, he died unto sin once: but in that he liveth, he liveth unto God. Likewise reckon ye also yourselves to be dead indeed unto sin, but alive unto God through Jesus Christ our Lord. Let not sin therefore reign in your mortal body, that ye should obey it in the lusts thereof. Neither yield ye your members as instruments of unrighteousness unto sin: but yield yourselves unto God, as those that are alive from the dead, and your members as instruments of righteousness unto God (Rom. 6:8-13).

Both Romans 6:3-13 and 1 Corinthians 6:13-15 express the same profound truth. It is more powerful than anything else to keep us from evil. It is more powerful than any moral consideration. When the believer's attention is focused on the Lord, he asks, "What would He want me to do?" This is the attitude of every believer who knows that he has been bought with a price, even the precious blood of Jesus.

Chapter 18

BELONGING TO CHRIST BEGETS POWER

In the previous chapter we have made a study of Paul's formula for deliverance from sin. In 1 Corinthians 6:16-18, Paul presents his closing arguments with which he is seeking to help these Christians in Corinth to be delivered from their habits of carnal sin. He is presenting to them a truth which has the power to deliver them and set them free. This power comes from the relationship of a believer to Christ.

In verse 9 Paul enumerates the vicious sins which are named among human beings: fornicators, idolators, adulterers, effeminate, abusers of themselves with mankind, thieves, covetous, drunkards, revilers, extortioners. What a grim catalog! But now Paul argues that human beings, evil though they are, can be delivered. This deliverance would come when they kept in mind at all times what Christ Jesus had done for them. The whole secret of deliverance for a believer from evil habits is in the realization that he belongs to Jesus Christ.

Suppose a man was going to town carrying fifty dollars of his employer's money in his pocket. As he goes along, he looks into store windows and sees things he would like to have. He will appreciate the things he sees, but he will not be tempted to buy them, because the fifty dollars he carries in his pocket is not his money. If it were, he could spend it. The temptation to spend it would be much greater if the money belonged to him. This is exactly what Paul pointed out to the Corinthians. He told them that they who had been purchased by the Lord Jesus Christ were no longer their own. In the same way that a person cannot spend money which does not belong to him, so believers are not free to commit evil.

This is Paul's great formula for refraining from fornication and any other sin. The believer's physical body is redeemed by the death of his Lord Jesus Christ. Christ paid the price physically to deliver him in his body. When someone comes to the Lord Jesus Christ in faith, the Holy Spirit works in his heart and takes charge of his body. The Spirit controls the body and inclines the believer Christward.

> What? know ye not that he which is joined to a harlot is one body? for two, saith he, shall be one flesh. But he that is joined unto the Lord is one spirit (1 Cor. 6:16-17).

If believers have received the Lord Jesus Christ into their hearts and have committed themselves to Him, His Spirit dwells in them, and they are one with Him.

In verse 18 Paul wrote, "Flee fornication." It is always interesting to notice how at times the Bible gives a clear, simple word. This imperative is direct and total.

> Flee fornication. Every sin that a man doeth is without the body; but he that committeth fornication sinneth against his own body (1 Cor. 6:18).

Paul did not discuss the consequences that follow gross sin. He appealed to the Corinthians to recognize the Christian principle that they were not their own. Involving their bodies in evil would be denying the truth of what Christ Jesus had done to redeem them.

The principle that our bodies are not our own can be applied in all aspects of living. Many people have gotten real help in being delivered from their appetites by suddenly realizing that the body they were indulging by overeating was in reality not theirs to abuse in this way. The same thing is true with drinking. Being convinced that his body belongs to Christ has been one of the most powerful considerations to keep a believer away from alcohol.

Inasmuch as the Lord Jesus belongs to believers and they are His, it follows that their eternal welfare and their relationship with God Himself come through faith in Him. His Holy Spirit will work in believers when they trust Him. Then they will not use their bodies, which belong to Him, for their own personal satisfaction. This is the great liberating principle in all personal conduct for believers. The Holy Spirit will call to our remembrance the terrible price our Lord paid to set us free. He will incline our hearts to Him, who loved us and gave Himself for us. Then as we yield ourselves to Christ, He will cleanse us and keep us from all evil.

Chapter 19

THE RESULT OF HAVING THE HOLY SPIRIT

In writing to the Corinthians, who were young believers, the apostle Paul had a twofold purpose. He had been away from them for some time, and in his absence certain problems had arisen in the congregation. He knew that the life of faith is much like a garden bearing fruit. First it needs to be cultivated. Then to have good fruit, it needs to have the weeds pulled. Paul in dealing with these new believers takes note of the fact that on the one hand there may have been a lack of spiritual growth because they were not being adequately nourished. Then also there may have been a situation where indolence and inactivity were the cause of spiritual immaturity.

It is also true that active, energetic people could act unwisely and make mistakes. This congregation of believers in the city of Corinth did not suffer from idleness or indifference. They suffered from error. These people were willing to be active and serve the Lord, but they were often unwise. Their conduct hurt their testimony and stunted their spiritual growth. In our previous study in 1 Corinthians 6 we have noted that Paul wrote of the action the congregation must take against the flagrant misconduct of one of their members. Then Paul warned these believers to beware of carnality and to flee fornication.

Continuing in this chapter, Paul summarizes and emphasizes his previous words when he writes, "What? know ye not that your body is the temple of the Holy Ghost" (1 Cor. 6:19). Again we are impressed with the fact that Paul does not harp on the sin itself. It would have been superfluous for him to tell a believer that to indulge in sinful acts is wrong. Discussing the evil itself would be to miss the deliverance which is in Christ Jesus.

Christ Jesus does not change one iota of the judgment of the law. In Him the law is to be fulfilled; but in Him also is the solution of the problem, namely, the deliverance from the bondage of sin. All this hinges on the fact that the body of a believer belongs to Christ. It is to be used to do His will. "Know ye not that your body is the temple of the Holy Ghost?"

The temple is the very place where the Holy Spirit dwells. In other words, our bodies are to be His dwelling. The Holy Spirit is the third person of the Godhead. In the King James Version, the term *Holy Ghost* is used. In the original Greek writing there is no difference between the words *Spirit* and *Ghost*. Personally, I use the word *Spirit* because of the common public reaction to the word *Ghost*. Yet in a sense the term *Holy Ghost* may bring more clearly to our minds that we are referring to a Person. To many people the words *Holy Spirit* clearly mean only a pious frame of mind. They find it difficult to think of the Spirit as a person.

Paul wrote that the body of believers is also the dwelling place of the third person of the Godhead. God's Spirit is in the believer. This is a profound, new experience. Ever since Pentecost the Holy Spirit is available to all believers. This means that He comes to be in them. ". . . the Holy Ghost which is in you, which ye have of God" (1 Cor. 6:19). The Holy Spirit is not something we can ever qualify for. We do not earn His presence by any effort on our part. God in His mercy gives Him to us: ". . . which ye have of God, and ye are not your own" (1 Cor. 6:19).

These words reemphasize the fact that we who are believers cannot do as we please with ourselves. For example, if a woman is sincerely a wife, she is not her own any more. If she starts acting on her own, it will cause tension, and that will cause trouble. The same is true of a man who is engaged as a servant. He is not his own boss any longer. Or if a man signs up in the army or the navy or the air force, he is no longer free to come and go and do as he wishes. Paul pointed out that this is the essence of the situation that will deliver a believer from self-indulgence.

In verse 20 we read:

> For ye are bought with a price: therefore glorify God in your
> body, and in your spirit, which are God's.

For the believer, a purchase has been made; and the price has already been paid. Christ Jesus shed His precious blood for us on Calvary. He bought us. "Therefore glorify God": work out His will fully in action and in spirit. In thoughts, purpose, and intent seek His glory. "Which are God's": both body and spirit belong to God. They are His not only because He created them, but also because He has redeemed them. Surely it should be our sincere desire to yield to Him both body and spirit, that He may have His way in us.

Chapter 20

PRACTICAL GUIDANCE IN THE
MARRIAGE RELATIONSHIP

In chapter 7 of his first letter to the Corinthians Paul wrote, "Now concerning the things whereof ye wrote unto me," by way of indicating that he would answer the questions that they, as a congregation, had asked him. He took each matter they presented to him in order and discussed and answered it in the light of God's Word.

The first of these questions relates to a problem which is of much concern all over the world even today, because it deals with disorders that affect marriage and the home. The first relationship man entered into was between Adam and Eve. Thus the first social situation to come into existence was the home. The home is fundamental to everything in life. The relationships between men and women can become critical because there is so much involved, such as personal appetite, personal vanity, personal desires, personal prestige, and personal security. All these personal affairs involve the home, the family, and everything that goes with it. This is also an area in which certain types of carnal sin are common.

In the King James Version Paul's opening words are, "It is good for a man not to touch a woman." Actually in this translation from the Greek several words are supplied. A better translation puts Paul's words in the form of a question. In all probability the Corinthians wrote to Paul asking this question: "Is it good for a man not to touch a woman?" Should there be no relationship between men and women at all? Some were evidently proposing this solution.

In explanation I would like to describe briefly Greek philosophy concerning this idea of living. The Greeks thought that everything done in the physical body was limited and

71

inadequate. While they did not know God as we do, they used the word *sin* the way we use it, meaning that anything inadequate was sinful and undesirable. They felt that acts of the physical body would result in evil, whereas things of the mind were desirable and adequate and would result in good. The Greeks desired to be intellectual and think things through until they were perfect. Putting thoughts into action, on the other hand, could spoil the perfection of the mind.

There are people today who hold the view that abstaining from all actions can solve problems. In other words, if we have trouble doing something, then we shouldn't do it. It is somewhat like saying that if we have trouble with weeds in the garden, it is best not to have a garden. This is not very practical. Someone must have a garden, even if others shrug it off and say, "Well, he has the garden and he has the weeds and the trouble." They do not consider the fact that they eat the produce from the garden.

This may seem ridiculous to us, but in some of the eastern countries of the world, there is the idea that if a person does nothing, he can certainly do no evil: therefore not doing anything is best. In one particular society there are those who are known as "holy men." These men do not work. They do absolutely nothing. How do they eat? People give to them. They give to them hoping to receive some blessing from these holy men who do no work, and thus do not get into trouble.

Though the marriage relationship can bring with it difficulties, it is still ordained of God. Speaking as a farmer, I would say it is true of life as a whole, including marriage, that to have good results takes work and effort. The more diligently we work at it, the better our garden will be, and the better our marriage will be. Some people would solve this matter by saying, "Stop the problem by stopping marriage." There are those who in order to be holy withdraw from the world to where they can be of no use to anyone.

> Nevertheless, to avoid fornication, let every man have his own wife, and let every woman have her own husband (1 Cor. 7:2).

Elsewhere in the New Testament we read, "Marriage is honourable . . . and the bed undefiled" (Heb. 13:4). Christians believe the relationship of marriage is intended to help out wholesome living.

> Let the husband render unto the wife due benevolence: and
> likewise also the wife unto the husband (1 Cor. 7:3).

Each spouse should extend kindness and consideration to the
other. This is not as when one pays a due bill. Each one should
give due attention, respect, and whatever else is needed to
enable both to live in a wholesome way.

> The wife hath not power of her own body, but the husband: and
> likewise also the husband hath not power of his own body, but
> the wife (1 Cor. 7:4).

In other words, husband and wife are dependent on one
another.

> Defraud ye not one the other, except it be with consent for a
> time, that ye may give yourselves to fasting and prayer; and
> come together again, that Satan tempt you not for your inconti-
> nency (1 Cor. 7:5).

Actually Paul is coming as close to giving a principle of freedom
in marriage as is found anywhere in the Bible. This principle of
conduct can guide husband and wife in their marriage relationship in order that it might be under control. If husband and
wife abstain from personal fellowship with each other, this
should be with mutual agreement for spiritual reasons, and it
should be moderated. Such a situation is practical but it is not
to be made permanent. In verse 6 Paul writes, "I speak this by
permission, and not of commandment." Paul is saying, "This is
my advice, but I do not insist upon it."

Chapter 21

THE PROBLEM OF MARRIAGE

In the greater portion of 1 Corinthians 7 Paul discusses principles that could guide believers in the realm of marriage and divorce. His comments are noteworthy because they reflect a broad tolerance and a real insight into the earthly character of marital matters. To say that marriage is earthly is not to say it is evil, but only to recognize that it can easily be corrupted.

In this passage Paul seems to reveal that he has no absolute guidance as to what the mind of the Lord is in the various situations he discusses. This would seem to imply that whereas the principles of integrity and responsibility are always important for a believer, the actual performance may vary because of difference in understanding and judgment. It seems possible that in matters of personal conduct what seems acceptable to one person's conscience might be unacceptable to another. But Paul emphasizes that each person should act in good conscience in whatever he or she does about his or her marriage situation.

For I would that all men were even as I myself (1 Cor. 7:7).

In 1 Corinthians 7:7-9 Paul expressed the wish that all believers were as free from the need for marital relations as he was. Some think this implies that either he was unmarried or a widower. But others think this may mean only that he did not need his wife to accompany him on his missionary journeys. In any case he was able to carry on his ministry without needing female companionship. However Paul recognized that not all men were like this, and so he recommended that those who needed female companionship should marry.

In verses 10-16 Paul writes to believers who are married and urges them to consider the marriage relationship as permanent throughout their earthly pilgrimage. They should not separate with any plan to remarry someone else. Then he addresses himself to couples where one is an unbeliever, and urged the believer in each case to be ready to keep the marriage unbroken. However, when the unbeliever departs, the believer is not to be in any bondage.

We do know there is neither marrying nor giving in marriage in heaven (Matt. 22:30); and this seems to confirm my understanding that marriage is an earthly arrangement. However, because the believer is a child of God, the marriage relationship is to be regarded as holy because he is holy. And if a believer is married to an unbeliever, the blessedness of the believer in Christ is shared graciously with the unbelieving companion.

> But as God hath distributed to every man, as the Lord hath called every one, so let him walk. And so ordain I in all churches (1 Cor. 7:17).

Paul felt that each believer should accept personal responsibility to serve God in the personal situation in which he was living when he came to Christ. He made it clear in emphasizing that if a convert had been circumcised (as a Jew), he should accept the fact that he was a converted Jew; and if he had not been circumcised (being a Gentile), he should accept the fact that he was not a Jew but a converted Gentile.

> Circumcision is nothing, and uncircumcision is nothing, but the keeping of the commandments of God (1 Cor. 7:19).

Once more Paul made it plain that the observance of any religious practice or the omission of any religious practice had no bearing on the blessedness of a soul. But obeying the guidance of God in His Word by His Spirit did make a difference.

What was true about observing religious practices was also true about personal circumstances. In Corinth some believers were slaves in bondage, while others were free men. Paul urged the believers to disregard their status. In belonging to Christ they were all slaves to Him, and yet were free from all men. Nevertheless, having mentioned slavery, Paul urges believers to avoid being "the servants of men," since they had been "bought with a price." Rather believers should accept as permanent whatever status they were in when they were called of God, and "therein abide with God."

In the latter portion of this chapter Paul discussed the whole matter of marriage in general terms. He was writing to believers who could depend on the providence and the grace of God in their living experiences. He did not want his comments to be taken as direct revelations of God's will, but he offered his own judgment as from "one that hath obtained mercy of the Lord to be faithful" (v. 25).

Apparently Paul believed that marriage was an optional condition, permissible under God, but not an unmixed blessing. Certainly it would be temporary, since life in this world is short compared to the eternal life believers have in Christ. But marriage would not be without liabilities. In marriage the believer would face the risk of divided interests: because he was a believer he would want to please the Lord, but being married he would want to please his wife. Paul pointed this out so the Corinthian believers might understand some of the problems that are involved in being married.

At the same time Paul understood that marriage could be helpful to some despite the problems. And he did not want any believer to feel it was a sin to marry. There were responsibilities involved in being married, and Paul wanted the believers to maintain their integrity with one another and before God.

> So then he that giveth her in marriage doeth well; but he that giveth her not in marriage doeth better (1 Cor. 7:38).

Paul was not dogmatic in setting forth his judgment, but he felt that what he had written was true:

> . . . and I think also that I have the Spirit of God (1 Cor. 7:40).

Chapter 22

OF EATING MEAT OFFERED TO IDOLS

In 1 Corinthians 8 Paul began a rather long discussion of a problem that had its roots in some of the pagan practices which were prevalent in Corinth. The believers who lived in Corinth were surrounded by pagan neighbors. There was always the temptation for them to share with their neighbors in popular pagan practices. It is much the same way in which we today live among worldly people. When I use the term *worldly people*, I do not mean to be unkind, nor am I making light of them. I merely recognize the fact that many persons naturally have their hearts and minds and consciousness filled with the things of this world. Believers, on the contrary, are related to another world.

How could these believers in Corinth living among pagan neighbors be tempted to act as their neighbors did? Surely they could not join them in matters of customs and worship. The pagan people had made gods of their own, and it was their custom and religion to worship these gods by offering them food offerings. They would take a platter of food to the temple and offer it to their god as a form of worship.

Recently, while traveling in the Orient, I was on the island of Taiwan, where I visited a Buddhist temple. While I was in the temple, a young Buddhist father came to worship his idol. He brought with him a large tray of prepared food. There was boiled pork, veal, and chicken. Then there were plates of vegetables, and other foods. All of this was placed before the idol as an offering. As we know, his god could not eat it. So in a day or two this man would return and take this food home to eat.

The people who practiced this had a feeling that such offerings were of special value. They believed that meat offered to an idol was better than other meat, so they expected a special blessing when they ate it. Even pagans would sometimes buy such meat in order to share in the blessing that had been bestowed on the meat by the idol. Believers in Corinth had shared in such customs before they came to faith in the Lord Jesus Christ. Now the question arose whether they should now partake of such meat when it was set before them by a pagan friend.

Should a believer eat meat that had been offered to idols? Some believers refused to eat this meat, for they felt that by eating it their testimony would be compromised. They feared that if they ate of the meat which had been offered to idols, it would imply that they still believed in idols. Other believers would eat the meat because they felt it was as good after it had been offered to idols as it had been before. This is why the Corinthians had written to the apostle Paul to ask him which practice was correct.

We can feel the significance of various contemporary issues that face us. There are things that people around us do in which we cannot join, even if they are our relatives and friends. The questions could come up, Should we as believers feel free to do as others do? What should control our conduct? Should we consider what effect our acts will have on others? These are the same things that Paul was considering.

> Now as touching things offered unto idols, we know that we all have knowledge. Knowledge puffeth up, but charity edifieth (1 Cor. 8:1).

Paul was saying, "We all understand about life, although our understanding may differ in some ways." Then Paul made a simple statement: "Knowledge puffeth up, but charity edifieth." This means that when we feel that we know and understand things, we are tempted to be proud and to look down on others. Feeling that someone else knows and understands less than we do puffs us up and builds up our own ego. On the other hand, if we are interested in the welfare of others, we will do our best to build up their confidence. When we do this, we will find that as we build up others, we will automatically be built up ourselves.

And if any man think that he knoweth any thing, he knoweth
nothing yet as he ought to know (1 Cor. 8:2).

That was a strong statement, but it was completely true. Paul
said to all who thought themselves wise and knowledgeable
that they were making a big mistake. They had the wrong idea.
Anyone who has not learned to love has not learned the most
basic essential of life. Of course some doctors know more than
other doctors, and some people drive a car better than other
people. But none of this should make a man proud and puffed
up.

But if any man love God, the same is known of him (1 Cor. 8:3).

To be able to truly love other people we must first love God.
Only then are we known to Him. Only then will we want to do
His will, serve Him, and seek to build up and encourage
others.

As concerning therefore the eating of those things that are
offered in sacrifice unto idols, we know that an idol is nothing in
the world, and that there is none other God but one. For though
there be that are called gods, whether in heaven or in earth, (as
there be gods many, and lords many,) but to us there is but one
God, the Father, of whom are all things, and we in him; and one
Lord Jesus Christ, by whom are all things, and we by him.
Howbeit there is not in every man that knowledge: for some
with conscience of the idol unto this hour eat it as a thing offered
unto an idol; and their conscience being weak is defiled. But
meat commendeth us not to God: for neither, if we eat, are we
the better; neither, if we eat not, are we the worse (1 Cor. 8:4-8).

Paul told the Corinthian believers that the meat which has
been offered to idols was just as good as it was before it was
placed before the idol because "the idol is nothing."

Chapter 23

DENIAL OF SELF FOR THE SAKE OF OTHERS

Before we go on with that portion of Paul's letter to the Corinthians that deals with the eating of meat which has been offered to idols, I would like to discuss some similar situations believers may face today. I hesitate to point out present circumstances that represent the same kind of problem, though I feel that this may be helpful in understanding the problems those early believers in Corinth faced.

For just a moment let us consider the issue of playing cards. Anyone could say, "Cards are nothing but pieces of pasteboard. So if we have fifty-two of those pieces of pasteboard, that's nothing." Now this may be true for some, but it is not true for everybody. There are some who feel that the very playing cards themselves have something evil about them. I know a number of people who would not allow a deck of playing cards to be brought into their homes. Others have cards lying around, feeling that one might as well get used to the idea that there is nothing to them.

Now in Corinth, among the believers, there were some who still believed that idols had real existence. They worshiped the true God but felt guilty in their consciences about eating meat that had been offered to idols. In this way, "their conscience being weak is defiled." In verse 8 Paul makes this general statement: "Meat commendeth us not to God." It is not the eating of meat or, for that matter, the playing of cards that makes the difference.

> . . . for neither, if we eat, are we the better; neither, if we eat not, are we the worse. But take heed lest by any means this liberty of yours become a stumbling block to them that are weak (1 Cor. 8:8-9).

Take, for instance, the matter of drinking beer. Many people feel that beer is just a stimulant, so why not drink it? Some believers do drink beer. In fact I have known some ministers who drink beer. They will do so just to show how free they are. Most of us will know that when a preacher acts in this way, he is showing a selfish lack of consideration for other people. "Take heed lest by any means this liberty of yours become a stumblingblock to them that are weak." Let us keep in mind that to those people who consider drinking beer to be wrong, it could well be wrong.

> For if any man see thee which hast knowledge sit at meat in the idol's temple, shall not the conscience of him which is weak be emboldened to eat those things which are offered to idols? (1 Cor. 8:10).

In these words Paul puts out a danger signal. Believers should beware lest some be tempted to act against their conscience when they see other believers "sit at meat in the idol's temple." It is like seeing a minister or any church member going into a bar and having a drink, or sitting with a group of people playing poker. There are some men for whom drinking beer is harmful, and they may begin to drink because others do it. Some men cannot resist gambling; if they see a church member playing poker, they will feel free to do it. Paul is asking:

> And through thy knowledge shall the weak brother perish, for whom Christ died? But when ye sin so against the brethren, and wound their weak conscience, ye sin against Christ (1 Cor. 8:11-12).

These are words of severe indictment. It seems evident that because a believer may feel clear in his conscience about doing certain things, that is not good enough.

There are two questions that should be kept in mind: How do our actions look to other people? and What do they think of our conduct? It will not do for a believer to say, "What I did was right for me, and if people do not like it, that is their problem." Wait a minute! This is something that takes mature thought. The fact that someone feels the believer is wrong should stop the believer in his tracks. "When ye sin so against the brethren, and wound their weak conscience, ye sin against Christ." This must be the guideline in the conduct of believers at all times.

> Wherefore, if meat make my brother to offend, I will eat no flesh while the world standeth, lest I make my brother to offend (1 Cor. 8:13).

It is possible for a believer to do something he feels is perfectly right, but by his act he may set an example that will encourage others to act against their conscience.

The principle involved here worked for me on one occasion in a significant way. It developed for me in the whole matter of driving my car on the highway. In my capacity as a minister I was often in a hurry to meet my appointments. It was possible for me to own a good car and keep it in good working condition. I was young and my reflexes were quick. I was a good driver and drove literally hundreds of thousands of miles before I ever had an accident. I often had a twinge of conscience about exceeding the posted speed limits, but this did not change my driving habits. Then one day I realized that by driving in this way, I was setting an example. Some other person, whose car or reflexes were not in as good a condition as mine were, could be following me and have an accident. When the impact of this came home to me, it slowed me down.

The impact of that truth has slowed me down to this day. When I act in a way that hurts other people or leads them into something that could hurt them, I am actually hurting Christ. As Christians we must decide how our actions may affect others and live accordingly, by the grace of God.

Chapter 24

THE PERSONAL TESTIMONY OF A MINISTER

Two vitally important considerations face every believer in the matter of personal conduct and its effect on other believers. The apostle Paul in discussing this subject is very positive in his views. In all our conduct as believers we must first be certain that what we are doing is right in our own judgment. Secondly, we should ask ourselves whether what we are doing is right or offensive to the conscience of others. The apostle Paul has affirmed that he himself would not do anything to offend the conscientious scruples of any other believer.

While I was a pastor in a certain city, I was invited to attend a wrestling match. As it turned out, I could not go and I told the man who had invited me that I had something else to do. In that city every Thursday night featured a wrestling match. So the following week he called and asked me to go with him on Thursday night. I told him that I was sorry, but I had something else I must do, which was the truth. Realizing that in all probability this man would ask me again, I arranged to have something to do on Thursday nights thereafter. After he had asked me several times, he said to me, "Preacher, I don't think that you want to go." So I told him with a smile, "Well, friend, if you put it that way, you're right." He turned on me quickly, "Why, you don't think there is anything wrong with wrestling, do you?" He happened to know that I used to be a boxer myself.

In response I told him that in my congregation were some dear elderly ladies. If they heard that their pastor attended a wrestling match, they would feel greatly disappointed and offended. Any one of these ladies could be on her deathbed at any time, and at such a time she would send for me. Somehow I would not feel right if I came straight from a wrestling match to visit someone who looked to me for words of comfort and assurance from the Word of God.

"Well," the man replied, "any of your members who object to wrestling are just narrow-minded. I would think as a believer you would be free to do as you please." This gave me the opportunity to tell him that living in obedience to Christ sets me absolutely free. He said, "You are not free to go to a wrestling match." I said easily, "You do not understand because you are not living in obedience to Christ. I am free from even wanting to go."

At another time I had a similar experience. I was raised on a farm where we boys used to race our farm horses. They were understandably slow, but we had fun seeing who could beat the other fellow's horse to the pasture. When horse racing was legalized in our state, and a new race track was built near our city, I really wanted to see a good horse race. So I wanted on my first day off to go and see a horse race. I had no desire to gamble; I just wanted to see it. I still do not feel that there is anything wrong with that. Then why wouldn't I go? I just did not feel that it would look right for a minister to attend a horse race.

Someone might say, "If your conscience does not bother you, it should be all right for you to go." No, that is the very point I am making. Just because my conscience is clear still does not make it right for me. What about other people? Some of them would think it was wrong for me a minister of the gospel to attend a horse race because of the environment. Their thinking it to be wrong would make it wrong for me to go.

In 1 Corinthians 9 Paul clarified his attitude in this matter of freedom to act.

> Am I not an apostle? am I not free? have I not seen Jesus Christ our Lord? are not ye my work in the Lord? If I be not an apostle unto others, yet doubtless I am to you: for the seal of mine apostleship are ye in the Lord (1 Cor. 9:1-2).

Here Paul gave proof of his apostleship and reminded the Corinthians of his effective ministry among them.

> Mine answer to them that do examine me is this, Have we not power to eat and to drink? (1 Cor. 9:3-4).

The implication was, of course, that Paul had the freedom to eat meat offered to idols and to drink wine, yet he did neither.

> Have we not power to lead about a sister, a wife, as well as other apostles, and as the brethren of the Lord, and Cephas? (1 Cor. 9:5).

In other words Paul is saying, "Am I not permitted to have a house and family?" Apparently Paul had neither a wife nor a family, although he knew he was free to have both.

Then Paul took up another matter that concerned him and Barnabas. Both of these men were great preachers who worked to support themselves. We may remember that every Jewish boy had to learn a trade, and Paul had been trained to be a tentmaker. He worked at this trade while he preached the gospel, and was mightily used of God. Now Paul asks:

> . . . have not we power to forbear working? Who goeth a warfare any time at his own charges? who planteth a vineyard, and eateth not of the fruit thereof? or who feedeth a flock, and eateth not of the milk of the flock? Say I these things as a man? or saith not the law the same also? (1 Cor. 9:6-8).

In other words, should not the man who is preaching the gospel live by the gospel?

> If we have sown unto you spiritual things, is it a great thing if we shall reap your carnal things? If others be partakers of this power over you, are not we rather? Nevertheless we have not used this power; but suffer all things, lest we should hinder the gospel of Christ (1 Cor. 9:11-12).

Paul asked, "If we supply the need of your souls, is it too much that you supply our bodily needs?" And yet the apostle, who had every right and freedom to receive support from them, did not accept it, "lest we should hinder the gospel of Christ." Here again we see that the first consideration of every believer is to do nothing that might hinder the spread of the gospel.

Chapter 25

SELF-DENIAL IN A MINISTER FOR THE SAKE OF THE GOSPEL

As we proceed with our study in the ninth chapter of Paul's First Epistle to the Corinthians, we find that he continued to emphasize the fact that believers should seek above all else to please God. He pointed out again that believers should not choose to act according to their own desires, nor even according to their own rights and privileges. A servant of Christ will be guided by a desire to please God and to be helpful to other people.

In this chapter Paul discussed his own procedure as a preacher. He reminded the Corinthians how both he and Barnabas actually worked with their hands to earn their own support, instead of depending upon the congregation in Corinth to supply it. This is one aspect of his ministry that was unusual. In Paul's Second Letter to the Corinthians, he writes about the fact that by working for his own support, he had not presented among them the usual ministry. He explained that he did this to advance the gospel. He did not want to be burdensome to them, in order not to give occasion for offense, that the preaching of the gospel might not be hindered among them. The apostle offered himself and discussed himself and presented himself as an example of acting under controlled restraint. He purposely did not do the things he had a right to do.

Paul expressed the general principle that it is right in the sight of God that they who preach the gospel should live by the gospel.

> Do ye not know that they which minister about holy things live of the things of the temple? and they which wait at the altar are partakers with the altar? (1 Cor. 9:13).

In the Old Testament the tribe of Levi was ordained to serve in the temple of God. They were given their own cities in which to dwell and received their living from those who came to worship, according to the law of God. They were appointed to "wait at the altar," which means to serve at the altar, as waiters in a restaurant wait on those who come to dine.

> Even so hath the Lord ordained that they which preach the gospel should live of the gospel (1 Cor. 9:14).

This was the will of God, and it certainly would have been Paul's privilege to take advantage of this.

> But I have used none of these things: neither have I written these things, that it should be so done unto me: for it were better for me to die, than that any man should make my glorying void (1 Cor. 9:15).

This was an illustration of the very thing Paul had been talking about. Paul was saying that he had a perfect right to expect that the believers in Corinth should support him. He did not exercise this right — there were special local reasons why he went out and earned his own living. He gloried in the fact that in order to advance the gospel, he had put himself under extra responsibility and strain. But Paul went on to say that he did not do this to receive the praise of men. He took no credit for himself for this self-denial.

> For though I preach the gospel, I have nothing to glory of: for necessity is laid upon me; yea, woe is unto me, if I preach not the gospel! (1 Cor. 9:16).

Here again Paul emphasized that he wanted neither praise nor credit for any self-denial on his part. He had an inner compulsion, a divine urgency, to preach the gospel.

> For if I do this thing willingly, I have a reward . . . (1 Cor. 9:17).

By this Paul meant that if he did gladly what the Lord wanted him to do, he would have a reward.

> . . . but if against my will, a dispensation of the gospel is committed unto me (1 Cor. 9:17).

Paul is saying, "If I find myself dissatisfied with my task, if deep down in my spirit I am not enthusiastic when preaching, woe is unto me." The literal translation of the word *dispensation* would be "house order," so this would mean "a special assignment is given unto me." This was a direct order from his Master: he must preach. Paul pointed out that a willingness to preach brought with it blessing.

Since Paul had preached the gospel with power, gladly and willingly, what would be the final outcome?

> What is my reward then? Verily that, when I preach the gospel,
> I may make the gospel of Christ without charge, that I abuse not
> my power in the gospel (1 Cor. 9:18).

To Paul this meant he should be an obedient and willing servant of the Lord Jesus Christ. His willingness to preach without pay in order to advocate the spreading of the gospel is an example of his self-control. It is an example of a disciplined use of liberty to the end that his preaching should not be hindered in any way. It is interesting to note that he was answerable to no man. He was free. No human being could tell him what to do. Whatever he did, he did unto the Lord and for His approval.

There are many Christians whose personal lives may seem quite ordinary. They have not been called to preach, and yet they can serve the Lord wherever they are. They may never receive any recognition or even expect it; however, they will receive God's blessing when they are inwardly willing and anxious to do the will of God in all they undertake and do.

Chapter 26

PAUL'S PROCEDURE IN SERVING CHRIST

In discussing the problem of liberty in conduct for a believer, the apostle gave personal testimony as to how he had been led to forego personal privileges that he might not leave a wrong impression with other believers. Now he testifies even more fully the frame of mind that he adopted to govern his own conduct.

> For though I be free from all men, yet have I made myself servant unto all, that I might gain the more (1 Cor. 9:19).

Paul knew he had been set free from ceremonial regulations by the death of Christ but he did not take this to mean that he had any license to act as he might want to act as a human being. He took himself in hand and made himself to be a servant to all men that he might win more souls to Christ. If he had allowed himself to act in ways that would irritate or offend others, he would have alienated some whom he might have won to the Lord.

> And unto the Jews I became as a Jew, that I might gain the Jews; to them that are under the law, as under the law, that I might gain them that are under the law; to them that are without law, as without law, (being not without law to God, but under the law to Christ,) that I might gain them that are without law. To the weak became I as weak, that I might gain the weak: I am made all things to all men, that I might by all means save some (1 Cor. 9:20-22).

Paul took the time to spell out exactly what he did so that the Corinthians would understand that he did not think any specific mode of conduct was either right or wrong. He was free to act one way or another, but what he did was under control: he did what he did "on purpose." He was willing to act like anyone he was with, but always with the same objective: he wanted to win souls to Christ.

When the Scripture says, "Whosoever will may come," the doors are being flung wide open so that anyone can come to Christ. The person who comes must follow the guidance of someone who knows the gospel. He will do this more readily if that other person acts in a manner similar to himself. Thus Paul artfully acted like a Jew when he was with Jews and like a Gentile when he was with Gentiles. But his purpose never varied: he wanted to win souls to Christ by sharing with them the gospel.

> And this I do for the gospel's sake, that I might be partaker thereof with you (1 Cor. 9:23).

Such conduct on the part of Paul involved self-discipline, which Paul described as being similar to the practice common to athletes in competitive sports. In the case of runners in a track event, it is known that only one can win in a race. The successful competitor is definitely self-controlled as the result of a regimen of self-discipline. Paul indicated that just as athletes control themselves to win a temporary crown, he disciplined himself that he might win an eternal crown.

Paul then changed the figure of speech from a track event to boxing. Just as a successful boxer controls his movements, even so Paul controlled his bodily activities, "buffeting" his body to bring it under control. Paul admitted frankly that he adopted this rigorous course of self-discipline because he did not want to be barren in his relationship with the Lord. It seems obvious that a believer has some responsibility in the matter of being fruitful in his service in the Lord.

This discussion in which Paul describes his own procedure as a servant of Christ follows in the context of his discussion of the problem of a believer's liberty to eat meat that had been publicly offered to pagan idols. Paul appreciated the freedom of the forgiven believer who knew the pagan idol had no real power, but he had testified to his own conduct when he considered the effect his actions might have in tempting some weaker brother to offend his own conscience.

> Wherefore, if meat make my brother to offend, I will eat no flesh while the world standeth, lest I make my brother to offend (1 Cor. 8:13).

After having pointed out he was as free as any other believer to act as he wanted to, Paul described the rigorous control he practiced on himself for the sake of his effectiveness among all men as a witness for Christ.

Chapter 27

THE BELIEVER MUST BE CAUTIOUS

Paul had first discussed the problem of a believer's liberty to eat meat offered to idols from the point of view of the believer's own understanding, and then had set forth his own witness in his own deliberate self-denial, in which he refused to allow himself any liberty in conduct that might cause some weaker brother to do wrong. Now in 1 Corinthians 10 Paul turned to the testimony of Scriptures for further insight into this problem.

In 1 Corinthians 8–10 Paul has advanced several opinions on the Exodus to show that there were Hebrews delivered from Egypt who did not continue in the blessing of God. Apparently Paul meant this historical reference to serve as a warning to believers in Corinth.

> Wherefore let him that thinketh he standeth take heed lest he fall (1 Cor. 10:12).

There seems to be no reason why any believer should ever feel that he is confronted by a situation that compels him to act out of the will of God. Undoubtedly, circumstances may put the believer in a difficult spot, but yielding to pressure to act out of the will of God is not necessary. God will have prepared the situation so that the believer can get out of it without compromising his testimony.

> There hath no temptation taken you but such as is common to man: but God is faithful, who will not suffer you to be tempted above that ye are able; but will with the temptation also make a way to escape, that ye may be able to bear it (1 Cor. 10:13).

In view of these considerations, which he had outlined to the believers in Corinth, Paul urged them to keep away from all pagan practices.

> Wherefore, my dearly beloved, flee from idolatry (1 Cor. 10:14).

He then appeals to their good common sense to see the importance of such procedure.

> I speak as to wise men; judge ye what I say (1 Cor. 10:15).

The very nature of the sacrament of the Lord's Supper should help them to see it is not fitting that any believer should eat meat offered to idols. When we eat the bread and drink the cup of blessing in the sacrament, we know that we are celebrating our communion in the body of Christ. Regardless of what we think of their idols or of their practices, the Gentiles offer their sacrifices as "to devils." When any believer shares in their worship, he is sharing in something offered to devils. And it does not make sense to be a partaker of the Lord's table and a partaker "of the table of devils."

> The cup of blessing which we bless, is it not the communion of the blood of Christ? The bread which we break, is it not the communion of the body of Christ? (1 Cor. 10:16).

> What say I then? that the idol is any thing, or that which is offered in sacrifice to idols is any thing? But I say, that the things which the Gentiles sacrifice, they sacrifice to devils, and not to God: and I would not that ye should have fellowship with devils. Ye cannot drink the cup of the Lord, and the cup of devils: ye cannot be partakers of the Lord's table, and of the table of devils (1 Cor. 10:19-21).

Paul warned the believers in Corinth that to share in the worship of the pagans was to be in danger of offending God.

> Do we provoke the Lord to jealousy? are we stronger than he? (1 Cor. 10:22).

Chapter 28

THE BELIEVER AND THE
OTHER MAN'S CONSCIENCE

In our previous chapter I have stressed the fact that the apostle Paul counsels the Corinthians again and again that their conduct should be blameless before the world. Now some people might feel that to be greatly concerned about the opinions of others shows a lack of sincerity. To them it would appear insincere to always do what others expect of them. I would like to comment on this, to show what is involved here.

Things can be right or wrong depending on the circumstances. For instance, if we went to church barefoot, or if the preacher went to the pulpit barefoot, we would say that was disrespectful. Yet there would be nothing wrong with a man being barefoot in his shower. A man could be properly or improperly dressed depending on the circumstances. How would he know? By looking around to see what was expected of him. In other words, a man will be guided in his conduct by what others think of it.

In 1 Corinthians 8-10 Paul has advanced several opinions on the subject of a believer's conduct. One of these was that nothing in itself is either bad or good. Then he points out that any act has value and meaning according to the intention of the person who does it. This makes the difference. Next he points out that a believer in Christ will conduct himself in such a way that others will not be offended. And finally, a believer will not be guided by what is right in his own eyes, when in doing so he hurts other people.

In 1 Corinthians 10:23-30 the apostle Paul writes some important regulations which all Christians should observe. In verse 12 of chapter 6 he writes, "All things are lawful unto me, but all things are not expedient: all things are lawful for me, but

I will not be brought under the power of any." In 10:23 there is a great similarity in the words, and yet Paul placed a different emphasis on them. In this instance he wrote: "All things are lawful for me, but all things are not expedient." So far his second statement is the same as the first, but then he wrote, "All things are lawful for me, but all things edify not." By this he means that all things do not build up or improve the soul in a spiritual way. A certain action may be valid and legitimate, but it may not be constructively helpful. It might be better to leave such an act undone.

> Let no man seek his own, but every man another's wealth (1 Cor. 10:24).

Paul wrote this general formula which covered all situations. This is the key to proper conduct. When we seek and do and plan for ourselves, we are sure to be disappointed. "Seek another's wealth." Seek what is good and helpful to the other person. By the grace of God, let us give up the idea of getting our own way. As we think about other people and seek their welfare, we will be blessed.

> Whatsoever is sold in the shambles, that eat, asking no question for conscience sake: for the earth is the Lord's and the fulness thereof (1 Cor. 10:25-26).

The word *shambles* means an "open market." Paul wrote that if in such an outdoor market meat is sold, there is no need to ask questions about it. The buyer need ask no questions as to where it came from. Is the meat good? Then he may buy it. When it was offered in public and no one else was interested, believers were to use their own judgment. This same rule holds true for believers in everything in life. However, this would not apply to doing anything foolish, or something that is wrong in the sight of God. Apart from that believers have total freedom to do as they like. They can wear a hat or go without one. They can wear shoes or go without them. They can do anything they want to.

> If any of them that believe not bid you to a feast, and ye be disposed to go; whatsoever is set before you, eat, asking no question for conscience sake (1 Cor. 10:27).

Surely these words spell out perfect liberty. If one who is not a believer in Christ invites a believer to a feast, the believer is to partake of the food set before him. He need not ask whether the meat which is being served had been offered to idols.

> But if any man say unto you, This is offered in sacrifice unto idols, eat not for his sake that showed it, and for conscience sake: for the earth is the Lord's, and the fulness thereof: conscience, I say, not thine own, but of the other (1 Cor. 10:28-29).

Notice Paul's reason: "For the earth is the Lord's, and the fulness thereof." Here is a wonderful spiritual principle that is most important. Because everything belongs to the Lord, a believer can take it or leave it. He can have it or do without it. He is free. "Conscience, I say, not thine own, but of the other." Paul clarifies this phrase by asking a question:

> For why is my liberty judged of another man's conscience? For if I by grace be a partaker, why am I evil spoken of for that which I give thanks? (1 Cor. 10:29-30).

As we consider this, we should note that our attitudes should be flexible, ready to meet any given situation. Believers are at complete liberty until their testimony as believers, whether by speech or by action, is affected. Then they are under total restraint, and they fit themselves into the situation in such a way as to cause no offense. This is not being hypocritical, when we conform in our conduct by considering other persons. We should keep in mind at all times that our way of life is under close scrutiny by others.

Chapter 29

PAUL'S DELIBERATE PROCEDURE

At the end of 1 Corinthians 10 Paul concludes his discussion about a believer's conduct. He has emphasized over and over that a believer's actions make a difference both to himself and to others. Interestingly enough, the difference is not because of what any activity is in itself. The difference lies in the reaction of others.

> Whether therefore ye eat, or drink, or whatsoever ye do, do all
> to the glory of God (1 Cor. 10:31).

We are so accustomed to saying these words that we are in danger of missing their great importance. We must not fail to note that when Paul says, "Whatsoever ye do, do all to the glory of God," he is urging believers not to allow themselves any personal interest. When we "do all to the glory of God," this means that we seek to please God in everything we do, and so we do not follow our own wishes and desires. Such a definite way of doing things is possible only for a crucified man.

Some believers are too immature in their faith to realize what this means. In writing to the Galatians, Paul wrote, "I am crucified with Christ," and "They that are Christ's have crucified the flesh with the affections and lusts." By such statements he is saying, "My ego is crucified. I have no personal interests now." In Romans 6:11 Paul wrote: "Likewise reckon ye also yourselves to be dead indeed unto sin, but alive unto God through Jesus Christ our Lord." We would all agree that a corpse does not care about what is going on. Someone will say, "A person could not live that way." But, he can. Or perhaps I should say, he can die that way. Paul wrote, "I am crucified with Christ: nevertheless I live; yet not I, but Christ liveth in me" (Gal. 2:20). Our Lord Jesus Christ said, "If any man will be my disciple, let him deny himself."

Conduct is a matter that includes not only the way you wear your hat, or what you wear; but it includes anything and everything you do. Conduct is evident in the way you live with your family, your neighbors, and your business associates. In everything the major consideration is self-denial.

When any situation or issue comes up, and the believer is face to face with some problem of conduct, his first safe rule is, "Thumbs down on himself." This is true even when his feelings and emotions become involved. No one else may know when one's "old self" takes over, but anything motivated by personal feeling will hurt the believer. His major consideration must still be self-denial. When he puts the glory of God first and puts himself out of the picture, he cannot be offended when he is badly treated. He can forget it. When he is made to look bad, he can forget it. In fact, this would solve all his problems of conduct. When believers do all to the glory of God, they have no trouble. So I would say he must yield, give up, give in, let go! He must be Christ's servant. It may work differently from what he expects, but it will be good if he trusts God and walks in His way.

> Give none offence, neither to the Jews, nor to the Gentiles, nor
> to the church of God (1 Cor. 10:32).

That's it! The believer will not hurt anyone's feelings. He will not hinder anyone in anything he says or does.

Paul writes: "Do not offend the Jews." They are people who have a cultural tradition. They respect certain days above others. Do not offend them. If we cannot agree with them, let's keep it to ourselves. "Nor to the Gentiles." The Gentiles are interested in personal value; they crave athletic distinction, fame, fortune, and so on. Perhaps this does not appeal to us, but it does to them. Do not offend them, belittle them, or laugh at them. "Nor to the church of God." This would concern spiritual issues. There are church members who feel strongly about evangelism or missions or their church program. Do not offend them.

Even as I please all men in all things, not seeking mine own profit, but the profit of many, that they may be saved (1 Cor. 10:33).

In the final analysis this must be our only consideration. Whatever we do, may we do it in order to turn others to the Lord. Only this bears fruit for eternity.

Chapter 30

GUIDANCE FOR PUBLIC CONDUCT

Before we begin our study of 1 Corinthians 11, I want to give you some background on the religious customs in pagan Corinth. The religious life of that community was centered around the pagan temples. These temples were administered largely by women. This in itself would seem acceptable enough except that in that part of the country their public conduct was notorious. These priestesses performed their temple rites in lewd and depraved ways. Actually it was so immoral and scandalous that many people who were not especially religious were offended by and disgusted at these so-called religious rites. Men and women everywhere felt a sense of aversion and disgust with the whole situation. This caused people to have a genuine skepticism about anything that was religious.

The Christian gospel has emancipated women wherever it is preached. Women all over the world have suffered, and in many countries still suffer, social bondage. There are parts of the world where certain social customs bind women to places of servitude. It has been characteristic of the Christian gospel to set women free both as individuals and as family members.

In Corinth this freedom from bondage that Christian women enjoyed was mistaken by outsiders of the church as being related to pagan license. Paul, who was aware of all this, offered the Christian women guidance. He gave them a reason for being careful in their public conduct, in order to avoid the stigma of a bad reputation. Because the priestesses of the pagan temples had become so notorious, any woman active in religion was in danger of being compared to the scandalous women in the temple.

Be ye followers of me, even as I also am of Christ (1 Cor. 11:1).

Here Paul made a direct appeal to these people to follow him as a guide. In effect he said, "Follow me, because I am following after the Lord."

Now I praise you, brethren, that ye remember me in all things, and keep the ordinances, as I delivered them to you (1 Cor. 11:2).

Paul gave a word of praise and encouragement to these believers who have kept the ordinances which the apostle had delivered to them. Next he set forth a general principle in the matter of the prominence of women in the church.

But I would have you know, that the head of every man is Christ; and the head of the woman is the man; and the head of Christ is God (1 Cor. 11:3).

I know there will be some women who will feel uneasy when they read that "the head of the woman is the man." They may interpret this to mean that they are being given an inferior position. But when we read, "the head of every man is Christ" and "the head of Christ is God," we see that the woman is not given an inferior position, but rather a *relational* position.

If there are a number of people going somewhere together, someone takes the lead, and the rest will follow. When Paul said, "The head of every man is Christ," this merely meant that Christ was in the lead and the man followed. "The head of the woman is the man." In a family situation the man must be expected to be the leader, and the woman as his helper by his side. Paul is not low-rating women. He is simply recognizing that in any social environment the man in the family takes the initiative.

Every man praying or prophesying, having his head covered, dishonoureth his head (1 Cor. 11:4).

The word *prophesying* in the New Testament means "preaching." For a man to take an active part in public services with his head covered would bring dishonor upon himself, according to the custom in Corinth.

But every woman that prayeth or prophesieth with her head uncovered dishonoureth her head: for that is even all one as if she were shaven (1 Cor. 11:5).

This was also the custom in Corinth. The men went bare-headed and the women wore hats. The general feeling was that when a woman wore a hat she would act like a woman, and this would be right in everyone's eyes.

> For if the woman be not covered, let her also be shorn: but if it be a shame for a woman to be shorn or shaven, let her be covered (1 Cor. 11:6).

Whenever we see the word *shame* we know that this is a human opinion, with God the word is *sin*. Paul concludes with a statement of the spiritual principle.

> For a man indeed ought not to cover his head, forasmuch as he is the image and glory of God: but the woman is the glory of the man (1 Cor. 11:7).

Chapter 31

THE SIGNIFICANCE OF PUBLIC CONDUCT

Before we continue our study in chapter 11 of 1 Corinthians, let me repeat a general comment on Paul's epistle as a whole. We have followed his writings of advice, instruction, and solution in regard to the problems the Corinthians faced, living as Christian believers in a pagan city. Someone may wonder why those who are members of Christ need instructions. In reply I would reemphasize that although Christian life begins in a moment, learning and growing in spiritual knowledge and wisdom is a lifetime process. The soul accepts Christ Jesus as Savior and Lord, then God sends His Holy Spirit into that soul. It is then that the believer learns in actual experience what is involved in putting off the old nature, the old man, and putting on the new.

The general truth is that this putting off of the old and putting on of the new can often be a painful uphill climb. Problems can occur in specific situations, as was happening in Corinth. The apostle Paul could have said at the very beginning, "Let the Lord Jesus have His way in your life." Actually he is saying this throughout his letter as he deals with the specific situations which had arisen in the lives of these young Christians: "Let Jesus Christ dwell in you; let Jesus Christ rule in you."

If there are divisions in the church, if there is toleration of open sin, let the Lord Jesus overrule in these matters. If there is quarrelsomeness, if there is carnal behavior, if there are problems between husbands and wives and questions of divorce arise, let Christ Jesus rule in that. Paul has in this epistle counseled in the matter of liberty in conduct: whether it is a matter of pleasing self, or whether consideration for others should come first. The solution to this problem, also, is to look to the Lord Jesus Christ. Seeking to please Him in all we do would solve every problem.

The situation with which Paul is dealing in this chapter includes a problem involving the place of women in the church. Apparently there was some question and opposition in Corinth in regard to women assuming prominent positions in the life of the congregation. Actually, there was no need for confusion in this matter, as so many people today seem to believe. Controversy based on this passage seems completely unwarranted. When we consider this passage as a whole, we will readily see that as far as public worship in Corinth was concerned, the men would be in charge, and the women were to dress and act like women. They were to help the men in their various assignments and duties.

Paul discussed the wearing of a covering on the head of women in public meetings, yet this does not teach that women ought not to pray or preach in public.

> But every woman that prayeth or prophesieth with her head uncovered dishonoureth her head: for that is even all one as if she were shaven (1 Cor. 11:5).

This verse only points out that when women pray or prophesy they are to wear a covering on their heads. The important emphasis to note here is that a woman is to be feminine. She is not to act like a man but like a woman. We have noted that in the rituals held in the pagan temple, women were unduly prominent over and above the man. They were also scandalous in their conduct. This caused many people to be uneasy about religion as a whole, and particularly in regard to the new liberty the Christian gospel gave to women. The gospel sets women free from bondage.

The matter of headcovering was a Corinthian custom. In our culture until some years ago we were accustomed to seeing dresses on women and trousers on men. We recognize that there have been cultural changes not only in the matter of clothes, but also in the matter of hair. Short hair on women and long hair on men becomes a matter of confusion, which I need not go into. Paul was concerned that the custom of Corinth should not be ignored by the believers.

Among the native Indians in America men wore long hair, but they were masculine. Chinese men braided their hair and wore gowns, and in their culture this certainly did not make them feminine. Paul would say, "Let the Chinese dress according to their custom, and the Indians according to their custom." In Corinth it was natural and proper for women to wear hats. This was the accepted practice in that city. Pauls summarized this when he wrote:

> But if any man seem to be contentious, we have no such custom, neither the churches of God (1 Cor. 11:16).

In other words, if anyone wants to make an issue of these things, let him remember that the church of God is free from all exterior customs. Believers conformed to them in order not to hinder the preaching of the gospel. They continued in these customs so as not to give offense to those outside the church. They did not want to be guilty of hindering the preaching of the gospel.

Chapter 32

RIGHT CONDUCT AT THE LORD'S SUPPER

The life of a believer involves problems arising out of individual judgments and attitudes and out of social relationships. An individual's personal conduct affects other persons, and this causes problems. And each believer's conduct is open before God. Because the believer is reconciled to God by the death of Jesus Christ His Son, the heavenly Father has a direct personal interest in the conduct of the believer. God wants the conduct of believers to honor His Son who gave Himself for them.

It was the custom of believers to share in a love feast in the company of the whole congregation. Apparently this took the form of a meal in which they all shared, and in the course of which the sacrament of communion with the Lord was celebrated. This sacrament would indicate the fellowship of the believers with the Lord and with each other.

In Corinth some unworthy conduct on the part of some of the believers marred the intended fellowship. This misconduct became so notorious that Paul heard about it. Paul did not seek out individual offenders but addressed his remarks to the whole congregation.

> Now in this that I declare unto you I praise you not, that ye come together not for the better, but for the worse. For first of all, when ye come together in the church, I hear that there be divisions among you; and I partly believe it. For there must be also heresies among you, that they which are approved may be made manifest among you (1 Cor. 11:17-19).

From Paul's remarks in this context, it would appear that heresies may be not only in doctrine, but also in practice.

It seems that the fault lay in not realizing the significance of the sacrament. Apparently some overlooked the sacred nature of the ceremony and took advantage of the common meal to indulge themselves in food and drink. To take such liberty in a fashion that showed disrespect to the intention of the sacrament was conduct that Paul could not accept.

> When ye come together therefore into one place, this is not to eat the Lord's supper. For in eating every one taketh before other his own supper: and one is hungry, and another is drunken. What? have ye not houses to eat and to drink in? or despise ye the church of God, and shame them that have not? What shall I say to you? shall I praise you in this? I praise you not (1 Cor. 11:20-22).

Paul then outlined in classic fashion the authentic description and interpretation of the sacrament. This has become the standard authorization throughout the church until this day.

> For I have received of the Lord that which also I delivered unto you, That the Lord Jesus the same night in which he was betrayed took bread: and when he had given thanks, he brake it, and said, Take, eat: this is my body, which is broken for you: this do in remembrance of me. After the same manner also he took the cup, when he had supped, saying, This cup is the new testament in my blood: this do ye, as oft as ye drink it, in remembrance of me. For as often as ye eat this bread, and drink this cup, ye do show the Lord's death till he come (1 Cor. 11:23-26).

In a stern tone of sharp judgment Paul discussed the serious nature of unworthy participation in the sacrament we have come to call the Lord's Supper.

> Wherefore whosoever shall eat this bread, and drink this cup of the Lord, unworthily, shall be guilty of the body and blood of the Lord. But let a man examine himself, and so let him eat of that bread, and drink of that cup. For he that eateth and drinketh unworthily, eateth and drinketh damnation to himself, not discerning the Lord's body (1 Cor. 11:27-29).

The worshiper should judge himself so that he can come in an acceptable mood of penitence; and he should heed the words of the institution of the sacrament when the Lord showed to Paul that the bread represented His broken body, and the cup His shed blood. To fail to do this would actually condemn the worshiper as he participated.

Paul tried to encourage the believers to judge themselves that they might be spared chastening from the Lord.

> For this cause many are weak and sickly among you, and many
> sleep. For if we would judge ourselves, we should not be
> judged. But when we are judged, we are chastened of the Lord,
> that we should not be condemned with the world (1 Cor. 11:30-
> 32).

Paul urged all believers to be careful to come to the love feast of
the congregation and the sacrament of communion with the
Lord with care and self-restraint. Paul recommended that if a
man was extremely hungry, he should eat at home before he
came to the communion service.

> Wherefore, my brethren, when ye come together to eat, tarry
> one for another. And if any man hunger, let him eat at home;
> that ye come not together unto condemnation. And the rest will
> I set in order when I come (1 Cor. 11:33-34).

Chapter 33

GIFTS ARE OF GOD

In the next three chapters of this epistle Paul discussed a major problem which harassed the church in Corinth, and which continues to appear as a problem even to this day. When a human being comes to faith in Jesus Christ and accepts Him as his personal Savior, God regenerates that person. The Lord spoke of this as being "born again" (John 3:3-7). Paul wrote:

> Therefore if any man be in Christ, he is a new creature: old things are passed away; behold, all things are become new (2 Cor. 5:17).

Into the regenerated heart God sends the Holy Spirit (Gal. 4:6-7). In His ministry in the hearts of believers, the Holy Spirit "gave gifts unto men" (Eph. 4:7-16). These gifts are called in the Greek language *charisma*, from which has been derived the contemporary word *charismatic*. A good description of a "gift" is "a divine enablement for service."

The whole matter of "gifts" continues to be the subject of much discussion in the church. The New Testament does not define the term in any clear fashion, but some aspects of the idea can be noted. Apparently not every believer is so endowed; and no case is presented of anyone who had all the gifts. It does appear however that some have received gifts. This would enable such believers to serve the body as a whole in a special way.

Possession of gifts did not make such believers mature, nor deliver them from human limitations. Apparently they were "comparing themselves with themselves" (2 Cor. 10:12) and, judging their personal "gift" to be better, became proud in self-esteem. This led to contentions among them, of which Paul had heard. Doubtless Paul realized how sincere persons could fall into such a trap through lack of understanding. In chapters 12–14 he made a careful effort to show the fallacy of such pride.

Paul began his discussion by reminding the Corinthian believers that they had been pagan worshipers of "dumb idols, even as ye were led." This meant that anything they now knew about Christ they had been told. Then he immediately emphasized that all believers worship Christ; and that no one can openly "say that Jesus is the Lord, but by the Holy Ghost." This puts down a basis for accepting as brethren *all* who confess Christ.

As Paul approached the problem that was causing contention, he pointed out both the condition which gave rise to the problem and the truth that pointed the way to solving it.

> Now there are diversities of gifts, but the same Spirit. And there are differences of administrations, but the same Lord. And there are diversities of operation, but it is the same God which worketh all in all (1 Cor. 12:4-6).

One basic fact is that people are different, but for believers the saving truth is that the one Lord is the sole director of all spiritual activity. Gifts, administrations, and operations will be multiform and varied, but all such are under the control and direction of "the same Spirit," "the same Lord," and "the same God." This insight would enable the Corinthians to understand that differences in gifts would never mean that they should be comparatively estimated for value.

Chapter 34

THE GIFTS OF THE SPIRIT

> But the manifestation of the Spirit is given to every man to profit withal (1 Cor. 12:7).

Paul, in 1 Corinthians 12, was dealing with the confusion which existed in the congregation at Corinth as a result of the various services individual believers performed, which differed from one another. Being immature and "babes in Christ," they failed to realize that all the different services are rendered in the will of the Lord and work together to achieve the same purpose. As a result of not realizing this, they began to compare themselves with one another and to prefer one over the other. This caused envy and vanity. It made some of them feel superior to others.

Men who have served in any branch of the armed forces know the feeling of superiority which one group feels over the other. This is quite natural, but when it is carried over into the church, it interferes with the testimony and the fellowship of believers. Some people are gifted as teachers. But it is not good when the teachers think that they are smarter and better than other people. Paul called attention to the fact that the Holy Spirit is the One who really matters and is of importance, since it is He who motivates men to serve God: "The manifestation of the Spirit is given to every man." Paul wants it clearly understood that it is the Spirit who enables some men to serve in one way and others in different capacities; yet all will be working together to bring about the will of God.

There is no record in the Bible of the Holy Spirit improving or equipping someone for personal gain or pleasure. No one ever received the Holy Spirit for personal enjoyment. The Holy Spirit motivates believers to serve others in the church.

This belongs to the very nature of God. In the Book of John we read that "God is love." John 3:16 tells us that "God so loved the world, that he gave his only begotten Son, that whosoever believeth in him should not perish, but have everlasting life." In love He saved mankind. In love He gives them His Holy Spirit.

In chapter 12 we find what is commonly referred to as the classic list of the gifts of the Spirit, which the Lord bestows upon believers.

> For to one is given by the Spirit the word of wisdom . . . (1 Cor. 12:8).

This means that some people are gifted by the Holy Spirit with the ability to counsel others wisely in any situation. A wise person is one who chooses the best means to an end, and then works to achieve it. Seeking anything but the best is not being wise.

> . . . to another the word of knowledge by the same Spirit (1 Cor. 12:8).

This does not mean that the Spirit will equip the mind with miscellaneous knowledge, but rather that He bestows on some the gift of being able to take what is revealed and to explain it to others. It refers to a certain capacity to realize the significance of any matter, and then to be able to share such knowledge competently and effectively with others. For example, if a father has a way of accenting the things that are worthwhile and guides his children in that direction, he is a wise father. If a mother has the ability to develop various skills in her children and awaken their interest in well-doing, she is a mother gifted "with the word of knowledge."

> To another faith by the same Spirit . . . (1 Cor. 12:9).

This does not refer to the initial faith that saves the soul, but rather the faith that achieves things. It would enable the believer to be conscious of the invisible world and to recognize God's hand in any situation. Such faith produces direct results. For example, consider some individuals who feel the need for an orphanage. They may not have an organization to put up the money, yet they would go ahead and build the orphanage, expecting to receive fifty thousand dollars a year towards its building and maintenance costs. They would trust that God would provide all their needs. God has in the past honored such faith. We have all heard of faith missions — missions operated by persons who have the capacity to understand the will of God and act in response to that. These are works of faith.

> . . . to another the gifts of healing by the same Spirit (1 Cor. 12:9).

When the apostle Paul wrote about gifts of healing, he did not refer to wisdom and understanding in the treatment of various illnesses by doctors and nurses. The gift of healing is a matter of being enabled by God's Spirit to pray earnestly and sincerely and to receive from Him what they ask in behalf of one who is ill.

Next Paul referred to the gifts of miracles, prophecy, and discerning spirits. The latter would mean the ability to discern between false and true prophets, based on the authority of God's Word. Next we read the words "divers kinds of tongues." Because this is a subject which causes much discussion, I will devote more time to it in a following chapter. The truth to note now is the fact that all these gifts, which Paul has enumerated, came from the same source, although each gift had a different function.

> But all these worketh that one and the selfsame Spirit, dividing to every man severally as he will (1 Cor. 12:11).

Surely this precludes all boasting on the part of believers since every ability is a gift of God and should be used to His honor and glory.

Chapter 35

MANY MEMBERS IN ONE BODY

In chapters 12–14 of 1 Corinthians, Paul continued to discuss the problem that was created by the fact that people differed in their gifts of service. Because some believers are still "babes in Christ," it is hard for them to realize that difference in emphasis and variety in service does not make one better than the other. We can be very grateful to the apostle Paul for his understanding as he deals with this problem. He does not start out by accusing anyone of doing wrong, nor does he infer that they are not true believers because they lack understanding in certain matters. Paul realizes so well that inexperienced young believers lack the wider, longer view.

Paul went on to show that there need not be any divisions, that this problem did not need to exist among them. He used a natural illustration of the human body to help them. Just because we have five fingers on each hand does not mean that the hand is divided into five parts. It seems that divisions over differences in procedure spring from individual pride. It is probably that divisions are caused by egotistical feeling. Each one starts thinking about himself, and that is sin. Paul did not discuss the matter from this point of view. He was more interested in helping people to a better understanding of the ways of God.

Believers should be able to accept the differences in other believers and the diversity of gifts bestowed on them by the Holy Spirit.

> To another the working of miracles; to another prophecy . . .
> (1 Cor. 12:10).

The working of miracles would be the gift of solving problems, and of getting divine help in times of trouble. Prophecy is the gift of preaching the gospel in such a way that the direct influence of the Holy Spirit is felt. This refers to the preachers who interpret the Word of God clearly. "Divers kinds of tongues" (1 Cor. 12:10) does not refer to the use of a foreign or strange language. Paul himself spoke several different languages, but this is not what he was talking about. He was talking about the kind of "speaking in tongues" that occurred in the early church. Another gift of the Spirit is "the interpretation of tongues." There are at least two of these gifts that I would not feel competent to explain nor to relate to our day. One is "the discerning of spirits," and the other is "the interpretation of tongues."

Paul clearly taught that the Holy Spirit uses each of these gifts. In verses 13-20 he was reasoning with the Corinthian believers. He explained to them that in the church there are many members who can all work together in the same way as the various organs of the human body function together. Paul wrote by way of introduction and emphasis the following verses:

> For by one Spirit are we all baptized into one body, whether we be Jews or Gentiles, whether we be bond or free; and have been all made to drink into one Spirit (1 Cor. 12:13).

Here Paul stresses the function and the presence of the Holy Spirit as the common denominator which unites all factions. When each denomination of the body of Christ functions in response to the Holy Spirit within, there is no inward division. Then outwardly there are no longer divisions as such, but a matter of different organs in one body.

> For the body is not one member, but many. If the foot shall say, Because I am not the hand, I am not of the body; is it therefore not of the body? And if the ear shall say, Because I am not the eye, I am not of the body; is it therefore not of the body? (1 Cor. 12:14-16).

Notice how many times in these two verses the "I" is used. This is the problem. Being conscious of differences between people should not encourage us to promote ourselves or to feel that we are the only ones who can do a certain task. Let us think this through and then keep it in our hearts and minds. Let us allow for the fact that someone might be "an ear," while someone else may be a "tongue." Let us just keep in mind that we do not need many tongues. We have two ears and two hands for every tongue. Thinking about this will help us understand the things Paul is saying to the Corinthians.

> If the whole body were an eye, where were the hearing? If the whole were hearing, where were the smelling? (1 Cor. 12:17).

Paul points out that the variation in functions actually increases the ability of the body.

> But now hath God set the members every one of them in the body, as it hath pleased him (1 Cor. 12:18).

The actual presence of each member is the will of God.

> And if they were all one member, where were the body? (1 Cor. 12:19).

One of the most marvelous structures in the whole world is the human hand, and yet in spite of the diverse functions of the fingers, it is just composed of bones, joints, sinews, and so forth. Paul bases his words of explanation on comparing the usefulness of the various organs of the body to the usefulness of every member of the congregation. He is telling them and us that we can be different and yet work together in the Lord.

Chapter 36

UNITY AMONG THE MEMBERS

No doubt every believer feels concern for another believer. He wants to be kind and generous and helpful. This is all good and yet it is inadequate. It is actually too limited. It is like saying that a man should try to keep his wife happy and contented in her home. We might even think that by keeping her happy he would be doing her a favor. Now this is not nearly the whole truth, nor the most important one. When we look a bit deeper into this matter, we realize that when a man is making his wife happy and contented in her home, he is actually making a better home for himself. He is taking care of what belongs to him, because his wife is a part of him. In other words, it is not nearly so much a matter of sentiment as it is a matter of good judgment and good sense. This is not selfishness in a bad way.

Let us consider a father who tries to keep his child healthy. Someone may say, "That is what he ought to do. A child deserves this care." In reality, a father will seek to keep his child healthy, not only for the sake of the child but for his own sake; because when the father keeps his child healthy, he is actually serving himself in a sensible way: he is serving the whole family.

The man who does things for others will automatically gain by this. Now someone may have the feeling that this causes selfishness. But is it selfish to eat good food and to keep oneself healthy and well? Surely no one would suggest that if a man tries to keep himself healthy and well, he is acting selfishly.

Now Paul projects this line of thought into the area of spiritual health, strength, and well-being. Paul argues that we will help fellow believers not only because we are concerned for them, but because they belong to us. They are a part of us just as the different members of the body belong together. The apostle points out that whatever hurts any part of the body hurts the whole body. Because I am a member of the body, what hurts the body hurts me. This is not a matter of selfishness; it is a natural, factual observation. The reason I will not drink poison is because it would kill me. The reason I try to avoid dangerous activities, like driving recklessly, or climbing in a dangerous spot, is because I might hurt myself. Is this selfishness, or is this good sense?

We read in the Bible that a man who loves his own wife loves his own flesh. There is nothing selfish about that. She belongs to him, and he has as much responsibility for her well-being as he has to keep himself healthy and well. On a larger scale Paul presents this idea to the believers in Corinth. They were confused and distressed because some prided themselves on being better than others. They acted as though they were doing something more important than others. The teachers felt themselves far more important than the people they were instructing, forgetting that the ability to teach was a gift from the Holy Spirit. Others with different gifts also exalted themselves, and this caused friction among them.

Even today in a congregation there may be a woman who is a good organizer and manager, who will automatically be put in charge of things. If she is not careful, she will begin to think that she is better than the other women, and others will feel that way too. In reality, the fact that she has been given an opportunity for service does not make her any better in the eyes of the Lord. Among believers there should be no divisions, no esteeming of some persons above others. The apostle Paul desired a spirit of unity among them, such as exists between members of the human body.

> And the eye cannot say unto the hand, I have no need of thee: nor again the head to the feet, I have no need of you. Nay, much more those members of the body, which seem to be more feeble, are necessary: and those members of the body, which we think to be less honourable, upon these we bestow more abundant honour; and our uncomely parts have more abundant comeliness. For our comely parts have no need: but God hath tempered the body together, having given more abundant hon-

our to that part which lacked: that there should be no schism in
the body (1 Cor. 12:21-25).

Here again Paul relates all believers together, like the members of the body are related to one another. There should not be even a tendency to separate from each other. No spirit of rivalry, no seeking for prestige, should exist among believers. Rivalry is never wholesome for morale. Even on a ball team it will not do to have the pitcher or the catcher or the shortstop feel that he is the most important man on the team. It is absolutely necessary for the best results that everyone on the team work together. If a man has a more prominent part to play, he will know that if it were not for the others helping him, he could not win the game. All nine players are needed, or there is no game. Similarly, believers cannot function independently from one another.

Paul makes it clear that there is no such thing as a partial or even sectional independence. To promote unity, every member must receive the same care and attention. Not all members are alike, but all are important and necessary in their own place. For instance, when we think of our eyesight, we are aware of the importance of our eyes. Yet it is true that we could lose one eye and still see. If through some misfortune we should lose both eyes, we can still think. So we at once realize the vital importance of the brain. Now the brain is unseen. It is so important that it is surrounded by a bone structure, which encloses it and protects it. In this way God has taken care of it.

Or let us consider the arm. It can be broken, or even cut off, but the heart goes on pumping blood through the body. The heart is enclosed in a rib cage. We do not see it, for God has planned it so that it is carefully protected. Surely every part of the human body has its own place of importance and usefulness, and each part is dependent on the other.

The apostle Paul climaxes his application of this truth by saying, "That there should be no schism in the body." This same dependence should be shown by believers. Only as believers have a realization of belonging together and working together can the gifts of the Holy Spirit bring blessing into their individual lives and their life as a congregation.

Chapter 37

GIFTS FOR SERVICE

In our study we have noted that the apostle Paul stressed the fact that all members of a church belong to the Lord. In His eyes those who do less important work are just as important as those who do the more significant work. This is obviously true. However we must admit that in the service of the Lord some are used in a more meaningful way than others. Some persons do not believe this. They are inclined to say that everything done as unto the Lord is of equal significance. This attitude is shown when in administering benevolent funds all the beneficiaries share equally. Many of us do not feel right about this. We cannot agree with their premise in this whole matter. We do not believe that one phase of service is as important as another.

The Bible reveals that there is a difference in the very nature of the work performed. Yet the first essential is that all should be done to the glory of God. In the Old Testament one of the sad stories is that of Esau and Jacob. Esau gave up his birthright, which would have brought with it God's richest blessing, for something to eat. He valued the blessing of God less than the food he wanted. He made a terrible mistake in doing this. The consequences of putting food ahead of God's blessing were so tragic that there was no way Esau could escape them.

By contrast we turn to the New Testament to read of the time when Jesus of Nazareth was in the desert and was tempted by Satan to make stones into bread. On this occasion He said, "Man shall not live by bread alone, but by every word that proceedeth out of the mouth of God" (Matt. 4:4). He put obedience to God above all else. When speaking of the rich man who had provided for all his wants, our Lord said, "For what shall it profit a man, if he shall gain the whole world, and lose his own soul?" (Mark 8:36). In these words He vividly presented the differences of temporal and eternal values, and the need for putting God first in all our considerations.

The apostle Paul had this in mind when he wrote to the Corinthians telling them that he had liberty to eat everything for which he had given thanks to God. Yet for the sake of those whose conscience would be offended by such an act on his part, he would eat no meat which had been offered to idols, "not while the world standeth." In other words, pleasing the Lord and being in His will must come before anything else.

In 1 Corinthians 12:28-31 Paul lists for the Corinthians the gifts of the Spirit. These gifts are given only to believers. Those who have not accepted the Lord as their Savior will never understand what I am talking about. To them my words may sound as though I were rationalizing in support of some theory. This would be because such people, as good as they may be, live in a different world from the one that Paul and the Corinthian believers and the believers of today live. These people lived in a world where they trusted in Jesus Christ. He had bought them for a price. He took care of them and watched over them.

These persons who lived day by day depending on the Lord received from Him certain enablement for service; certain gifts were given to them. Paul discussed these gifts with them, explaining to them that these gifts vary, so that they are of greater or less importance. In verse 28 Paul gave a classic rating of spiritual gifts. Nowhere else in the New Testament are they so clearly defined. "And God hath set some in the church, first apostles": these were the authorized interpreters of the gospel; "secondarily prophets": these are the preachers that proclaim the Word of God, showing the people how they may come to faith in Jesus Christ by believing and receiving the gospel; "thirdly teachers": who explain the Word of God and its manifold truths; "after that miracles": when the gospel had been interpreted and preached and taught, it was followed by the performance of miracles and wonders by the power of God; "then gifts of healings": this does not refer to medical healing, but rather to healing in answer to prayer. Many believers have experienced the healing hand of God in answer to their prayers, for with God all things are possible. He will do, according to His will, that which is best for us.

"Helps" refers to persons who have the ability to see the needs of others and to respond to them. They possess the understanding as well as the heart to do just what will bring the greatest assistance to those in need. "Governments" refers to persons who have a gift of planning and arranging and directing. Persons who have this gift should realize that such ability is given to them in trust. They are supposed to exercise this gift in the Lord for the sake of others. Last on this list we read: "diversities of tongues." This does not mean the ability to speak many languages as the disciples did on the day of Pentecost, where every man heard the gospel preached in his own native tongue. The speaking in "divers tongues" could not be understood and needed interpreting in order to edify other believers. This is the naming of the gifts given to believers by the Holy Spirit.

> Are all apostles? are all prophets? are all teachers? are all work-
> ers of miracles? Have all the gifts of healing? do all speak with
> tongues? do all interpret? But covet earnestly the best gifts: and
> yet show I unto you a more excellent way (1 Cor. 12:29-31).

Chapter 38

GIFTS ARE NOT ENOUGH

In his discussion of spiritual gifts the apostle Paul first recognized that such gifts are given to believers for the benefit of other believers. He pointed out that while such gifts differ from each other, they are not to be compared and evaluated as if their possession made some believers better than others. Apparently the gifts themselves differ in importance, and Paul submitted a list of the gifts in order of their respective importance (1 Cor. 12:28); but then he pointed out that their possession is not a valid basis for comparison of spiritual achievement. After urging them to seek earnestly the best gifts, Paul told them there was a better way to excel than to have any of the gifts.

> Though I speak with the tongues of men and of angels, and have not charity, I am become as sounding brass, or a tinkling cymbal. And though I have the gift of prophecy, and understand all mysteries, and all knowledge; and though I have all faith, so that I could remove mountains, and have not charity, I am nothing. And though I bestow all my goods to feed the poor, and though I give my body to be burned, and have not charity, it profiteth me nothing (1 Cor. 13:1-3).

In these words the apostle pointed out that even if a believer exercised any of the gifts even in a great fashion, but lacked charity, his actions would have no spiritual significance. The one element essential to add quality to any action or behavior is charity, or love.

Paul then extolled the characteristics of charity that make any behavior excellent.

> Charity suffereth long, and is kind; charity envieth not; charity vaunteth not itself, is not puffed up, doth not behave itself unseemly, seeketh not her own, is not easily provoked, thinketh

123

> no evil; rejoiceth not in iniquity, but rejoiceth in the truth;
> beareth all things, believeth all things, hopeth all things, en-
> dureth all things (1 Cor. 13:4-7).

The exercise of the various gifts will be temporary, whereas charity is continuous. It will never fade out or quit. Even when the believer is hurt or offended, charity will suffer long and be kind. Charity maintains good will toward others. It does not envy others nor boil over with jealousy. It is not boastful or proud. It is not conceited and it does not have any grand opinion of itself. Charity does not act improperly or rudely. It does not scheme to advance its own ideas nor to get its own way. Charity is not quick to take offense and is not looking for faults in others. Charity is never happy when someone does something wrong, but is always glad when things happen as they should. Charity will put up with anything that is done and will always trust the good intentions of others. Charity expects things to work out as they should and persists patiently to the very end. In this description the Corinthians could judge themselves for contention and quarrelsomeness. It would be obvious that charity was lacking in their own hearts.

Paul then continued his discussion about charity by pointing out that it will never diminish. He emphasized the importance of this fact by contrasting the fact that the gifts with which they have been endowed are operative for a limited time only.

> Charity never faileth: but whether there be prophecies, they
> shall fail; whether there be tongues, they shall cease; whether
> there be knowledge, it shall vanish away. For we know in part,
> and we prophesy in part (1 Cor. 13:8-9).

In so many words Paul pointed out that the function of the gifts is for a limited time: prophecies shall fail; tongues shall cease; knowledge shall vanish away. All human thinking deals with limited ideas; only the Word of God is eternal and infinite. This being true, the believer will commit himself to the promises of God, and not put too much confidence in the words or the works of man.

> But when that which is perfect is come, then that which is in part
> shall be done away. When I was a child, I spake as a child, I
> understood as a child, I thought as a child: but when I became a
> man, I put away childish things. For now we see through a glass,

darkly; but then face to face: now I know in part; but then shall I
know even as also I am known (1 Cor. 13:10-12).

Paul used several illustrations to enable the Corinthians to
realize that something better than possessing gifts for service
was going to be their experience. Since gifts in themselves
dealt with only a part of their whole life, Paul pointed out that
when something which affected their total experience (such as
charity) became theirs, then the attention to gifts would be
dropped. Paul used his own development from childhood to
maturity as an illustration of what would happen spiritually. He
began his life as a child and acted as a child, but when he
became a man he put away childish things. This seems to
indicate that interest in gifts for service and in comparing one
with another actually belongs to the stage of being "babes in
Christ," whereas the demonstration of charity belongs to the
stage of maturity.

Paul then went on to say that there is progression also in
understanding truth. First we see only dimly and imperfectly
as one would see when looking at the reflection of reality in a
mirror; but later one would see truth completely as it is in
reality. Then the imperfect concepts would be put away for the
actual reality. Again this seems to imply that being interested
in gifts will be set aside when charity is present.

Chapter 39

LOVE IS THE GREATEST

Probably one of the most famous verses of Scripture is found in chapter 13 of 1 Corinthians:

> And now abideth faith, hope, charity, these three; but the greatest of these is charity (1 Cor. 13:13).

First of all, I want to call attention to the context in which these words were written. In this letter to the Corinthians Paul has been dealing with many problems which had beset these young believers. He has pointed out to them that if they could have understood all that is involved in the gospel, these problems that troubled them need never have arisen. In chapters 12–14 we find that much of the confusion and tension which existed among them was due to contention because of comparisons and envyings over the varied gifts which God had given to them. The apostle Paul did not criticize the Corinthians for their immature behavior. He refrained from expressing any derogatory judgment. He showed sympathetic but realistic recognition of their problem. He analyzed their situation and presented to them the way they could follow to eliminate their problem.

Paul pointed out to the Corinthians that to become mature, intelligent believers, they should not try to excel each other in the matter of service. This kind of attitude could never result in healthy spiritual growth. He pointed out again that it was not the persons who are most capable and competent in putting their gifts to work who are most important. It is the inner intention and purpose on the part of those who serve that is most vital in the sight of God.

Paul emphasized that to attain an attitude of acceptable service, love must be the keynote in everything. The words *faith*, *hope*, and *charity* are so often used and yet they are not so readily explained. I would say that they are three manifestations of the Spirit. Faith, hope, and charity must be manifested in our actions as believers. When we respond to the revealed will of God and to His promises, by receiving them as true, that is faith.

The word *faith* has a secondary meaning. We may speak of the faith of a believer in Christ, or the faith of a Methodist or a Baptist, but the word *faith* as Paul used it has to do with the actual function involved. It is an act of our will as we respond willingly to the revealed promises of God.

Hope is an attitude of the heart. In faith the emphasis was on self and a conscious commitment to God. Hope is the firm expectation that God will keep His promises. Here the emphasis is on God, that He will keep His Word. There is also a secondary meaning for the word *hope*. We may speak of the hope of a believer in Christ, or we may speak about the "blessed hope," in which we refer to a certain expectation that God will fulfill according to His promises. But primarily, as Paul uses the word *hope* in this chapter, it has to do with our anticipation becoming reality as we trust God.

Charity and *love*, in this context, mean the same thing. They refer to actively seeking the welfare and happiness of others. When we do anything for the sake of someone else, we do it in love. When we do things for our own sake, we are acting selfishly. There is also a secondary meaning of this word *love*. We can speak of love as manifested in deed and word, but it is not the meaning of the word *love* which is implied here. So far as love in itself is concerned, it is primarily the motivation that causes us to express ourselves in deeds and acts which will bring happiness to others.

> And now abideth faith, hope, charity, these three; but the greatest of these is charity (1 Cor. 13:13).

The apostle Paul gives us no explanation as to why charity is the greatest. Perhaps it is because love is included in both faith and hope. In other words, only as we believe in God, does it become possible for us to desire to do for others. "We love him, because he first loved us." One follows the other. First God loved us, then we love Him; and because we love Him, we love others. So we can see that love is grounded in faith.

It is because we believe that we love. The same thing is true of hope. We can love because we have the sure hope that God will do according to His promises in our behalf. We read about the Lord Jesus Christ,

> Who for the joy that was set before him endured the cross, despising the shame, and is set down at the right hand of the throne of God (Heb. 12:2).

Many people say that when Christ Jesus died for us, He manifested God's love for us. This is true. It is also true that He died for us in the confidence of what God would do, which is "hope." So actually "faith, hope, and love" are not separate but rather are related to one another. Of the three, it is love which constitutes a believer's likeness to God. For this reason it is the greatest of God's gifts to His children. Love actually encompasses faith and hope as it activates Christians to live to the glory of God and to the strengthening and comfort of other believers.

Chapter 40

PROPHESYING IS BETTER

In 1 Corinthians 13 the apostle Paul pointed out that love/charity must be the basis for believers' attitudes towards others. And now he goes on,

> Follow after charity, and desire spiritual gifts, but rather that ye may prophesy (1 Cor. 14:1).

"Follow after charity." In other words, pursue love and desire it, because everyone may have it. Not everyone will be an apostle or a preacher. Not everyone will be a teacher or be able to help in a governing capacity. Not everyone will have faith to perform miracles or gifts of healing. Not everyone will speak with tongues. But everyone can have faith and hope and charity.

In chapter 12 Paul discussed the gifts of the Spirit, which only some may have. But in chapter 13 he discussed the fruits of the Spirit which everyone could and should have. Everyone should seek to cultivate and nurture faith and hope and charity as much as possible. Paul said that regardless of our capacity for service, our ability or our lack of it, we can have love. When we want to do everything possible to help and strengthen others, then we will have that love which comes from God.

"And desire spiritual gifts." There is nothing wrong with gifts. We should be willing to serve in any way. "But rather that ye may prophesy." Prophesying is a matter of interpreting the Scriptures and communicating their meaning to others. Paul urges that of all the various gifts, we should seek above all else the gift of witnessing the truth of the gospel to other people.

> For he that speaketh in an unknown tongue speaketh not unto men, but unto God . . . (1 Cor. 14:2).

Anyone who has been present at a meeting where people speak with "tongues" will know that what they say will not be understood. The assumption is that God will understand. So the person who is speaking in tongues is not helping those who hear him. He is speaking, as it were, to God: "for no man understandeth him; howbeit in the spirit he speaketh mysteries." Paul recognized that such a man may in the Spirit refer to things that are hidden from the world. They may even be things hidden from his own consciousness. God alone is able to judge what is being said.

> But he that prophesieth speaketh unto men to edification, and exhortation, and comfort (1 Cor. 14:3).

Although these words are not in comman usage, their meaning is not obscure. Actually the word *edification* means "building up," and he who explains the meaning of the Scripture builds men up. He builds up their faith. Faith, we are told in the Bible, "cometh by hearing, and hearing by the word of God." The more we understand God's Word, the stronger our faith will be, the more we will believe. We will believe that Christ Jesus died for our sins and that He was raised from the dead. We will believe that God gives His Holy Spirit to work in us to bring us into closer fellowship with Him. He will give us faith to believe that as we die to self, we can be free from sin. We will have faith to know that God can raise us, after dying to self, to newness of life. Then doing His will and walking in His way will be the desires of our hearts. All this His Holy Spirit will work in us as we grow in faith and knowledge of His Word. This is why those who have the gift of preaching and teaching should do it with simplicity of words, so plainly that none can miss the message of the gospel, so that all may grow in faith.

"And exhortation" means to incite to action. When I think about exhortation, I think of an exhorter, a cheerleader who leads a crowd at a football game, calling out words of encouragement and inspiration to their team. In a similar way a preacher urges people on to receive the gospel. This is not always done with a loud voice, nor necessarily with undue feeling. It is chiefly a matter of conveying the urgency of the message and the need for response on the part of the people. This can be done quietly and calmly as well as with much feeling and enthusiasm. The main object is that the truth of the gospel should move men toward God.

"And comfort": This is a very real service. Here the apostle Paul indicated that the Scriptures, when clearly explained, will actually bring comfort into the hearts and lives of believers. Often someone may say, "Be ye comforted"; but that is not enough. Telling anyone to "be comforted" is like telling a frightened child, "Don't be afraid," without giving any reason for assurance. To comfort someone does not mean simply to say, "Now take it easy; everything will be fine." How can the disturbed person know this? If we really want to comfort someone, we must give him something positive and helpful.

Consider a person who feels that he has sinned to a point where God will never forgive him. We could comfort such a one by showing him the Scriptures that say, "Though your sins be as scarlet, they shall be as white as snow; though they be red like crimson, they shall be as wool" (Isa. 1:18). These are words that will bring comfort and assurance. This is preaching; this is prophesying. We go to those who sorrow and mourn, who have lost a loved one. A minister can comfort bereaved parents who have lost a child. He can assure them that the child has fallen asleep in Jesus and that Almighty God will care for him. These are words of comfort for all believers.

> He that speaketh in an unknown tongue edifieth himself; but he that prophesieth edifieth the church (1 Cor. 14:4).

Here the comparison is clearly stated. The person who speaks with an unknown tongue puts the focus on himself; it is always less than good enough. But a person who prophesies edifies the church. His message focuses on others. This is always good, and this is what ought to be done.

> I would that ye all spake with tongues, but rather that ye prophesied: for greater is he that prophesieth than he that speaketh with tongues . . . (1 Cor. 14:5).

This is something we should keep in mind when we hear people talking about "speaking in tongues." Let us remember that the person who teaches and preaches in an intelligent way, helping others to understand the Scriptures, is greater than the person who speaks with tongues.

Chapter 41

PREACHING SHOULD BE IN PLAIN TALK

No one is born with gospel beliefs and convictions. No one is born with faith in Christ. These things are not a part of the natural man. The Bible says, "Faith cometh by hearing, and hearing by the word of God" (Rom. 10:17). It is true that "whosoever shall call upon the name of the Lord shall be saved," but in this context Paul went on to ask this question:

> How then shall they call on him in whom they have not believed? and how shall they believe in him of whom they have not heard? and how shall they hear without a preacher? (Rom. 10:14).

The word *hear*, of course, includes the idea of understanding.

The revelation of God comes in the gospel, and in this case, referring to the preached Word of God. In the Old Testament we read how God revealed Himself and His will to the prophets. In the New Testament He is revealed in and by His Son, the Lord Jesus Christ. It is the Bible alone which must be the textbook if men would learn about God and His plan for mankind.

Paul has pointed out in 1 Corinthians how believers can help each other by the gifts of the Spirit which have been given to them. We have noted that the most important gift of all is the gift of prophecy. Now in verses 6-11 Paul makes a great plea urging on preachers the practical necessity for plain talk. There must be clarity of expression in preaching and teaching and praying so that other people will be moved to accept the message which is presented to them.

> Now, brethren, if I come unto you speaking with tongues, what shall I profit you, except I shall speak to you either by revelation, or by knowledge, or by prophesying, or by doctrine? (1 Cor. 14:6).

If I do not communicate to you something that is meaningful so that you may understand the revelation of God, you will know no more than you did before I spoke. If I do not interpret the Scripture so that you understand it better, what good is my preaching? "What shall I profit you?" Today, especially in the field of education, we hear a lot of talk about wordless communication, imageless thought. These terms mean little, not nearly as much as they imply. I do not question that one can communicate in a limited way by gesture, posture, and visual aids. If people get on their knees, this means something. If they close their eyes or raise their eyes toward heaven this could mean something. When people find themselves in an atmosphere of reverence and worship, this inclines them to dwell on the things of God. People are even influenced by the mood of those about them, whether it is somber or joyful. However, none of this is a valid way of communicating the gospel.

To tell about the gospel we need speech; we need words. God Himself comes to us in words that must be understood by the mind. Therefore it is not difficult to realize why Paul says, "What shall it profit you, if you do not understand what I am saying?"

> And even things without life giving sound, whether pipe or harp, except they give a distinction in the sounds, how shall it be known what is piped or harped? (1 Cor. 14:7).

Today we would say if the organ or the piano do not produce distinctive sounds, how could we recognize a tune? If this is true of inanimate objects like an organ or a piano, how much more true it is with a human being. There has to be something definite said. Just talk or just syllables do not mean a thing. Words have to mean something. Baby talk will not do. We must use intelligent talk and plain talk so we can be understood.

> For if the trumpet give an uncertain sound, who shall prepare himself to the battle? (1 Cor. 14:8).

This sounds almost like a proverb. If a soldier does not know whether to advance or retreat because the trumpet makes an uncertain sound, what is he going to do? Even so, church services ought to be conducted in such a way that people can understand what is being preached.

> So likewise ye, except ye utter by the tongue words easy to be understood, how shall it be known what is spoken? for ye shall speak into the air (1 Cor. 14:9).

Plain talk is essential. The very words preachers use should be easily understood. Every true preacher has the Bible in his hands, and not one of the men who preach is unfamiliar with these words in 1 Corinthians 14. So if a preacher gets up to preach using an abundance of words that do not really mean anything, he is answerable to God. God will judge him. This passage of Scripture makes it abundantly clear that the preaching of the gospel must be readily understood by all who hear it. Of course it is important that a preacher's language be logical, well organized, well arranged, and well developed. However if the whole presentation is not easily understood, it falls short of the whole purpose of preaching.

Some years ago in thinking about this matter, I came across something I have often recalled. The average perception of an American audience is on the level of a twelve-year-old boy. Any preacher would be smart to take note of this and preach accordingly. Once when I was preparing a series of books of "Plain Talk" on Bible truths, I mentioned that I planned to prepare something we could offer to the mission field so that native believers might understand the Bible better. One of the local pastors heard me say this and said, "Fine, when you get that book published, please let me know. I want my church officers to have it so that they can follow through."

> There are, it may be, so many kinds of voices in the world, and none of them is without signification. Therefore if I know not the meaning of the voice, I shall be unto him that speaketh a barbarian, and he that speaketh shall be a barbarian unto me (1 Cor. 14:10-11).

If the words spoken are unintelligible, it is as though we were foreigners and strangers to one another. May the preaching of the gospel never be hindered by an overabundance of words.

Chapter 42

ALL PUBLIC WORSHIP SHOULD BE
IN PLAIN TALK

We have followed the apostle Paul in his discussion of the various gifts for service which the Corinthian believers had received from the Lord. Nine such gifts were enumerated in chapter 12, and in chapter 14 Paul discusses one gift in particular at some length. Apparently this gift had caused more dissension and trouble in Corinth than any of the others. This gift was "speaking in tongues."

The apostle Paul offered no opposition to speaking with tongues. He was quite ready to accept this as a valid expression of an inward power from the Lord. However Paul was concerned that this gift of tongues should be controlled. In listing all the gifts for service according to their importance (1 Cor. 12:28), he puts this one last. And yet it received the most attention. Why? Because it appeared that this gift could be dangerous and harmful. It could cause divisions among people and could create tension and stir up resentment among believers.

Paul took time to explain that no gift of the Holy Spirit should be the cause of trouble. Paul placed practical limitations on the use of tongues. Some believers today who have experienced this phenomenon of speaking with tongues are quite concerned about it. Other believers think it is absolutely wrong to speak with tongues, because they see nothing to it. Some are concerned that if they spoke with tongues, they would be put out of the church to which they belong. It will be helpful to remember how Paul deals with this gift.

> Even so ye, forasmuch as ye are zealous of spiritual gifts, seek
> that ye may excel to the edifying of the church (1 Cor. 14:12).

Paul recognized that in Corinth some of the believers were

zealous to serve in a sophisticated way, with great intellectual significance. They preferred to think that when speaking with tongues, they evidenced the grace and the presence of God in an exceptional measure. Because the church would not be edified by unintelligible words, Paul wrote:

> Wherefore let him that speaketh in an unknown tongue pray that he may interpret. For if I pray in an unknown tongue, my spirit prayeth, but my understanding is unfruitful (1 Cor. 14:13-14).

This brings to our attention something of great importance, namely that our understanding of the gospel demands plain words and plain talk. This ties in with what the apostle Paul is saying: "If I pray in an unknown tongue, my spirit prayeth." No one will question or condemn such prayer. "But my understanding is unfruitful," because human understanding depends so much on words.

> What is it then? I will pray with the spirit, and I will pray with the understanding also: I will sing with the spirit, and I will sing with the understanding also (1 Cor. 14:15).

This is very important. When we listen to anthems and songs by our church choir, it is not just the rhythm and the tempo, but also the words and their meaning that bring blessing. This is why Paul says that he will both pray and sing "with understanding also." Every choir ought to recognize this, and every choir director should read this verse again and again.

> Else when thou shalt bless with the spirit, how shall he that occupieth the room of the unlearned say Amen at thy giving of thanks, seeing he understandeth not what thou sayest? (1 Cor. 14:16).

A public service is held so that other people can participate. A person who praises God in public expects others to join him. One who sings in public sings so that other people can join him. But how can others join in our worship service if they cannot understand what is preached or prayed or sung? This is what the apostle Paul is stressing. If people in their hearts join in public prayer, how can they say "Amen," if they do not understand the prayer? How can they join in the singing if the words are foreign to them? For the sake of other people who are present in the service, there must be perfect understanding of every word that is spoken or sung.

> For thou verily givest thanks well, but the other is not edified
> (1 Cor. 14:17).

This is Paul's burden throughout this discussion. "In everything, in the use of every God-given gift, think of others. How are they affected?" Paul emphasized his own attitude:

> I thank my God, I speak with tongues more than ye all: yet in the church I had rather speak five words with my understanding, that by my voice I might teach others also, than ten thousand words in an unknown tongue (1 Cor. 14:18-19).

This is something that should be kept in mind by every preacher and particularly by people who lead in prayer. Public prayers should be spoken clearly, slowly, and plainly so that everyone persent may pray along in their hearts. We should pray in such a way that someone who is present for the first time will be moved to pray also and be blessed.

Chapter 43

PUBLIC WORSHIP SERVICES SHOULD
BE ORDERLY

Paul concluded his long discussion of spiritual gifts with an appeal to the Corinthian believers' responsible understanding. At no time did he say that "speaking with tongues" was wrong, but he did want to challenge them to be intelligent when they practiced this gift.

> Brethren, be not children in understanding: howbeit in malice
> be ye children, but in understanding be men (1 Cor. 14:20).

Turning to Old Testament Scripture, Paul showed that the phenomenon of messengers speaking with "other tongues" would occur, but the purpose of this was to be a sign for unbelievers. On the other hand, prophesying was for the sake of believers.

> In the law it is written, With men of other tongues and other lips
> will I speak unto this people; and yet for all that will they not
> hear me, saith the Lord. Wherefore tongues are for a sign, not to
> them that believe, but to them that believe not: but prophesying
> serveth not for them that believe not, but for them which
> believe (1 Cor. 14:21-22).

Apparently public services of worship should be conducted with the possible presence of an unbeliever in mind. It will be important that the whole procedure commend itself to the attention and judgment of the unbeliever. When the unbeliever is favorably impressed and instructed in the course of the service, he will more readily recognize the truth of God.

> If therefore the whole church be come together into one place,
> and all speak with tongues, and there come in those that are
> unlearned, or unbelievers, will they not say that ye are mad?
> But if all prophesy, and there come in one that believeth not, or
> one unlearned, he is convinced of all, he is judged of all: and thus

are the secrets of his heart made manifest; and so falling down on his face he will worship God, and report that God is in you of a truth (1 Cor. 14:23-25).

Because of the importance of careful conduct in public worship services Paul suggested an orderly procedure (1 Cor. 14:26-31). He urged that the believers control themselves to maintain an atmosphere of peace. A basic principle to be kept in mind is that such self-control is possible in the Lord.

And the spirits of the prophets are subject to the prophets. For God is not the author of confusion, but of peace, as in all churches of the saints (1 Cor. 14:32-33).

Continuing his admonition that public worship services should be conducted in peaceful fashion, Paul advised believing women to refrain from vocal participation. This may have had a primarily local bearing because the notorious activity of women in the pagan temples was a scandal in Corinth. Paul may have had in mind that public decorum on the part of women who believed in Christ would improve the testimony of the gospel in that city. That Paul did not forbid women to share in public worship services seems to be revealed in his writings elsewhere (Phil. 4:3).

Paul did not take time in any effort to prove the authenticity of his treatment of this whole problem. Rather he challenged any person claiming to belong to Christ to admit the testimony of the Holy Spirit in his own heart as to the truth of Paul's comments. If any reader were not inwardly taught of God, Paul made no effort to convince that person.

The final admonition is based on the whole discussion. Apparently believers by their attitudes can influence their own endowment with helpful gifts; but no one should forbid those who have the lesser gifts to exercise them. And all this is deliberately designed to promote peace among the brethren.

What? came the word of God out from you? or came it unto you only? If any man think himself to be a prophet, or spiritual, let him acknowledge that the things that I write unto you are the commandments of the Lord. But if any man be ignorant, let him be ignorant. Wherefore, brethren, covet to prophesy, and forbid not to speak with tongues. Let all things be done decently and in order (1 Cor. 14:36-40).

Chapter 44

THE GOSPEL IS BASED ON THE
RESURRECTION

In 1 Corinthians 15 Paul wrote his most comprehensive discussion of the doctrine of resurrection from the dead. He was concerned that the Corinthians should be aware of the significance of the resurrection for their own spiritual experience in order that they might in faith live in the newness of life, which is provided in Christ Jesus. These believers were evidently babes in Christ, which helped to account for their contentions (1 Cor. 3:1-3). Apparently Paul felt that they needed to be reminded and confirmed in their understanding that in the resurrection they would live in the newness of life, forsaking old ways of living (2 Cor. 5:17). What he had to say about Christ's resurrection was really part of the gospel story:

> For I delivered unto you first of all that which I also received, how that Christ died for our sins according to the scriptures; and that he was buried, and that he rose again the third day according to the scriptures: and that he was seen of Cephas, then of the twelve: after that, he was seen of above five hundred brethren at once; of whom the greater part remain unto this present, but some are fallen asleep. After that, he was seen of James; then of all the apostles. And last of all he was seen of me also, as of one born out of due time (1 Cor. 15:3-8).

Paul considered himself as "the least of the apostles," but understood that "by the grace of God I am what I am," and could say that he "laboured more abundantly than they all." He preached the same message the other apostles preached, and that was what the Corinthians had believed. That message affirmed that Jesus was "alive" (Acts 25:19).

Apparently some in Corinth were saying there is no resurrection of the body, and Paul met such ideas in open contradic-

140

tion. He linked the resurrection of the believers with the resurrection of Christ Jesus. If Christ was raised from the dead, then the believers will be raised; but if there is no resurrection from the dead for the believers, then Christ was not raised from the dead. In that case the gospel is false and the Corinthians are yet in their sins. This would be the logical conclusion, but Paul had no doubt about the resurrection of Christ Jesus.

> But now is Christ risen from the dead, and become the firstfruits of them that slept (1 Cor. 15:20).

When Paul wrote of Christ being the "firstfruits," he meant that Christ's resurrection was an example, a sample of what will follow. If we went to a peach orchard and found the first ripe peach, that would be a sample of what the whole orchard would produce. In that sense, the firstfruits, the first full ripe fruit, is the sample of all that will come after it. In like manner Christ Jesus risen from the dead is a sample of all others who will be raised from the dead.

> For since by man came death, by man came also the resurrection of the dead (1 Cor. 15:21).

Having within us the life and the sin of Adam, we also share in the death of Adam. "By man came also the resurrection of the dead." Jesus of Nazareth, by His resurrection, in the form of a man, will through His righteousness bring all who belong to Him into the resurrection from the dead.

> For as in Adam all die, even so in Christ shall all be made alive. But every man in his own order: Christ the firstfruits; afterward they that are Christ's at his coming (1 Cor. 15:22-23).

He is the One who goes first; afterward those who belong to Him, who have been born again in the Spirit, will be raised like Him. "They are Christ's at his coming."

> Then cometh the end, when he shall have delivered up the kingdom to God, even the Father; when he shall have put down all rule and all authority and power (1 Cor. 15:24).

In Psalm 8:6 we find these words: "Thou madest him to have dominion over the works of thy hands; thou hast put all things under his feet." This refers to the Son of God, our Lord, who, when His work was completed, returned all rule and authority and power to the Father.

> For he must reign, till he hath put all enemies under his feet
> (1 Cor. 15:25).

In other words, Jesus Christ will absolutely accomplish the purpose of God.

> The last enemy that shall be destroyed is death (1 Cor. 15:26).

Christ Jesus our Lord overcame death in and by His resurrection from the dead.

> For he hath put all things under his feet. But when he saith all
> things are put under him, it is manifest that he is excepted,
> which did put all things under him. And when all things shall be
> subdued unto him, then shall the Son also himself be subject
> unto him that put all things under him, that God may be all in all
> (1 Cor. 15:27-28).

These verses are a description of the arrangement that exists in the Godhead itself. In the plan of God, Jesus Christ was in control of all creation until His work here was completed and death was defeated. Then all things would be delivered to the Father, and the Son also becomes subject to the Father.

> Else what shall they do which are baptized for the dead, if the
> dead rise not at all? why are they then baptized for the dead?
> (1 Cor. 15:29).

It is strange how many different interpretations have been offered for this verse. I will suggest that this verse is most meaningful when we consider that "dead" refers to the death of the old nature, the old man in us. In other words, why make an open profession of having accepted Jesus Christ as our Savior and Lord if we are still just the human beings we were before?

> And why stand we in jeopardy every hour? (1 Cor. 15:30).

Paul is saying, "Why endure suffering and constant danger except for your faith and your hope of the resurrection?"

> I protest by your rejoicing which I have in Christ Jesus our Lord,
> I die daily (1 Cor. 15:31).

Here the word *die* points to self-denial. Paul was willing to stake the joy which was his, because he had led the Corinthians to faith in the Lord Jesus Christ, upon the truth that believing means the daily dying to self.

If after the manner of men I have fought with beasts at Ephesus, what advantageth it me, if the dead rise not? . . . (1 Cor. 15:32).

The expression "after the manner of men" means "as an ordinary human being." In other words, Paul asked, "If I do this thing in my human strength, where is my hope of the resurrection? Risking my body in the arena against lions is an advantage to me only when I believe that I will be raised from the dead."

In the following verse Paul shows the demoralizing thoughts that can follow when believers doubt the resurrection and try to accomplish something in human strength alone. "Let us eat and drink; for tomorrow we die." If there is no hope of the resurrection, all else is vain.

Be not deceived: evil communications corrupt good manners. Awake to righteousness, and sin not; for some have not the knowledge of God: I speak this to your shame (1 Cor. 15:33-34).

These are words of warning and counsel. "Do not let those who have no knowledge of God, who doubt the resurrection, corrupt your faith and your way of life in Christ Jesus. Follow after righteousness which is in Him and deny yourselves, for the certain hope of the resurrection is yours." In other words, the resurrection of the body is necessary for the gospel that Paul is preaching. It is the very cornerstone of Christian hope and faith.

Chapter 45

THE RESURRECTION BODY

The resurrection of the body is a truth that is hard to grasp. Even when Jesus of Nazareth was raised from the dead and identified Himself before His disciples by showing them His hands, His feet, and His side, they found it hard to believe the evidence of their own senses. The Resurrection goes beyond our common understanding. It challenges our careful consideration. To those who doubt the reality of God and the gospel of the Lord Jesus Christ, the Resurrection will seem fantastic. To us that know that God is almighty and that Jesus Christ is the Son of God and our Savior, the Resurrection is not only possible, but real and reasonable.

> But some man will say, How are the dead raised up? and with what body do they come? (1 Cor. 15:35).

How often has this question been asked? How wonderful that the Scriptures contain the answer.

> Thou fool, that which thou sowest is not quickened, except it die (1 Cor. 15:36).

"Thou fool" could be translated, *"Thou foolish one,* are you so naive that you do not know that which you sow is not quickened, except it die?" Paul is using the illustration of wheat being put into the ground and then springing up in the newness of life. He is pointing out that the seed of wheat sown into the ground can produce nothing, until it in itself disintegrates.

> For if we have been planted together in the likeness of his death, we shall be also in the likeness of his resurrection (Rom. 6:5).

"Planted together" contains this same idea of the seed being

144

put into the ground. It is only as the seed in the ground dies that out of it come the stalk and the green blade, which do not resemble the kernel of wheat that was put in the ground. And yet the identity is constant.

> And that which thou sowest, thou sowest not that body that shall be, but bare grain, it may chance of wheat, or of some other grain: but God giveth it a body as it hath pleased him, and to every seed his own body (1 Cor. 15:37-38).

It is God who causes the green stalk to grow up out of the kernel of grain, which was put into the ground to die for this purpose.

> . . . it doth not yet appear what we shall be: but we know that, when he shall appear, we shall be like him; for we shall see him as he is (1 John 3:2).

This clearly indicates that we will be different when we are raised from the dead. In the four Gospels and in the Book of Acts we are told that the risen body of our Lord Jesus Christ had a different nature. The kernel put into the ground was wheat and the green stalk is wheat, but they have a different appearance.

> All flesh is not the same flesh: but there is one kind of flesh of men, another flesh of beasts, another of fishes, and another of birds (1 Cor. 15:39).

Just because the body is flesh it can still be different, depending on its composition and substance. Similarly, it depends on what was planted in the ground that determines what will come out of the ground.

> There are also celestial bodies, and bodies terrestrial: but the glory of the celestial is one, and the glory of the terrestrial is another. There is one glory of the sun, and another glory of the moon, and another glory of the stars: for one star differeth from another star in glory (1 Cor. 15:40-41).

Celestial means "heavenly," and *terrestrial* refers to the "earthly." There are heavenly bodies and earthly bodies. Paul clearly indicated that the body we have here on earth is only in some respects the body we will have in the resurrection. Our resurrected body will be constituted of different "stuff." It will not be made of the same substance as our natural body.

> So also is the resurrection of the dead. It is sown in corruption; it is raised in incorruption (1 Cor. 15:42).

The body that is put into the ground in death is a decaying and corrupting body. In fact, even while we live in our human body, the tissues are wasting away and being replaced by new ones all the time. That is the way it is with ourselves. It is, in a way, actually living and dying at the same time. This is why our natural body can decay and is called corruptible. But the new body that will be ours in the resurrection can't decay. It is eternal. Just like the one is mortal and the other is eternal, so "it is sown in corruption, it is raised [in the resurrection] in incorruption." "It is sown in dishonor" — the natural body that is sown has the germ of death in it — "it is raised in glory." The spiritual body is free from all weakness. Each of us as a human physical being will die. Our bodies sown in weakness will be raised in power. Everyone who is a new creature in Christ Jesus has a nature in him that has the power to live eternally; it is immortal.

> It is sown a natural body; it is raised a spiritual body. There is a natural body, and there is a spiritual body (1 Cor. 15:44).

I want to call attention to the concept of "a spiritual body." This is strange to us. Commonly speaking, in our ordinary use of the word *spiritual*, we do not associate it with a body such as we have. We should not say however that a spirit cannot have a body. We know that when our Lord Jesus Christ arose from the dead, He was raised in the Spirit, but He had a body. He was raised in a body that had corporeality, which means that it had a *corpus*, a body. It was a body that could be seen and handled, and yet it was not natural. It was not human flesh; the substance it was made of was spiritual, not earthly. It was not made of carbon, oxygen, and hydrogen, etc. It was not made of the dust that would return to dust and ashes that would return to ashes. It was made of matter that was eternal, which will never die.

Chapter 46

THE HEAVENLY BODY

In our last study we considered the wonderful truth of the resurrection of the dead. In 1 Corinthians 15:45 we read that the whole truth of the resurrection of the body points forward to heaven into the very presence of God. In the meantime, while we are here on earth, we will look ahead with confidence and joy to the day when our mortal bodies will be changed.

> And so it is written, The first man Adam was made a living soul; the last Adam was made a quickening spirit (1 Cor. 15:45).

Now the "first Adam" is the one God created in the Garden of Eden. The "last Adam" refers to Jesus of Nazareth. We read here that "the first Adam was made a living soul." That is to say that he was a living being, someone with self-consciousness, with an ego, with an identity of his own. He was a living person and all his children would be just the way he was. "The last Adam," Jesus of Nazareth, "was made a quickening spirit." He was, after the Resurrection, more than a living human being of flesh and bone and muscle and nerves. He was something more than that. In His resurrection from the dead His spiritual body was not hampered by any of the limitations of His mortal body.

> Howbeit that was not first which is spiritual, but that which is natural; and afterward that which is spiritual (1 Cor. 15:46).

God made Adam of the dust of the earth. But of the children of Adam, "as many as received Him [Christ Jesus]," He made of them children of God. So the first is that which is natural, afterward that which is spiritual. We call the natural birth the "first birth." Being made the children of God through faith in Jesus Christ we call the "second birth."

147

> The first man is of the earth, earthy: the second man is the Lord
> from heaven (1 Cor. 15:47).

When Paul wrote "The first man is of the earth, earthy," he was saying again that Adam was made of the dust of the ground, and that he was therefore of that substance and nature. "The second man is the Lord from heaven" means that the second man, Jesus of Nazareth, was born as the Son of God. It is true that He came into this world in human form, but He was the Son of God from heaven.

> As is the earthy, such are they also that are earthy: and as is the
> heavenly, such are they also that are heavenly (1 Cor. 15:48).

This repeats for emphasis the same thought that all the descendants of Adam are of the earth as he was. Those who have believed in Jesus Christ, those who have been born again, are the children of the heavenly.

> And as we have borne the image of the earthy, we shall also bear
> the image of the heavenly (1 Cor. 15:49).

These are actually words of promise that we who bear the likeness of the natural will, because we are born again in Christ Jesus, be raised in His likeness. This naturally does not relate to human likeness in any way. Rather, as we are born again, we will have His disposition to "please the Father in all things."

> Now this I say, brethren, that flesh and blood cannot inherit the
> kingdom of God; neither doth corruption inherit incorruption
> (1 Cor. 15:50).

This is a dogmatic, categoric statement. It is positive and puts a sweeping end to the discussion. "Flesh and blood cannot inherit the kingdom of God." No human being in his own physical, sociological human nature can enter into the kingdom of God. Surely this illuminating truth should be taught and preached, instead of trying to get unregenerated human beings to do what the Scripture demands only of the children of God. Out of a corruptible body can never spring eternal, incorruptible beings.

> Behold, I show you a mystery . . . (1 Cor. 15:51).

Paul means by this statement that he would reveal a hidden truth, something that was true all the time and yet something which had not been seen. It is mysterious in the sense that electricity in a copper wire is a mystery. We cannot see it, but it is there. It is the underground oil in an oilfield. We can grow corn in the field, but underneath is oil, which is hidden. This is what Paul means by mystery — not something strange or abnormal, but something that exists and yet is out of sight. He is saying, "I am going to show you something that does not appear on the surface."

> We shall not all sleep, but we shall all be changed (1 Cor. 15:51).

Not everyone is going to pass through the experience of physical death, but all believers will pass through the experience of personal change, and this will be an absolute change. The body of the person who dies in the flesh will return to dust. The body the believer receives in the resurrection will be different from the body which returned to the dust. It will be as different as the brown kernel of wheat is to the green stalk which appears.

This truth applies equally to those believers who are living on earth when our Lord Jesus Christ returns.

> In a moment, in the twinkling of an eye, at the last trump: for the trumpet shall sound, and the dead shall be raised incorruptible, and we shall be changed (1 Cor. 15:52).

We can readily understand that the dead will be raised to life, and that they will have different bodies from the ones that were put into the ground. The resurrected bodies will be fashioned of something eternal and incorruptible. Those believers who are alive on earth at the time of the return of our Lord Jesus Christ will be suddenly transformed, in an instant of time. Their bodies will become spiritual bodies like the body of our Lord after His resurrection.

> For this corruptible must put on incorruption, and this mortal must put on immortality. So when this corruptible shall have put on incorruption, and this mortal shall have put on immortality, then shall be brought to pass the saying that is written, Death is swallowed up in victory. O death, where is thy sting? O grave, where is thy victory? The sting of death is sin; and the strength of sin is the law. But thanks be to God, which giveth us the victory through our Lord Jesus Christ (1 Cor. 15:53-57).

This tremendous change will actually take place.

Therefore, my beloved brethren, be ye steadfast, unmovable, always abounding in the work of the Lord, forasmuch as ye know that your labour is not in vain in the Lord (1 Cor. 15:58).

By the grace and power of God all believers will live again, a life that is eternal.

Chapter 47

PLANNING AHEAD

In 1 Corinthians 16 Paul wrote in a practical way about what is commonly referred to as "the guidance of the Holy Spirit." There are some believers who feel that it is wrong to make any plans because they believe that they should just be ready to act as the Spirit leads them. They claim that it is spiritually wise to move along as they are led and when they are led.

Once I had a friend who was a young preacher. He had a tendency when preaching to his congregation to say practically the same thing every Sunday. When he preached, he came back to the same things and kept emphasizing them over and over. In that city we ministers sent our sermon topics to the newspapers in order that they might publish them for each succeeding Sunday. The copy of the various sermon topics had to be in the newspaper office on Tuesday. I noticed that this young man never announced a sermon topic. Occasionally I mentioned this to him, hoping that if he published his sermon topic he would do a better, more organized job on Sunday, preaching something that would have more body to it.

One day this young preacher took me aside and explained why he would not publish his sermon topics. He said, "I want to be led by the Spirit. Suppose I announced on Tuesday what I would preach on the next Sunday, and when Sunday came, the Spirit would lead me to preach on something else. Then what would I do?" I replied, "Did it ever occur to you that the Spirit might lead you before Sunday, so that you could prepare yourself?" He never did comprehend that. Yet actually planning and preparing one's sermons is a mark of diligence. Preparation of this kind is only giving our work the attention it deserves.

151

If a woman has to prepare meals for her family, part of her work is planning her menus ahead of time. A good cook would know on Monday what she will serve on Tuesday, and so on through the week. Surely her meals will be better and less expensive when she plans them in advance.

Jesus of Nazareth taught about this matter of preparedness.

> And there went great multitudes with him: and he turned, and said unto them, If any man come to me, and hate not his father, and mother, and wife, and children, and brethren, and sisters, yea, and his own life also, he cannot be my disciple. And whosoever doth not bear his cross, and come after me, cannot be my disciple (Luke 14:25-27).

Here our Lord was instructing those who were following him that to be His disciple one must first purpose in his heart the things he intends to do. He is to think things through.

> For which of you, intending to build a tower, sitteth not down first, and counteth the cost, whether he have sufficient to finish it? Lest haply, after he hath laid the foundation, and is not able to finish it, all that behold it begin to mock him, saying, This man began to build, and was not able to finish. Or what king, going to make war against another king, sitteth not down first, and consulteth whether he be able with ten thousand to meet him that cometh against him with twenty thousand? Or else, while the other is yet a great way off, he sendeth an ambassage, and desireth conditions of peace. So likewise, whosoever he be of you that forsaketh not all that he hath, he cannot be my disciple (Luke 14:28-33).

Jesus was teaching here that deliberate, intelligent, purposeful planning is essential to discipleship. In our Lord's service planning the program is actually part of spiritual control.

In 1 Corinthians 16 we will find recorded several instances of this very thing I have been discussing. Paul wrote concerning money that would be given to charity:

> Now concerning the collection for the saints, as I have given order to the churches of Galatia, even so do ye. Upon the first day of the week let every one of you lay by him in store, as God hath prospered him, that there be no gatherings when I come (1 Cor. 16:1-2).

"Take up your collections now, before I come, so that when I come, we can make use of it." Surely this also points to careful planning. Sometimes church members think that budgeting finances in the affairs of the church is not spiritual, but this is not true. I believe that plans may be made depending on God's support; but we need to know what we are doing, and we should plan accordingly.

Paul, in speaking of the money being collected for the poor, said, "Upon the first day of the week." I have been asked whether Sunday is the first day of the week. We call it "the Lord's Day," and this is evidently the day on which the church in Corinth met for worship. This meant that they met one day out of the seven. The word *Sabbath* means "one-seventh." It also means "rest." Both of these ideas stemmed from the first great illustration of the Sabbath, at the time of the creation. God made the world in six days, and on the seventh day, one in seven, He rested. So here we see the word *seventh* and the word *rest* combined in the word *Sabbath*. When believers speak of the first day of the week, they still have their "seventh" day set apart. Believers worship God on the first day of the week, and on the strength and the blessing they receive on this day of rest they go for six days.

"Upon the first day of the week" the believers in Corinth came together to worship, and to take up their collection for charity. Paul left the details of the planning in their hands.

> And when I come, whomsoever ye shall approve by your letters, them will I send to bring your liberality unto Jerusalem (1 Cor. 16:3).

The Corinthians themselves were the ones to choose who should be sent to Jerusalem with the money.

> And if it be meet that I go also, they shall go with me (1 Cor. 16:4).

If it turned out that Paul was to go to Jerusalem at the same time, they could all go together. What a wonderful experience it would be for a young Christian to travel in the company of one of the great apostles! Yet Paul puts no emphasis on himself, even though he was the man who had been so mightily used of God in their behalf.

> Now I will come unto you, when I shall pass through Macedonia: for I do pass through Macedonia. And it may be that I will abide, yea, and winter with you, that ye may bring me on my journey whithersoever I go (1 Cor. 16:5-6).

All of this indicates looking forward to the future and planning for it. Here we find no slothful folding of the hands, but energetic, dedicated, orderly planning, subject to the will of God and redounding to His glory.

> For I will not see you now by the way; but I trust to tarry a while with you, if the Lord permit. But I will tarry at Ephesus until Pentecost. For a great door and effectual is opened unto me, and there are many adversaries (1 Cor. 16:7-9).

Despite his great affection for the Corinthian believers Paul could not visit them at this time, but he hoped to spend some time with them later if this was in the Lord's will for him. Evidently Paul planned his schedule but always under the Lord's guidance. He expected to spend some time at Ephesus where he faced a great opportunity and would encounter much opposition.

> Now if Timothy come, see that he may be with you without fear: for he worketh the work of the Lord, as I also do. Let no man therefore despise him: but conduct him forth in peace, that he may come unto me: for I look for him with the brethren (1 Cor. 16:10-11).

Paul looked upon Timothy as his own son in the faith. He asked the Corinthian believers to receive Timothy with respect because he was a true servant of the Lord, and to help him on his journey that he might join Paul.

> As touching our brother Apollos, I greatly desired him to come unto you with the brethren: but his will was not at all to come at this time; but he will come when he shall have convenient time (1 Cor. 16:12).

Apollos had been one of the preachers over whom divisions had occurred in Corinth (1:12; 3:22). It has been noted that this comment by Paul indicated that Apollos did not want to visit these believers who were preferring him in a divisive way. It can be seen that Paul urged him to visit Corinth despite this tension, but Apollos humbly declined "to come at this time." This reference seems to reflect the fine fellowship between Paul and Apollos, as it shows that ministers do have an option about going here or there in their travels.

Paul concluded his epistle with strong exhortation:

> Watch ye, stand fast in the faith, quit you like men, be strong.
> Let all your things be done with charity (1 Cor. 16:13-14).

After he had conveyed personal greetings from individuals and from other congregations, Paul bluntly challenged each person with the claim of the Lord Jesus Christ.

> If any man love not the Lord Jesus Christ, let him be Anathema Maranatha (1 Cor. 16:22).

Personal commitment and loyal service to Christ Jesus was the prerequisite Paul demanded of any person who wanted to have fellowship with him.

Second
Corinthians

Chapter 48

A PASTOR'S CONCERN FOR HIS PEOPLE

Paul, an apostle of Jesus Christ by the will of God, and Timothy our brother, unto the church of God which is at Corinth, with all the saints which are in all Achaia: Grace be to you and peace from God our Father, and from the Lord Jesus Christ (2 Cor. 1:1-2).

The Epistles to the Corinthians were written by a pastor to his former congregation. Before this time Paul had come to the city of Corinth and had been used in calling these people together in their faith in the Lord Jesus Christ. Paul ministered among them for months. He wanted them to grow in their Christian experience and in faith; he yearned over his congregation as a nurse cares for her patients or as a father cares for his children.

First Corinthians presents one correction after another of blemishes or faults. The Corinthian Christians were new believers who believed in the Lord Jesus Christ. They were following Him, but were doing many things contrary to the gospel. There may be a child in your home who is doing things that are contrary to your wishes, but he is still your child.

All men are born as natural human beings; believers are born again. They are to develop into spiritual persons as children of God. All believers have in themselves two principles: flesh and spirit. We have naturally our earthly parents; but we also have a heavenly parent: Almighty God. Flesh can be good or bad, but it is always natural, following the principles and laws of nature. We read that flesh and blood shall not inherit the kingdom of God. The Lord Jesus Christ said about the flesh, "You must be born again." That which is of the flesh is flesh and that which is born of the Spirit is spirit. The person born in the flesh must be born again. The other element in every believer we call the spirit: the Spirit is from God. This is heavenly in origin and is good in its character. It is the spiritual element in the believer.

Paul wrote that "if any man be in Christ, he is a new creature." Every sincere believer has in him something that is quite new. As many as are led by the Spirit of God are the sons of God. They are not those who merely talk about it, or those who claim to have it, but they are the people who are led by the Spirit of God who are the sons of God.

Each believer has both these elements in him. In every believer there is the natural element, which is human in nature and social in character, so that he is a social being among others. This is the flesh. And every believer has his spiritual being: he is godly because of the Spirit who is within him. We read in Galatians that the "flesh lusteth against the Spirit, and the Spirit against the flesh: and these are contrary the one to the other: so that ye cannot do the things that ye would" (Gal. 5:17).

Every believer has an inner conflict in him between the flesh and the spirit. While in the Orient a few years ago, I was asked by one of the native pastors if it is true that there is in the life of a believer both flesh and the spirit, even though flesh and spirit are contrary to one another. I told him that was certainly true. He said in that case there would be continuing conflict, which would be psychologically bad. It is important that a person should find peace and rest, but how could a believer who has within him both flesh and spirit ever arrive at peace within himself?

His question reminded me of something I had seen in the fields of that country. Farmers often used large water buffaloes as their main source of power. I noticed these buffaloes needed to be guided, usually by ten- or twelve-year-old boys who sometimes rode one of the animals. The buffalo preferred to lie in a pool of water and stay cool; the boy wanted him to work because his boss was watching. With the boy on the buffalo, there was a situation of relative peace. But if the buffalo were on top and the boy on the bottom, there would be conflict. So it is with the flesh and the spirit. If the spirit is in control, so that a person is led by the Spirit of God, the person can have peace and quietness in his soul. But if he is led by the flesh, his actions produce conflict.

Thus, in the heart of the believer, one principle must prevail. John the Baptist spoke of it: "He must increase, but I must decrease" (John 3:30). And that is the way it will be inside of a believer's heart: the things of the Lord must gain ascendancy and the things of the flesh must diminish.

Paul followed a practical procedure in leading these people in this matter, and we can apply it to ourselves. Natural man looks around and sees things he would like to have to make himself feel important. But those things are of the flesh and could lead into sin. As a believer, a person has in his heart (created by the Spirit of God) a disposition to want to please the Lord. The believer should feed the Spirit with the Word of God and deny the flesh, which will get weaker and weaker. Paul wrote 2 Corinthians to encourage believers to grow spiritually, urging them to deny their flesh. This is what we will be considering in this study, asking the Lord to guide us so that we can grow in grace and in knowledge.

Chapter 49

THE SUFFERING OF A BELIEVER CAN BE
A BLESSING TO OTHERS

> Blessed be God, even the Father of our Lord Jesus Christ, the
> Father of mercies, and the God of all comfort; who comforteth us
> in all our tribulation, that we may be able to comfort them which
> are in any trouble, by the comfort wherewith we ourselves are
> comforted of God (2 Cor. 1:3-4).

This is a most remarkable statement. In it we find what a true
believer will look like. When Paul describes a true believer,
the first things he notes are the blessing of God on the believer's daily affairs and comfort when the believer has trouble.

It is when we have trouble that we take note of things.
Unfortunately, this is a human characteristic. When everything is going well, it is easy to forget about God and to let
things go. But it is when we have trouble and suffering that we
stop, look, and listen. At no time is God so real or His grace so
precious as when we are in trouble and He helps us. It is then
that the heart feels the wonderful comfort of God and is filled
with thanksgiving and praise to the God of all grace.

In this passage Paul emphasizes a dimension, an aspect of
suffering, which can bring real blessing. In the days of Abraham, the Lord said, "I will bless thee and make thee a blessing." Here Paul is saying that God will comfort the believer so
that he can comfort others. The believer finds that God will
forgive sin and that He wants believers to forgive those who sin
against them. When the believer is lonely, he finds that the
Lord will stand by; and God wants believers to stand by other
lonely people, so that they can learn about God.

The believer who has suffered doubt finds assurance in
Scripture; then God wants him to go to other pople who are
doubting and study the Bible with them to help them in their
doubts. When Paul discusses the matter of trouble, he is

delving into something that is as common as mankind, because "man is born unto trouble, as the sparks fly upward" (Job 5:7). Everyone has trouble. The Lord Jesus said, "In the world ye shall have tribulation: but be of good cheer; I have overcome the world" (John 16:33). And just as God helps believers overcome the world, He wants them to help others overcome the world in the same way.

> For as the sufferings of Christ abound in us, so our consolation also aboundeth by Christ. And whether we be afflicted, it is for your consolation and salvation, which is effectual in the enduring of the same sufferings which we also suffer: or whether we be comforted, it is for your consolation and salvation. And our hope of you is steadfast, knowing, that as ye are partakers of the sufferings, so shall ye be also of the consolation (2 Cor. 1:5-7).

This is what Paul writes to these believers regarding their personal affairs. The sufferings of Christ will be their experience, but they will also have the consolation of Christ. Whatever the sorrow and pain, the believer brings them to the Lord Jesus Christ. He will bear the believer's infirmities in Himself and carry them away, and the believer shall be delivered. Do you want to be a true believer, to actually grow as a believer? The blessing will come to you and then through you to other people.

Let us remember again the geography of the Holy Land: the Jordan River flows down into the Sea of Galilee, then out into the Dead Sea. As the river flows through the Sea of Galilee, the water is sweet and wholesome. It flows into the Dead Sea but never flows out, and there it becomes a salty brine, a lake in which nothing grows. That is why it is called the Dead Sea. The human heart is like that. If I am blessed, I must give out the blessing; if I am blessed but never give out the blessing, I will be like a cistern in which the water becomes rancid. In order to have sweet water that is usable, it must be running water.

Paul says, "Whether we be afflicted, it is for your consolation and salvation, which is effectual in the enduring of the same sufferings which we also suffer: or whether we be comforted, it is for your consolation and salvation" (v. 6). Regardless of what happened to Paul, it was designed for the Corinthians. Believers should know that regardless of what happens to them, everything is designed for other people who will benefit by seeing and receiving help. In like manner, no matter what joy or gladness there may be, it is for others also.

Some years ago our family had a baby boy who was very dear to our hearts. God took that boy to Himself. It was a severe blow, and for many years our hearts were tender over the loss of that boy. Even to this day we remember him with a sense of sorrow and loss. But God spoke to our hearts in that experience, and told us that He would be with us and would bless us. We were given this verse of Scripture: "Thy lovingkindness is better than life" (Ps. 63:3). That verse, through our testimony, has proved to be a source of blessing to many others.

A believer will keep in mind that Almighty God knows what is happening to him, is watching over him, and is touched with all the feelings of his infirmities. Just as surely as the believer enters into suffering, God will see him through. Then the believer can be of help to others. In many ways this is the main function of the believer — to help others know God and trust Him.

Chapter 50

THE BASIS FOR CONFIDENCE

The apostle Paul knew what it meant to walk in the will of God. He was like a man who steps into a ditch and gets wet: he knows what it is like to be covered with water, and he can talk about it. Paul knew what it was like to walk in the Lord (he had done it), and he had experiences of trusting in God. Because of this he could write this epistle.

In this Second Epistle to the Corinthians the first aspect that Paul discussed about living in faith was the assurance that God wants His people to be comforted in trouble. Paul pointed out the principle that God blesses those who believe in Him that they may comfort others. Paul now presents an example of this blessing.

> For we would not, brethren, have you ignorant of our trouble which came to us in Asia, that we were pressed out of measure, above strength, insomuch that we despaired even of life: but we had the sentence of death in ourselves, that we should not trust in ourselves, but in God which raiseth the dead: who delivered us from so great a death, and doth deliver: in whom we trust that he will yet deliver us; ye also helping together by prayer for us, that for the gift bestowed upon us by the means of many persons thanks may be given by many on our behalf. For our rejoicing is this, the testimony of our conscience, that in simplicity and godly sincerity, not with fleshly wisdom, but by the grace of God, we have had our conversation in the world, and more abundantly to you-ward (2 Cor. 1:8-12).

When Paul left the city of Corinth he went to the city of Ephesus, which was in a part of what we know as Asia Minor. He stayed and preached there two years. Toward the end of that time there were people in the city of Ephesus who learned that when the Ephesians became believers in Christ they no longer worshiped in the heathen temples. Thus they did not buy the silver trinkets, the images of the goddess Diana; and this meant that the silversmiths were losing their trade. Therefore the silversmiths stirred up a riot so great that there was danger for Paul's life. It is written in the Book of Acts that when Paul wanted to go to the rioters and explain to them what he was doing, his own followers would not let him, because they feared for his life. Paul did not in himself have the strength to overcome the danger of that violent mob, but he trusted in God. "But we had the sentence of death in ourselves, that we should not trust in ourselves, but in God which raiseth the dead" (2 Cor. 1:9). Paul did not think he in himself was that strong, but he was confident in God's strength.

In this incident we can see that a person who wants to live in obedience to Christ will remember what God has done for him. The believer may have trouble and he may suffer loss (even loss of life), but he will not be everlastingly destroyed. Paul had confidence that God would watch over him in this trouble.

When we read, "Ye also helping together by prayer for us" (v. 11), it brings to our mind that Paul took courage not only from his trust in God, but also from knowing that his fellow believers were praying for him. They had proven their interest by helping him, not only praying for him but by contributing to his support: ". . . that for the gift bestowed upon us by the means of many persons thanks may be given by many on our behalf." They had helped him with money.

As we read on we have further proof of Paul's honesty and spiritual conduct: "For our rejoicing is this, the testimony of our conscience." Paul knew his own heart in this matter. He kept in mind, "that in simplicity and godly sincerity [Paul lived his life openly], not with fleshly wisdom [he did not make up his mind according to human or personal ideas], but by the grace of God [he acted according to the promises of God], we have had our conversation [that is, our manner of life], in the world, and more abundantly to you-ward [this is the reason why we live this way]."

In this simple outline we have the formula for living. Paul emphasized that a believer could follow this if he wanted confidence in the day of trouble. In case you are having serious trouble, think of these things and remember that Christ died for us.

Chapter 51

THE BASIS OF A BELIEVER'S CONFIDENCE

How often we have been uncertain and fearful of tomorrow! But that shows that we have good sense. Death will certainly come, and no one knows when; but it is not necessary for the believer to be burdened with such uncertainty. He may not know what will happen, but he can know who will be there. I may not know how things will turn out but

> I know whom I have believed, and am persuaded that he is able to keep that which I have committed unto him against that day (2 Tim. 1:12).

Nothing that will happen tomorrow is unknown to God.

In 2 Corinthians, when writing about a life of faith, Paul uses himself as an example:

> For we write none other things unto you, than what ye read or acknowledge; and I trust ye shall acknowledge even to the end; as also ye have acknowledged us in part, that we are your rejoicing, even as ye also are ours in the day of the Lord Jesus (2 Cor. 1:13-14).

Paul is looking ahead with sure confidence, knowing that God is in heaven and that Christ died, rose again, ascended into heaven, and is now there praying for us.

One reason why Paul is so confident is that he is sure these believers will stand by him, and this is one big factor in the confidence and courage of all: the fellowship of other believers. Some years ago, during World War II, an incident occurred at sea. Apparently a troop ship had been torpedoed and was sinking. There were not enough lifeboats for all of the men on board. Four chaplains aboard stood together, gave up their places in the lifeboat, and went down with the ship, arm in arm. I have often been strengthened as I remembered that.

> And in this confidence I was minded to come unto you before,
> that ye might have a second benefit; and to pass by you into
> Macedonia, and to come again out of Macedonia unto you, and
> of you to be brought on my way toward Judea (2 Cor. 1:15-16).

Paul planned to go to Corinth and then to go on from there in
his journeys. His coming would have been a blessing to them.
He had been there before, and they had received a benefit;
now he would come again, and they would have a second
benefit. He knew if he came and talked about the Lord and
explained the gospel to them, it would strengthen them.

> When I therefore was thus minded, did I use lightness? or the
> things that I purpose, do I purpose according to the flesh, that
> with me there should be yea, yea, and nay, nay? (2 Cor. 1:17).

Paul is confident because he is counting on help from the Lord;
he did not make his plans on human judgment, and now he is
confident because the Lord would carry out His promises.

> But as God is true, our word toward you was not yea and nay.
> For the Son of God, Jesus Christ, who was preached among you
> by us, even by me and Silvanus and Timothy, was not yea and
> nay, but in him was yea (2 Cor. 1:18-19).

In other words, there was nothing tentative about the will of
the Lord Jesus Christ; nothing merely suggestive about the
gospel. It was a positive message, dynamic in its effect on
people and sure about the Lord Jesus. There was no saying *if* or
maybe. "If God be for us, who can be against us?" As we live
our Christian life, expectantly, we can be sure that God is in
heaven on the throne, watching over us and ever mindful of our
needs.

Paul had implicit confidence in his planning because of the
integrity of his purpose: he was serving Christ. He had been
helped in this way before, "Hitherto hath the Lord helped us,"
and he believed that the Lord would help him further. He had
implicit confidence in Christ Jesus because he was following
the guidance of the Spirit, not of self or of man. His plans were
not conclusions of his own personal judgment as to whether
this was feasible or practical. He was led in his planning by the
promises of God with implicit confidence that He was able to
do it. When we put our whole trust in the living Lord, we too
will be strengthened, moving forward with confidence.

Chapter 52

THE GLORY OF GOD

If you have ever felt afraid that you cannot hold out as a believer — or if you are not a believer in Christ and are holding back from committing yourself to God right now because you are afraid you will not be able to hold out — then I have something to say to you. The apostle Paul sets forth the grounds for a basic confidence in the work of God:

> For all the promises of God in him are yea, and in him Amen, unto the glory of God by us. Now he which stablisheth us with you in Christ, and hath anointed us, is God; who hath also sealed us, and given the earnest of the Spirit in our hearts (2 Cor. 1:20-22).

Think of these amazing words! What are the promises of God that are absolutely sure in Christ Jesus? The forgiveness of sin is certainly promised to everyone who believes, also the regeneration of the soul — you will be born again — and adoption as a child of God — you will be adopted into the family of God when you believe in Him.

> But as many as received him, to them gave he power to become the sons of God, even to them that believe on his name (John 1:12).

The receiving of the Holy Spirit is a promise of God. It was a promise to Abraham, and God will give it to everyone who believes in Him. There will be grace to live by. Believers are surrounded by sinful people, and they have sin in themselves; but where sin abounds, grace will much more abound. Another promise is that they will be kept by the power of God. And again, God will work in them to nurture, to enable them to grow in faith and in knowledge. And finally, He will bring them to Himself. These are absolute promises.

169

All of these promises of God in Christ Jesus are "yea"! Straightforward *yes;* not a wishy-washy *maybe.* "And in him Amen, unto the glory of God by us." The glory of God would be the fulfillment of God's plan, what He really set out to do, as we read the whole story of the Bible. God set out to create and prepare a whole company of brethren among whom the Lord Jesus Christ would be first. He would forever be the firstborn among many brethren. God created man in His own image. Then God proceeded to deal with man and to regenerate him and make him into His own image as a child of God; until finally the Lord Jesus and all those who believe in Him will be with God forever. The fulfillment of His plan and these promises point forward to that. Believers are the trophies of God's great program; they are the results of His grace and mercy in Christ Jesus. The "glory of God by us" means that God will "get the job done" according to the way He planned it, in the way He deals with us.

Chapter 53

THE CONFIDENCE OF A BELIEVER

Now he which stablisheth us with you in Christ, and hath anointed us, is God (2 Cor. 1:21).

This emphasizes again the work of God, with the basic truth that everything is in Christ Jesus. The word *stablisheth* is not commonly used today. Instead we say *establishes*. An establishment is something that has been set up on a solid basis. This matter of "stablishing us with you in Christ" is like setting out a plant in a garden. One needs to prepare the soil carefully, often using fertilizer to give it an extra boost when it starts growing, and using plenty of water to get the roots into the soil quickly; then packing it firmly and sheltering it from wind and rain until the roots start to grow in the ground. When the plant becomes settled, it is established.

When a person becomes a believer, he accepts the Lord Jesus Christ as his Savior, and he yields himself to God. There are truths to learn; and the more he learns about God's ways, the stronger his faith will be. The believer will be rooted in Christ, and he will be developing in Him. The One who makes this sure — "He which stablisheth us" — is God. He then makes the believer sure about his relationship with Christ by giving peace in his heart. God actually works in the believer and keeps him by answering his prayers. The believer can feel the assurance that he really does belong to God because when he talks to Him, God responds. God reminds the believer of what Christ has done by dying on Calvary, by going into heaven, by sending the Holy Spirit, and by encouraging the believer through communion with other believers. In all these ways the believer is encouraged and strengthened to believe that he really does belong in Christ. So he is established in Him.

171

"And hath anointed us": the anointing is receiving the Holy Spirit to serve. Paul recognized that he was an instrument to be used by the Holy Spirit, who "hath also sealed us." The sealing of the believer is in receiving the Holy Spirit. It is like the stamp that confirms a contract. A person signs a contract; and when he puts his signature on it, it is then sealed. When this seal is stamped on it, the contract is confirmed. When God gives the Holy Spirit to the believer, he definitely indicates that the believer does belong to Him. "And given the earnest of the Spirit in our hearts": this is the down payment of the things of heaven.

The ultimate plan of God is to have the believer in heaven with the Lord in unbroken communion. This is offered to the believer in the gospel, and made sure to him by the presence of the Holy Spirit in his heart. The true believer can rest in the plan of God to bless him, to keep him, to use him, and to bring him to glory. "If God be for us, who can be against us?"

Chapter 54

PAUL'S CONCERN FOR THE SPIRITUAL GROWTH OF HIS FOLLOWERS

Sometimes it is easy to be more impressed by a human being than by God Himself. Consider how a family prepares to receive an important guest. Isn't it true that elaborate preparations are made, manners checked on, and every detail worked out? What does a believer understand about where God is? Isn't it true that God is right there by us always? As a believer I should keep in mind that every day in every place I am, I should take off my shoes, for the place where I am standing is holy ground.

When I was in Taiwan some time ago I had the privilege of visiting among some Chinese people, and I learned to take off my shoes as I entered a house, and to walk in the slippers they provided for me. This was a matter of courtesy. Similarly believers should mentally take off their shoes continually, because they are standing in the very presence of God.

It is human to be impressed by people, but this can lead us astray. In the last two verses of chapter 1 we see that the apostle Paul is concerned that his importance should not be overestimated as a minister. He did have authority as a minister of the gospel in Corinth; he had preached the gospel there, and people had believed, looking to him as one who spoke the truth. He had, in a real sense, spoken the oracles of God. Although it may have been out of proportion — and Paul realized they were giving him far too much attention — it was indeed real. They looked upon Paul as their leader. But this is the frame of mind that can lead one astray. Paul did not come to the church when there was a crisis. Paul stayed away because if he had come, they would have asked him to solve their problem. Had he suggested something, they would have accepted his advice without prayerful consideration.

Paul did not want their problems to be solved that way. He wanted them to turn to God, so he stayed away until they looked to God. He had no intention of having dominion over their faith. He simply did not believe that any human being should be lord over any other human being. The believers in Corinth would have given him this prestige because he was a great preacher. He had preached the gospel there which had led to their salvation. Naturally they looked up to him for that. But Paul denied any interest in being considered their true leader.

The history of the Christian church is marked by just such views. It is surprising how some have accepted the idea that the minister of the gospel has some special authority in the Word of God. It is not true. The idea that the minister can be the judge of the heart, or that a priest can decide what the Spirit of God will do, is out of all proportion. Although there is human willingness to grant unusual prestige to the minister, to give him a higher place of authority over the Word of God, and to practically worship the pastor, that is not the truth as revealed in the New Testament.

In Old Testament days this was the issue at stake with Samuel, who ministered among the Israelites as a priest following Eli. Samuel had been the judge over the whole country. In his old age the people came to him and said they wanted a king, but Samuel was against it. He said, "You have a king; you have God." You will remember how the Lord led Samuel to yield to their request, though it was unfortunate. Paul did not want to encourage their "hero worship," but the fact was that he had dominion over them. So he stayed away in the time of their controversy in order not to become involved.

Paul was concerned about the Corinthians' faith, as would be true of all worthy pastors. He did plan to come and help them to set things straight.

> Moreover I call God for a record upon my soul, that to spare you
> I came not as yet unto Corinth. Not for that we have dominion
> over your faith, but are helpers of your joy: for by faith ye stand
> (2 Cor. 1:23-24).

Paul is saying that he wants them to know absolutely that this is true, that the reason he did not come to Corinth was that he wanted to spare them. He did not want them to be overly impressed with his presence, and he wanted to give them time and liberty to work through it between themselves and God. He did not want to impose upon them or to have final dominion over their faith. The faith a believer has will lead him into joy, but this joy can be hindered by various things. It will come as the fruit of the Spirit, but the Spirit will lead believers along the lines of the Word of God.

Paul coveted this joy for his people, and he was willing to come and help, but he did not want them to overestimate his importance. To let them overestimate his importance would actually hinder the work of the Spirit in them. It is true the Spirit will work in hearts through believing in the promises of God, and the fruit of the Spirit is love, joy, and peace, et al., but no human being tells us about that. It comes from God. We read the Word of God, and the Holy Spirit shows us the meaning of it. People can help us. Paul was willing to help his people, even as believers should be willing to help each other.

Chapter 55

HOW TO DEAL WITH A SINNING BROTHER

We have noticed that a true believer should have joy. This is the fruit he should promote in himself for his own blessing and to enable him to help others. Paul now offers his own conduct as an example.

> But I determined this with myself, that I would not come again to you in heaviness. For if I make you sorry, who is he then that maketh me glad, but the same which is made sorry by me? (2 Cor. 2:1-2).

Paul was receiving personal encouragement from the Corinthians, and they were, in their faithfulness, a blessing to him. He hated to think that he should be the one who would cause them to feel badly when they were making him feel so good.

> And I wrote this same unto you, lest, when I came, I should have sorrow from them of whom I ought to rejoice; having confidence in you all, that my joy is the joy of you all. For out of much affliction and anguish of heart I wrote unto you with many tears; not that ye should be grieved, but that ye might know the love which I have more abundantly unto you (2 Cor. 2:3-4).

We remember that in the first epistle the apostle Paul drew attention to sin that was tolerated in the church, and he urgently pointed out that this would hurt all of them. They needed to discipline the sinning person. Now he makes it clear that when he wrote to them he was deeply burdened. He tells them the sinning person grieved him, but there were others in the church who did not grieve him, so he did not hold all of them responsible for the conduct of the sinning person.

> But if any have caused grief, he hath not grieved me, but in part: that I may not overcharge you all. Sufficient to such a man is this punishment, which was inflicted of many. So that contrariwise ye ought rather to forgive him, and comfort him, lest perhaps

such a one should be swallowed up with overmuch sorrow. Wherefore I beseech you that ye would confirm your love toward him. For to this end also did I write, that I might know the proof of you, whether ye be obedient in all things. To whom ye forgive any thing, I forgive also: for if I forgave any thing, to whom I forgave it, for your sakes forgave I it in the person of Christ; lest Satan should get an advantage of us: for we are not ignorant of his devices (2 Cor. 2:5-11).

The general tone of the early part of this passage conveys this simple truth: Paul would not impose his own grief on them. He felt badly, and if he had come to them at that time he would have shown it; but he did not want to make them feel badly so he stayed away. It is always a chilling experience to have a killjoy in your midst. On the other hand, the Bible says, "A merry heart doeth good like a medicine."

There is significant truth implied in Paul's words: Some people in real trouble are nevertheless cheerful; others are just the opposite. There are times we must shed tears, but Paul would suggest we do it in private. Paul communicated his grief to these people by letter. They needed to know that he cared deeply about their trouble because he loved them.

The one who sinned was to be disciplined, but when the disciplining was completed, punishment should not be prolonged. The focus should be on the sin (and it should be dealt with), but never upon the sinner. He should be kept. After judgment and punishment, mercy and grace should follow in order that they might be right in God's sight.

In the exodus of Israel there was an incident when Miriam criticized Moses. Because of her criticism she was stricken with leprosy. She asked Moses to pray for her and he did. Her sins were forgiven, but Israel made no progress during that time. For seven days they stood still until Miriam was restored. It is significant that if there is tension between believers, no progress is made until the tension subsides. The true believer will make sure the other person understands that he is forgiven. Paul wrote that they should confirm their love toward him, making sure he knew they had truly forgiven him. To prolong an atmosphere of criticism or judgment is unwise, and believers should keep this in mind. To hold anything over someone is not good, "lest Satan should get an advantage of us: for we are not ignorant of his devices."

When a person has been criticized, judged, and condemned, he is naturally upset. That is when Satan begins to tempt him to be discouraged, to say, "It is just no use"; to be rebellious, "Why are they always picking on me?"; and to keep the wounds sore by saying, "He still holds it against me." The sun should not go down on his wrath; he should get over it. Let the criticizing person know that he is over it. The criticized person should ask the critic to help him. The true believer will try to promote a strong fellowship by being careful to see that differences of opinion and even criticism are not to be allowed to cloud the spirit over a long time. He should get it over with, so that the other person can enter into the sunshine again and be blessed.

Chapter 56

PAUL'S ATTITUDE IN PREACHING
THE GOSPEL

In 2 Corinthians Paul is telling his own story to show how he lived, how he made decisions, and how he worked in the Lord.

> Furthermore, when I came to Troas to preach Christ's gospel, and a door was opened unto me of the Lord, I had no rest in my spirit, because I found not Titus my brother: but taking my leave of them, I went from thence into Macedonia. Now thanks be unto God, which always causeth us to triumph in Christ, and maketh manifest the savor of his knowledge by us in every place. For we are unto God a sweet savor of Christ, in them that are saved, and in them that perish: to the one we are the savor of death unto death; and to the other the savor of life unto life. And who is sufficient for these things? For we are not as many, which corrupt the word of God: but as of sincerity, but as of God, in the sight of God speak we in Christ (2 Cor. 2:12-17).

Here is a combination of personal intention and of God's intervention; a combination of the individual doing what he wants to do, and of God helping him and doing what only He could do. Paul came to preach and the Lord opened the door; Paul did not try to open the door himself. All who preach or teach or witness need to learn from this. We have to wait for our opportunities until the Lord opens the door.

The decision to move on and preach in another place was based on Paul's personal feeling. God used Paul just the way he was. Here Paul acted the way he personally felt. Although he was in a place that was opened to him by the Lord, he was restless and upset, because he did not find his fellow worker, whom he called "Titus, my brother."

Titus was a Greek, and because of this Paul would not let the Jews circumcise him. We know the alienation that existed between Jews and Greeks: they had no dealings with each other. Yet here Paul is reaching over this cultural barrier and actually calling this uncircumcised Gentile his brother. Titus was a believer in Christ, and that made him a brother of Paul.

Paul then moved on into Macedonia, and the Lord providentially opened the door for him to preach there at Troas. In that place Paul expressed his own personal feelings. Christians can have their feelings and still be in the will of God. Paul seemed to be perfectly free and independent, yet he was by no means a loner. He was undoubtedly in constant companionship with Christ, his Lord, by the Holy Spirit; but he also needed human comradeship. He made a point of moving his place of service so that he could find the fellowship of other workers. When he did not find Titus there at Troas, he did not stay.

In Macedonia he found an opportunity to serve the Lord, and it seems that what happened there was the kind of thing Paul recognized as God overruling in His own will to His own glory. Guided by his own inner need of the company of his fellow worker Titus, Paul went into Macedonia, and there he was used of God to spread the gospel. Everywhere he went, people got the taste of Christ, "the savor of the knowledge of God."

The word *savor* is like taste or fragrance. Paul was a sweet fragrance to God in the way he personally testified for Christ. Paul understood all men to belong to one of two classes: those who are saved and those who perish. The true believer causes everyone to think of God, but people do not all think the same thoughts. The life a believer lives makes some people think of death, but makes other people think of heaven. Paul recognized this as being a great responsibility, and he trembled when he thought of his own weakness, saying, "Who is sufficient for these things?"

This is the cry of everyone who witnesses for Christ. Paul then expressed the basic confidence of the witness:

> For we are not as many, which corrupt the word of God: but as of sincerity, but as of God, in the sight of God speak we in Christ (2 Cor. 2:17).

He had the integrity of his own conscience. There was no pretense in Paul's preaching. It was simple talk about what he knew because of his own experience. He believed in Jesus Christ as the Son of God; he believed in the Scriptures and in the resurrection of the dead. He believed in the return of the Lord, and he let these things be known everywhere.

Chapter 57

THE MARKS OF A TRUE BELIEVER

You may ask, When would a preacher be commended as an effective minister, another man a good farmer, or another a good doctor? The answer is: By their fruits you shall know them. Would souls won to Christ be the only evidence of a true minister of the gospel? I think the answer to that would have to be that you could not tell for sure. A true believing woman is not always able to win her husband or children to the Lord. It was said about Jesus of Nazareth, "he did not many mighty works there because of their unbelief." Some seed will fall by the wayside; some will fall in stony ground; and some will fall in thorny ground. Only some of the seed falls in good ground.

A young man was recently concerned about his ministry in a certain church because, in the course of a year, he had won very few new members to his church. In his county 90 percent of the people were already committed to some church. As I told him, a fisherman may be a good fisherman, but on occasion he may go out with his fishing equipment and catch no fish. Why? There were no fish in the lake. When a man takes the pastorate of a congregation, he is limited in a certain sense to that particular church. It may be that in that particular place the fish are "not biting"; and if that is the case, he will not be able to show results. The same can be true of a wife and mother: her husband or children may act in open rebellion to her wishes. In the long run, by the grace of God, her testimony may bear some fruit, but she may go through long periods of distress and frustration, with no evidence that she is making any impression on them.

At the same time, there will be some results which are

evident, regardless of whether anyone is won to the Lord or
not. There will be fruits of the Spirit. A certain woman had a
profound spiritual experience in which she rejoiced. While
talking to her pastor, she asked how she could tell the folks at
home that the Lord was with her. He told her she would not
have to tell them; they would just know. And Paul, in writing to
the Corinthians, drew their attention to the fact that the results
in their own experience of hearing him preach were evidence
enough of his authenticity as a minister. Certain results had
taken place in them as they listened to him, which showed that
he was a true minister of the gospel.

There is further evidence of a believer in Christ.

> Do we begin again to commend ourselves? or need we, as some
> others, epistles of commendation to you, or letters of commen-
> dation from you? Ye are our epistle written in our hearts, known
> and read of all men: forasmuch as ye are manifestly declared to
> be the epistle of Christ ministered by us, written not with ink,
> but with the Spirit of the living God; not in tables of stone, but in
> fleshy tables of the heart. And such trust have we through Christ
> to God-ward: not that we are sufficient of ourselves to think any
> thing as of ourselves; but our sufficiency is of God; who also hath
> made us able ministers of the new testament; not of the letter,
> but of the spirit: for the letter killeth, but the spirit giveth life
> (2 Cor. 3:1-6).

Here the apostle Paul is saying that the Corinthian believers
were the evidence of the authenticity of his own spiritual
experience. They had listened to him preach and had been
affected; they were epistles of Christ, known and read by all
men. Every believer is actually an epistle of Christ. You and I
are, as it were, like a letter written for people to read. Although
there may be days when it seems to be like a letter written with
a lead pencil. I suspect there are times when some will have the
feeling that the writing was blurred badly by something we
did.

What are some of the things we see in a true believer? We
see in him peace of mind and joy. This person has been
delivered from bondage. He has pleasure in worship, in praying and singing and in Bible study. There is love toward other
men, and he seeks the welfare of others. He is sympathetic
with his peers and has respect for those in authority; he is
considerate of all men and is charitable to those who do not

have what they need. If he is steadfast and humble consistently, you can be sure that man is working under God. If he is generous, giving cheerfully, you know that is not human nature, but that it is from God. If he is devout and prays, you have evidence; and if every now and then he tells you about his faith or asks you to come to church, you will know you are looking at a true believer. What you see in him is the result of his faith in God because what he does and the way he acts is the overflow from his heart.

How can any person be that way? It will not be in his own strength or wisdom. This is "Christ in you the hope of glory." It is the help of God that makes what he does adequate for the situation.

Chapter 58

THE GRACE OF GOD IS THE
BETTER DYNAMIC

The apostle Paul is recognized throughout history as a master minister of Christ; if you want to know what a true believer is like, you should study the life, experiences, testimony, and works of Paul. He lived among the Jewish people with great tradition. The Jews have been a great people in the history of the world. They have produced leaders like Moses, Joshua, David, Samuel, and many other giants of faith. Though small in number and often weak in military strength, they have nonetheless accomplished amazing feats, having achieved in the course of history a notable performance. Paul preached a new way of living that the prophets of the Old Testament had predicted would come: a life style of obedience and walking with God.

In this study we shall notice that there are two general motivations for conduct: On the one hand I do what I do because I have to; I am forced to do it. On the other hand I do what I do because I am inspired to do it. In the first place I do what I do when I have to do it either to achieve a certain result, such as if I want to escape punishment or to please others, or the situation may have certain requirements I must meet. On the other hand, I may act as I do because I want to . I may want to please someone or simply to express myself. In the course of the history of God's people both of these motivations were felt. The first one comes out of the history of Israel; the law declares what is right: If you do this, you will be blessed. The second way comes from the testimony and the work of the Lord Jesus Christ, and we speak of it as the gospel. We act this way because it is a privilege and because it is pleasing to God. We act a certain way because we have been blessed.

Doing what I have to do is natural. It makes sense to human beings. "Whatsoever a man soweth that shall he also reap" is the principle of the law, and it prevails throughout the world among all peoples. The second way of doing things is truly spiritual: I receive what I have because God gives it to me. When thinking in terms of "I do what I have to do because it is necessary," I receive wages, and the Bible tells us the wages of sin is death. When I do what I do because I want to be pleasing to God, I receive life. The gift of God is eternal life through Jesus Christ our Lord.

This contrast can be seen everywhere. Regardless of where I work, my job has certain requirements, and I must meet them. Some people have to be on the job a certain number of hours; they measure the time and watch the clock closely. Others work at their job because they want to and because it pleases God. As another example, think about courtesy: a person may be polite because it is politic. Notice the relationship in these words: *polite* and *politic*. One is polite because it pays off. On the other hand, he can be courteous because he is gracious; he really wants to please people.

Everyone recognizes that we will do more when we want to than we will do if we have to. Both of these ways of doing things are set forth in Scripture, and Paul referred to them. He knew both kinds of motivation, having been brought up in the law and then saved by Christ. He was born again into the new way of doing things — the gospel — and he was totally committed to it. The following words seem quite obscure, but with this background perhaps the passage will be more meaningful.

> But if the ministration of death, written and engraven in stones, was glorious, so that the children of Israel could not steadfastly behold the face of Moses for the glory of his countenance; which glory was to be done away: how shall not the ministration of the spirit be rather glorious? (2 Cor. 3:7-8).

Here Paul contrasts the ministration of death and the ministration of the Spirit. When we read this in its context, it is clear that by the "ministration of death" he meant the law. "The soul that sinneth, it shall die" and "All have sinned and come short of the glory of God." This is what a man has to preach if he preaches the law. And that was glorious because it was the truth. They could tell that when they saw the face of Moses after he had been on the Mount. His face was so glorious the people could not look upon it.

Now the ministry of the Spirit — presenting the things of Christ Jesus, telling about His forgiveness, His grace, and His regeneration by the Holy Spirit — would be rather glorious, not so much in Paul as in his people, in their fruit. Look at verse 9:

> For if the ministration of condemnation be glory, much more doth the ministration of righteousness exceed in glory.

The result of teaching the law is to arouse guilt, but the result of teaching the gospel is to promote righteousness in living.

In view of the results, the teaching of the law pales into insignificance in comparison with the teaching of grace.

> For if that which is done away was glorious, much more that which remaineth is glorious (2 Cor. 3:11).

"That which is done away" is the old covenant: the law which was passed away. "That which remaineth" is the new covenant: the grace of God which is eternal. Now we ask ourselves: Shall we serve Him because we must or because we want to in response to what He has done for us?

Chapter 59

THE PRINCIPLE OF GROWTH IN A BELIEVER

Certain words and phrases we read in the Bible can be illuminated by the Holy Spirit with special emphasis conveying important truths about Christ in you. The unbelieving person can read God's Word and not see the truth of Christ, but a person whose heart is yielded to the Lord — who has accepted Christ and been born again — has a new life in Him. He sees truth in the Scriptures. The casual reader would never see it; but the believing, spirit-filled heart would be sensitive to this truth.

Some years ago, when a person sent his clothing to a laundry, the workers would be able to identify it, although the owner would not see any marks. They had put certain invisible marks on his clothes that only their machinery could detect. This truth was illustrated when our Lord Jesus was here on earth. When He was walking through the streets of Jerusalem, in the cities and towns of Palestine, thousands of people saw Him as Jesus of Nazareth but never saw Him as Lord. It was as though they were blinded. They did not see the glory. John says, "The world knoweth us not because it knew him not." The world does not now fully appreciate those who are the children of God because they did not believe Him then, who was the Son of God.

> Seeing then that we have such hope, we use great plainness of speech: and not as Moses, which put a veil over his face, that the children of Israel could not steadfastly look to the end of that which is abolished: but their minds were blinded: for until this day remaineth the same veil untaken away in the reading of the old testament; which veil is done away in Christ. But even unto this day, when Moses is read, the veil is upon their heart. Nevertheless, when it shall turn to the Lord, the veil shall be

> taken away. Now the Lord is that Spirit: and where the Spirit of
> the Lord is, there is liberty. But we all, with open face beholding
> as in a glass the glory of the Lord, are changed into the same
> image from glory to glory, even as by the Spirit of the Lord
> (2 Cor. 3:12-18).

What does a veil do? It blurs. One cannot see clearly through it
for it blots out the image. Moses went up to Mt. Sinai and
remained there for forty days in the presence of the Lord,
receiving the law of God written on tablets of stone. When he
came down, his face shone so radiantly the people could not
look upon it. He had to cover his face with a veil. He was not
aware of it, but they could see it. This veil persists even now
over the heart of the Jew.

Who is the Jew in the New Testament? He is the interested,
informed believer in the Word of God. It is a cultural term,
referring to people who know about these things, but who have
never accepted Christ personally. Such persons are in our
churches. They deny the fact that the body of Jesus Christ was
raised from the dead. That truth is like a bright light which they
do not want to look at. They do not want to discuss if He is alive
today. They would not want to say He is not, but they also
would not want to say He is. Is He coming again? They will
seek excuses not to talk about it. Remember, "Nevertheless,
when it shall turn to the Lord, the veil shall be taken away."
Despite their unbelief, there is hope for such persons.

When the soul comes to know the Lord Jesus Christ as
Savior, this will all be cleared up.

> Now the Lord is that Spirit: and where the Spirit of the Lord is,
> there is liberty. But we all, with open face beholding as in a glass
> the glory of the Lord, are changed into the same image from
> glory to glory, even as by the Spirit of the Lord (2 Cor. 3:17-18).

This language is based on the use of a mirror. A mirror may be
only plain glass or burnished metal. If you focus it right, you
can look into the mirror and see the face of a friend; if you turn it
another way you can see some bright lights or flowers or
whatever the mirror is focused on. Paul is suggesting that we
are like that. We look into the Bible, and there is shown to us
the face of Jesus Christ, and we see that face for ourselves.
There are many different ways of expressing this. Various
translators have tried to explain the meaning of these verses as

there is something here not easily grasped at once. Someone has said that looking at Jesus Christ will save, but gazing upon Him sanctifies. "We all, with open face beholding as in a glass the glory of the Lord [looking into this mirror], are changed into the same image from glory to glory, even as by the Spirit of the Lord." To gaze upon the face of Jesus Christ means that the believer will grow in holiness.

Chapter 60

PAUL WAS HONEST IN HIS PREACHING

Do you have any idea why Paul could be as bold and plain-spoken as he was in his preaching? The answer is simple. He had nothing to hide; he just told the truth. Something had happened within himself, and to this he openly testified. It is not always easy to find light shining in these words:

> Therefore, seeing we have this ministry, as we have received mercy, we faint not; but have renounced the hidden things of dishonesty, not walking in craftiness, nor handling the word of God deceitfully; but by manifestation of the truth commending ourselves to every man's conscience in the sight of God. But if our gospel be hid, it is hid to them that are lost: in whom the god of this world hath blinded the minds of them which believe not, lest the light of the glorious gospel of Christ, who is the image of God, should shine unto them. For we preach not ourselves, but Christ Jesus the Lord; and ourselves your servants for Jesus' sake. For God, who commanded the light to shine out of darkness, hath shined in our hearts, to give the light of the knowledge of the glory of God in the face of Jesus Christ (2 Cor. 4:1-6).

Paul had been enabled to see the truth about Jesus Christ, and he could talk openly about it. Because these things were real to him, he could say, "We faint not." There was never slackening in what Paul had to say because of doubt. The things of Christ were to him like a precious gem in the hands of a jeweler. They were continually showing forth new light, with new splendor and new glory. And because Paul had this truth in personal experience, having put his trust in Jesus Christ, he had been reconciled to God, saved, and given the peace of God.

". . . but have renounced the hidden things of dishonesty." In his preaching Paul made a special point of emphasizing his honesty. He wanted to claim before the whole world that he

191

was not putting on an act, but that he was telling the truth. This may raise the question why some people seem to prefer ritual in public worship. Ritual may be performed faithfully and sincerely, yet it can be used as a fence behind which the worshiper hides.

It was my privilege not long ago to take part in a prayer meeting in a lawyer's office during the noon hour. Among the group I remember one man especially, who in his prayer humbled me as I listened to him. He prayed so simply and was so genuinely sincere. He told the truth, saying, "I thank Thee, God, for being good to me, for being kind and forgiving. You know I don't always do right, and maybe I did wrong this morning, but You know that if I did, I did not mean to. I would like to do everything right before Thee." My heart just opened up.

Paul could say he "renounced the hidden things of dishonesty, not walking in craftiness." Paul claimed openly there was nothing tricky or clever about his testimony before the world. Sadly enough, some people do walk cleverly in their religious life. Often when a congregation has listened to a prospective minister preach and have heard nothing that was wrong or subversive, they call him, only to learn later that he did not really believe what they had *thought* he believed.

Paul went on to say, "Nor handling the word of God deceitfully." This is also a common practice: quoting Scripture just because the words seem to fit, even though the speaker does not believe the Bible. That is deceitful. Paul did not handle the Word of God deceitfully. "By manifestation of the truth" means openly demonstrating what is claimed. "Commending ourselves to every man's conscience in the sight of God" means acting honestly because no one would ever doubt a genuine believer.

"If our gospel be hid" meant that Paul stressed the importance of living our lives openly for people to see. Paul said, "The god of this world hath blinded the minds of them which believe not." Here is the tragedy. Those who do not believe are often blinded by circumstances. Many people say they do not believe because of contradictions in the Bible, yet they have never read it. They say such things because they have been blinded.

"For we preach not ourselves, but Christ Jesus the Lord." It is difficult at times for a minister to remember in giving his message that he is talking about the Lord. "For God, who commanded the light to shine out of darkness, hath shined in our hearts, to give the light of the knowledge of the glory of God in the face of Jesus Christ." Paul said there was something about his coming to faith that was much like the creation of the world. Before the creation everything was shapeless, chaotic, and dark, and God said, "Let there be light." After God had thus acted, the believer could best bear his testimony in the open daylight of common honesty. If a person really believes, he should say so.

Chapter 61

SUFFERING IS INVOLVED IN SERVING
THE LORD

Paul's experience in the Lord as a sinner, believing in Almighty God through Jesus Christ, is classic for all believers. It is the classic experience of the believer being an example for others to follow. Every believer is a witness. The question is whether he will be a good or a poor witness. If a person is a believer in the Lord Jesus Christ, his home is in the right spot where he can begin to witness. If he is a member of a church, in one way or another he is making a profession of faith in Jesus Christ. The same would be true in any business relationship.

Paul told the Corinthians how God had worked to keep him humble. Because Paul had much to say about God when he talked about the gospel, it would have been natural for people to think that Paul was someone special. This was what Paul had in mind when he made these comments:

> But we have this treasure in earthen vessels, that the excellency
> of the power may be of God, and not of us (2 Cor. 4:7).

The water the servant is offering may be in a battered dipper, but we do not drink the cup; we drink the water. The expression *earthen vessels* refers to vessels made of pottery. One could say, "We have this treasure in crackable pottery." For that is what you and I are when we are witnessing for the Lord.

There is a strong tendency in the church to focus attention on the preacher. If one feels that he is getting no benefit from the church, he blames the preacher; if he feels he is getting a lot out of the church, he credits the preacher. On one hand he may blame the preacher when the preacher is really not responsible and does not deserve the blame, and on the other hand he may praise the preacher when he is not responsible and does not deserve the credit.

Because of this God sees fit to allow His ministers to have trouble. This is the way Paul put it:

> We are troubled on every side, yet not distressed; we are perplexed, but not in despair; persecuted, but not forsaken; cast down, but not destroyed; always bearing about in the body the dying of the Lord Jesus, that the life also of Jesus might be made manifest in our body. For we which live are alway delivered unto death for Jesus' sake, that the life also of Jesus might be made manifest in our mortal flesh. So then death worketh in us, but life in you (2 Cor. 4:8-12).

Paul took his troubles in stride. He was perplexed but not in despair. He never thought of giving up. He knew that people would hurt him and persecute him, but he knew also the Lord would not let him go. He related his suffering to Christ Jesus. He understood that if he wanted to show Christ in his conduct, then he would be identified with Christ. Paul knew how the Lord Jesus Christ lived. The servant is not greater than his Master. Jesus of Nazareth suffered and was raised from the dead, so Paul expected that he would suffer that he might be raised from the dead. If a person would show meekness, he must endure injustice. Not in every experience as a human being did Paul have this, but enough happened in which he suffered because he was a believer. This is a general principle for all believers.

> For we which live are alway delivered unto death for Jesus' sake, that the life also of Jesus might be made manifest in our mortal flesh (2 Cor. 4:11).

Paul rarely uses the name *Jesus* by itself, but here he does because he is referring to the human body of Jesus of Nazareth. There is a functional value in suffering: it makes a difference to others when the minister suffers.

> So then death worketh in us, but life in you (2 Cor. 4:12).

Believers do not have to invite this kind of suffering: it will come; and when it comes in the will of God, they can be sure it will pay off in other people being able to believe because of them.

It was said of the Lord Jesus Christ:

. . . who for the joy that was set before him endured the cross, despising the shame, and is set down at the right hand of the throne of God (Heb. 12:2).

A believer endures the suffering, because this is the way others can be shown about Christ that they, too, might come to believe.

Chapter 62

THE SECRET OF PAUL'S STRENGTH

Do you think it makes any difference to believers whether or not heaven is real? According to Paul it makes a great deal of difference in this world to the person who believes whether heaven is real. Having referred to his own experiences of hardship, Paul emphasizes that the strength to endure was derived from the confidence he had in the reality of the invisible things of God. He knew that he in himself did not have the strength to perform all his daily duties and responsibility in Christ Jesus. He was serving the Lord, and in so doing he was called upon to endure much suffering and to face many trials. In his case he was strong throughout. Now he points out that this strength was not in himself, but because he had confidence in the reality of the invisible things of God.

> We having the same spirit of faith, according as it is written, I believed, and therefore have I spoken; we also believe, and therefore speak (2 Cor. 4:13).

In the Old Testament days one of the witnesses to God made this remark, "I believed, and therefore have I spoken." Now Paul says, "I am standing in that same tradition." Those who truly believe in God and have dealings with Him can speak out. Paul continued:

> Knowing that he which raised up the Lord Jesus shall raise up us also by Jesus, and shall present us with you (2 Cor. 4:14).

Paul expected to be raised from the dead by the power of God just as Christ Jesus was raised from the dead. Paul's experiences of suffering were cases of dying daily; but every time he died in Christ Jesus, God raised him from the dead. He had resurrection experience, and this was based on the resurrection of the Lord Jesus as we find it in 1 Corinthians 15. This event happened once at Calvary, but the principle is operative every time a believer suffers for Christ's sake.

> For all things are for your sakes, that the abundant grace might through the thanksgiving of many redound to the glory of God (2 Cor. 4:15).

Here is the real reason for all that happens in the world: that the plan of God for believers in the Lord Jesus Christ can actually be carried out. Since this is the plan of God, Paul took courage as he continued his work and had strength to believe and to serve.

> For which cause we faint not; but though our outward man perish, yet the inward man is renewed day by day (2 Cor. 4:16).

Paul would admit that trouble and suffering could involve death, but his confidence was unshaken because of the prospect that God could raise the dead.

This may seem far removed from daily living, but it need not be so for the believer; this calls for continual exercise of faith. Paul described his own procedure:

> For our light affliction, which is but for a moment, worketh for us a far more exceeding and eternal weight of glory (2 Cor. 4:17).

This language needs to be understood. When Paul speaks about his "light affliction," he is referring to all the troubles he had: when enemies stoned him and left him for dead, and when they beat him. When he looked back, it did not seem to him those things were really very great. This expression "weight of glory" actually refers to a kind of medal or medallion that victors in a contest would win. If a person won a wrestling match, he would receive a medal. Paul knew his troubles were the basis on which he would receive a great medallion in glory, a far greater and eternal prize. He practiced looking at the invisible reality of this fact. This world's affairs he called "light affliction," and this world's time he called "but for a moment."

> While we look not at the things which are seen, but at the things which are not seen: for the things which are seen are temporal; but the things which are not seen are eternal (2 Cor. 4:18).

I wish I could share this with every believer who is trying to live in obedience to the Lord. We are not thinking about the luxuries of life, nor even the necessities or goals. Life makes excessive demands when we try to get into a position where we can earn a good salary in order to have everything we want. Many people, when confronted with a decision, will often ask what they will get out of it. But Paul said that when he was dealing with people, he did not look at the things of this world but at the things which are not seen: a relationship with God, the fact that heaven is real right now, and the fact that Jesus Christ is in the presence of God, praying for us. Paul looked at the spiritual world, because the things which are seen are temporal, but the things which are not seen are eternal. They are not sensed by the senses; they are heavenly and will not fade away.

This was the secret of Paul's strength that kept him faithful and zealous. This can be the secret of your personal experience that will keep you steadfast and earnest in everything you do. You can practice looking into the face of the Lord Jesus Christ at all times.

Chapter 63

THE BELIEVER'S HOPE ABOUT HIS BODY

The basic confidence a believer in Christ can cherish is the assurance from God that he has a home in heaven. How can a believer in Christ be satisfied and strong if he can look forward only to life in this world? Some years ago when teaching in seminary I was openly challenged in class for emphasizing the importance of heaven. I was quoting Paul, "If in this life only we have hope in Christ, we are of all men most miserable" (1 Cor. 15:19). One student claimed that being a believer was so self-satisfying it was worth it even if there was no future. That is not what Paul felt. If there is not life after this one, then suffering for Christ now will not be fulfilled. There are people who suffer for Christ unto death: they are called into the presence of judges, found guilty, given an opportunity to recant their faith, and, refusing, they are burned at the stake.

Believers may, for the sake of serving the Lord and doing what is pleasing in the sight of God, demonstrate before all men how gracious He is and deny themselves. They will not seek anything for themselves. If there were not another world in which this could be vindicated, then it would be a burden. The Scripture reports that Jesus of Nazareth was aware of His assured future, "Who for the joy that was set before him endured the cross, despising the shame, and is set down at the right hand of the throne of God" (Heb. 12:2).

During the years I have spent in colleges, universities, and in seminary, I have been with students, many of whom sneer at anything that sounds like otherworldliness. Frequently they talked about those of us who are "trying to escape." Now I have nothing against escaping. In the army I was in charge of a hospital detail at the time the flu epidemic first struck North America and men were dying every day. I contracted flu myself, and the doctor who was giving the best medical advice they had in those days told me exactly what to do. I followed his orders and I escaped death.

Many people feel that when believers turn to God in heaven away from the world, this is a cowardly retreat. A believer turns to God — yes; but he will come back into a situation with the power of God. Paul could refer to his own steadfast courage and purpose because he was a stalwart believer in Christ. He explained that his steadfastness was not because he liked to suffer, nor was it because the suffering would be less when he was steadfast, but it was because he knew his suffering was not in vain in the Lord.

> Therefore, my beloved brethren, be ye steadfast, unmovable, always abounding in the work of the Lord, forasmuch as ye know that your labour is not in vain in the Lord (1 Cor. 15:58).

You will win before God because you have all eternity in which God can make this thing right.

> For we know that if our earthly house of this tabernacle were dissolved, we have a building of God, a house not made with hands, eternal in the heavens. For in this we groan, earnestly desiring to be clothed upon with our house which is from heaven: if so be that being clothed we shall not be found naked (2 Cor. 5:1-3).

My present body is called a house because I live in it and a tabernacle because it is temporary, like a tent. If it were dissolved, I as a believer have a building of God. Actually, in ways that cannot be expressed, believers look forward to heaven, to a time when things will be right. That will be a time when we will become what we could be and what we will be in Christ Jesus.

> For we that are in this tabernacle do groan, being burdened: not for that we would be unclothed, but clothed upon, that mortality might be swallowed up of life (2 Cor. 5:4).

It isn't that we want to quit living; it is that we would just like to live with all the power of God. We would like to have the body that is prepared for us in heaven.

> Now he that hath wrought us for the selfsame thing is God, who
> also hath given unto us the earnest of the Spirit (2 Cor. 5:5).

The One who has made us so that we will want this is God. We would like to be someplace where there is no sorrow, no hurt, and no separation; and that is what is in heaven.

God has also given us the "earnest of the Spirit," the down payment of heaven, which is the Holy Spirit Himself in our hearts. There is one thing on earth that will never be changed in all eternity: it is the fellowship with God that believers have through the Spirit.

> Therefore we are always confident, knowing that, whilst we are
> at home in the body, we are absent from the Lord (2 Cor. 5:6).

Someday we will be with Him, and then we shall have those things that have been promised.

Chapter 64

THE AMBITION OF A BELIEVER

We might say in truth that since believers in Christ trust everything to God, they are not seeking earthly wealth. They are not seeking power nor are they seeking pleasure above everything else. If that is true, wouldn't it follow that they need not strive about anything? The Scriptures advise: "Seekest thou great things for thyself? seek them not" (Jer. 45:5). Believers are, in fact, committed to deny themselves. John the Baptist admonished, "He must increase, but I must decrease." Heaven will be provided for believers: we do not have to buy it or work for it. We are just strangers here, pilgrims in this land. It does not make sense to be ambitious; as a believer there is no need to struggle, because as far as this world is concerned, we are not collecting anything.

Is the believer's prospect, then, just one of standing pat or drifting along? Let us notice Paul's confession about his personal life:

> (For we walk by faith, not by sight:) We are confident, I say, and willing rather to be absent from the body, and to be present with the Lord. Wherefore we labour, that, whether present or absent, we may be accepted of him (2 Cor. 5:7-9).

Labor is a strong word. It can be literally translated: "Therefore we agonize; we work hard." It has been translated in another version with the phrase, "ambitious to be well pleasing in His sight." In different places we find that Paul testified that he had ambition in connection with his daily life:

> And every man that striveth for the mastery is temperate in all things. Now they do it to obtain a corruptible crown; but we an incorruptible. I therefore so run, not as uncertainly; so fight I, not as one that beateth the air: but I keep under my body, and

> bring it into subjection: lest that by any means, when I have
> preached to others, I myself should be a castaway (1 Cor.
> 9:25-27).

Paul indicated that he was like an athlete in competition and he
described his spiritual life in that comparison.

> But what things were gain to me, those I counted loss for Christ.
> Yea doubtless, and I count all things but loss for the excellency of
> the knowledge of Christ Jesus my Lord: for whom I have suf-
> fered the loss of all things, and do count them but dung, that I
> may win Christ, and be found in him, not having mine own
> righteousness, which is of the law, but that which is through the
> faith of Christ, the righteousness which is of God by faith: that I
> may know him, and the power of his resurrection, and the
> fellowship of his sufferings, being made conformable unto his
> death; if by any means I might attain unto the resurrection of
> the dead. Not as though I had already attained, either were
> already perfect: but I follow after, if that I may apprehend that
> for which also I am apprehended of Christ Jesus. Brethren, I
> count not myself to have apprehended: but this one thing I do,
> forgetting those things which are behind, and reaching forth
> unto those things which are before, I press toward the mark for
> the prize of the high calling of God in Christ Jesus (Phil. 3:7-14).

Paul is telling us here how living in faith can go on. The
knowledgeable believer is ambitious to be well-pleasing in the
sight of God. His proper attitude toward himself is one of
repentance, always willing to confess to God how much he
needs His grace. His attitude toward Christ Jesus involves
believing in Him, trusting Him, and calling on Him. In his
attitude toward his deeds, the believer is ready at all times to
confess sin, knowing that "If we confess our sins, he is faithful
and just to forgive us our sins, and to cleanse us from all
unrighteousness" (1 John 1:9). He really wants to open his
heart and mind to the Holy Spirit of God, and he seeks to learn
more about Him. And the believer is obedient: he studies how
to best achieve obedience.

Then, too, the believer's attitude toward the lost is important. The Lord Jesus came to seek and to save that which is lost;
and as He was sent, so He sends us. In the believer's attitude
toward the Bible, he will read and study it. He wants to know
more about it, because this will draw him nearer to God. In
other words, in every way "ambitious to be well-pleasing" is a
matter of the heart's attitude toward God. And so Paul says,

"Wherefore we labour, that, whether present or absent, we may be accepted of him" (2 Cor. 5:9). The wonderful thing for you and for me is that the Holy Spirit will move us to be ambitious and well-pleasing in His sight.

Chapter 65

KNOWING THE JUDGMENT OF GOD
MOTIVATES CONDUCT

The believer in Christ expects to meet God face to face; he will be appraised, evaluated, or, shall I say, judged by God.

> For we must all appear before the judgment seat of Christ; that every one may receive the things done in his body, according to that he hath done, whether it be good or bad. Knowing therefore the terror of the Lord, we persuade men; but we are made manifest unto God; and I trust also are made manifest in your consciences. For we commend not ourselves again unto you, but give you occasion to glory on our behalf, that ye may have somewhat to answer them which glory in appearance, and not in heart. For whether we be beside ourselves, it is to God: or whether we be sober, it is for your cause (2 Cor. 5:10-13).

Here again Paul is describing his own personal attitude. How often a person will say, "God is my Judge." God knows and cares about what is going on, and in His righteousness He is judging what is acceptable and what is not acceptable.

God the Father has committed all judgment to the Son. When we use the word *God* in referring to the whole Godhead, we say that God is the Judge of all the earth. But when we specifically consider the three persons of the Trinity, we recognize that it is the Lord Jesus Christ who will come to judge the living and the dead.

When Paul writes that we must all stand before the judgment seat of Christ, by "all" he includes everyone. Will everyone be judged at one time? I am not sure, though I don't believe so. In Revelation 20 we read about the great white throne where all men are brought before God in judgment. But at that time another book is opened called the Book of Life, and those whose names are written therein are those who have believed in the Lord and accepted the grace of God.

There is a special list of those who, we would say, have settled their case out of court. It is as though a time had been set when all people would be brought into the presence of the court to answer for certain delinquencies. Their cases would be taken up one by one and judgment pronounced. These sentences would be executed on that particular judgment day. But at that time there would be some names of people who had done wrong who would not appear because they had settled out of court, having come ahead of time, confessed their wrongs, had their fines paid, and their cases had been recorded as having been settled.

Even so, they actually come before the judgment seat: "That every one may receive the things done in his body" — that they may see the results and consequences of their own personal conduct in this world: "According to that he hath done, whether it be good or bad." We do not know if this means that all judging will be done at one time, if there will be one moment in which the full consequences and punishment of a person's conduct will be poured upon him at one particular moment. When the Scriptures speak about the things of God, they leave out all concepts of time and space. We read that there will be two resurrections — one of the just and one of the unjust — but whether they will occur simultaneously we do not know.

Let me assure you that everyone, believer and unbeliever alike, will stand before Christ Jesus to answer for the deeds done in the body. What a wonderful thought that the believer can stand with confidence, knowing that the Lord Himself has paid his bill.

> For we commend not ourselves again unto you, but give you
> occasion to glory on our behalf . . . (2 Cor. 5:12).

Paul told the believers that they should not be striving to gain their own approval or confidence; Paul simply told what God had done so they could rejoice with him. Paul lived in a way that glorified the Lord — this was the basic mark of his living. This is characteristic of the mature Christian — nothing for self. Paul demonstrated that it is possible to live totally committed to the Lord.

Chapter 66

BELIEVERS ARE RECONCILED TO GOD
FOR A PURPOSE

Can you understand what would make a man preach to
people who do not listen and talk to people who really do not
want to hear about the Lord?

All believers in Christ face discouragement and opposition
from time to time. A person whose only thought is to do what is
pleasing to God and helpful to others exposes himself to opposition and discouragement. What can keep such a man faithful
to his course, and how can he possibly overcome the disposition in himself to retaliate? People usually act as they do for
some obvious reason. First, there is the simple reaction you
have if a person were to stick a pin in you — you jump. Often
you react in direct response to things: a cold wind is blowing
so you button up your coat; there is a pleasant smile on someone's face, so you smile at him; you are hungry so you
look for something to eat. This is the way conduct is affected
by your situation, and you respond to it according to that
situation.

Sometimes people do what they do for reasons that do not
arise out of the immediate situation. Perhaps something happened in their past that causes them to act in a certain way; or
maybe something that will happen in the future causes them to
act as they do. For instance, we think of a young person in
college: his parents are away; he lives by himself. Something
comes up that this person realizes is not right. Now why would
he refuse to do something that promises pleasure and/or profit? It may be because of something that happened long ago:
maybe he accepted the Lord Jesus Christ as his Savior; or
perhaps when this temptation is being faced, someone was
praying for him. And it may be he knows he will stand in the

presence of God to answer for every deed done in the body, and it is this knowledge that deters him.

This would be the case of a person acting with what I would call sufficient reason. Motivation for action is usually grounded in a certain attitude, and this may be inspired by certain goals or aims. We expect a mother to be thoughtful of and careful for her child. She may not have adopted any formal judgment about this, but from the bottom of her heart her love for her child causes her to do certain things. The motivation she has to look after the child is her love and her desire to see the child benefited. A bride may not sign a declaration that she will do what is pleasing to her bridegroom, but because she loves him, there are certain things she will do naturally. Her attitude toward her bridegroom governs the motivation of her conduct.

Paul was a good example of a mature believer in Christ. The mature believer realizes he has been bought with a price, and commits himself to serve and please his Lord. This accounts for the things he does.

> For the love of Christ constraineth us; because we thus judge, that if one died for all, then were all dead: and that he died for all, that they which live should not henceforth live unto themselves, but unto him which died for them, and rose again (2 Cor. 5:14-15).

We are inwardly impelled by the love which moved Christ to give Himself for sinners. Love does not mean that He delighted in or admired sinners. The love of Christ might be better understood as being grounded in His compassion; He was touched by the feeling of their infirmities. Paul affirmed that he was inwardly impelled by this love of Christ. All were dead in trespasses and sins, and Christ Jesus died to deliver them; Paul therefore decided the fact that He died for all makes it imperative that they who live because of that death, and receive that grace from God, should henceforth live not unto themselves.

Because this was true Paul wrote:

> Wherefore henceforth know we no man after the flesh: yea, though we have known Christ after the flesh, yet now henceforth know we him no more (2 Cor. 5:16).

Believers no longer esteem or despise people because of their human aspects. Before Paul was a believer, he had thought of

Jesus of Nazareth as a man after the flesh; but now he did not think of Him that way any more. When you think of a person, you esteem him as you see him to be: one is a man, another is a woman; that one is rich, this one is poor. Paul would say he did not pay attention to any of these things. Believers do not esteem anyone according to his human qualities; they see him and think of him as a creature of God.

> Therefore if any man be in Christ, he is a new creature: old
> things are passed away; behold, all things are become new
> (2 Cor. 5:17).

All things are of God. They originate in Him, who has reconciled believers to Himself through Jesus Christ. That He said He would accept believers is not merely a matter of words but an actual operation of reorientation. He reconciled believers to Himself, and He has given to them the ministry of reconciliation. He called believers to function in promoting this reconciliation, actually turning people to Him.

> To wit, that God was in Christ, reconciling the world unto
> himself, not imputing their trespasses unto them; and hath
> committed unto us the word of reconciliation (2 Cor. 5:19).

God was in Christ not only in His power, but even more basically in His purpose. By removing the barrier, arranging to remove their sins, His promise was to forgive all believers through Christ Jesus. This is now their function in the world — to tell the children of men that salvation is nigh, that the way is open for them to come to God.

Chapter 67

AMBASSADORS FOR CHRIST

How easy it is for us to fall into a snare when we think about what the church should tell the world or a preacher tell his people! How easy it is to get the idea that the preacher should tell his people what they should do, and that believers should challenge others to get right with God! I often think that those of us who preach give the impression that the whole matter of living the life of faith is performing certain duties according to certain commands. As we try to learn how a mature believer should live, it is good for us to remember that no one is born with faith in Christ. We know that being saved depends on our believing in the Lord Jesus Christ. No one is born with this faith; it must be acquired. Faith needs to be true and to grow more and more. It can be weak or strong. Faith comes from the Word of God: Paul wrote, "Faith cometh by hearing, and hearing by the word of God" (Rom. 10:17).

In the Scriptures it is revealed that the believer is brought to understand that the soul must confront the living God. There must be between the individual soul and the living God what we call a "thou-me" relationship.

> . . . he that cometh to God must believe that he is, and that he is
> a rewarder of them that diligently seek him (Heb. 11:6).

The soul that wants the blessing of God must recognize not only the reality of God but also the grace of God. No one can arrive at this by himself or by looking inwardly. No one in his own consciousness can imagine or speculate as to what this truth is. God must reveal Himself and His plan to man; He can do far more than we can ask or think. No human being by himself can ever imagine the grace of God. The only people who ever believed in the Lord Jesus Christ were those who heard the gospel.

Even today there are people who earnestly and sincerely seek the solution to their problems in their own understanding. They talk together, reason together, plan together, agree on things together, and have the feeling that together they can find out what is true. These people need to realize that no man by searching can find God. Such persons, by looking into each other's hearts, will never get to know God. "He that hath seen me hath seen the Father" (John 14:9). It is not possible for anyone to come to God except through the Lord Jesus Christ: "I am the door: by me if any man enter in, he shall be saved" (John 10:9); and "I am the way, the truth, and the life; no man cometh unto the Father, but by me" (John 14:6). The individual soul needs to know that Christ Jesus came not to condemn the world but that the world through Him might be saved; therefore, the believer does not seek men to tell them that they are lost, as much as he seeks them that they may know salvation is prepared and ready. He does not need to do anything to convince them they are lost; what they need to know is the way out.

Many people shun the public worship of God. They do not want to talk about God or Christ Jesus, and they do not want to talk about being saved. This is a sign of their inner conviction: they know they are not right within themselves. They know they are out of touch with God, and they are afraid of Him. No one is ever glad to see his executioner. God is the Judge, and many want to stay away. This aspect of reality is true. Men have sinned and are condemned, but it is also gloriously true that God is merciful and has prepared a salvation for all who will believe.

This is what the Christian wants to tell all men: God is prepared to save to the uttermost those who come to Him by Christ Jesus.

> Now then we are ambassadors for Christ, as though God did beseech you by us: we pray you in Christ's stead, be ye reconciled to God. For he hath made him to be sin for us, who knew no sin; that we might be made the righteousness of God in him (2 Cor. 5:20-21).

Did you notice what the messenger goes forth to tell? There is no mention here about what the sinner should do: there is no work to perform, no special thing to do. It is for him to know that he can be reconciled to God.

We might pause here to reflect that it is God who beseeches people, and then to observe how Christ does this beseeching.

> Come unto me, all ye that labour and are heavy laden, and I will give you rest (Matt. 11:28).

This promises rest and relief from strain and distress. We remember also how, when the woman was brought before Him in sin, He said, "Neither do I condemn thee: go, and sin no more" (John 8:11). He was graciously releasing her from obligations. "Him that cometh to me I will in no wise cast out" (John 6:37).

When Jesus of Nazareth was calling men to Himself, He taught them that turning to God requires no prerequisites or preparation; these things have been done for them. The message that goes out to all the world is: All things are now ready. Paul restates what God has done to prepare this salvation and to provide it for those who will believe. Almighty God counted Jesus of Nazareth as if He were a sinner that He might count me as if I were a saint. He treated Him as a sinner that He might treat me as a son, a saint. He bestowed upon Him my guilt that He might bestow upon me His glory. Yes, that is amazing!

Of course, Jesus did not deserve that kind of treatment; it is equally true that I do not deserve this kind of treatment. I should never be treated as a saint. But we remember how Paul said, "For ye know the grace of our Lord Jesus Christ, that, though he was rich, yet for your sakes he became poor, that ye through his poverty might be rich" (2 Cor. 8:9).

This is the story believers have to tell. This is what they are speaking of to the whole world when they call on people to be reconciled to God. This is God's amazing plan: if sinners will come to Him and put their trust in Him, He will transfer to them the righteousness of the Lord Jesus Christ. This is what parents try to tell their children: "Put your trust in God. He will forgive you; He will keep you." Ministers, missionaries, and teachers go forth telling everyone how the Lord Jesus could say, "I gave Myself for thee," and then ask, "What hast thou given for Me?"

Chapter 68

THE TESTIMONY OF A TRUE BELIEVER

The apostle Paul emphasizes that a mature servant of God, a believer who really understands what it means to trust in the Lord Jesus Christ, will try to live in a manner that befits the name of Christ. This kind of yielding to the Lord will show up not so much in results of what he does as in the consequences to himself. Actually, the results are largely dependent on circumstances: sometimes results are good and sometimes they are poor. When a man goes fishing, he takes along his fishing tackle and his bait, but the number of fish he will catch depends somewhat on how many fish are in the lake and whether or not they are biting. The number of fish he catches is not necessarily an index of what kind of fisherman he is.

So we say that in spiritual work, results are largely dependent on circumstances. Even if a pastor comes to a certain church and a hundred members are added to its membership, that may not be a good index of what kind of pastor he is. Another man may be called to a church, be there all year long, and get only twenty people to join; but perhaps there were no more than twenty available. Again, as far as the actual indication of a person's life is concerned, results are largely dependent on circumstances. Results are not always a good index of quality.

The question is not, How much did I accomplish? That is often quite misleading. What did it cost me? is a better clue to my part in an activity. Paul is greatly concerned that the Corinthian believers should be careful of their conduct. And when Paul talks about himself, he is talking about things that happened to him, not the results he produced in the community.

> We then, as workers together with him, beseech you also that ye receive not the grace of God in vain. (For he saith, I have heard thee in a time accepted, and in the day of salvation have I succored thee: behold, now is the accepted time; behold, now is the day of salvation.) (2 Cor. 6:1-2).

Paul looked at the present time as *the* opportunity to witness. He was eager that the Corinthians should be worthy of their confidence and testimony for God, right where they lived, so he set himself up as an example and undertook to show them what it was like.

> Giving no offence in any thing, that the ministry be not blamed (2 Cor. 6:3).

Paul was careful not to give anyone cause to stumble. He knew that the minister, or any person who was telling the gospel story, would be carefully observed and criticized regarding his conduct. He should be dependable and give a good report of himself. He should be careful not to give offense with reference to his dress, his speech, and his manner. And this he would do for the sake of the gospel.

> But in all things approving ourselves as the ministers of God, in much patience, in afflictions, in necessities, in distresses (2 Cor. 6:4).

By staying right in there and not quitting, by enduring persecution, by doing things that were needed, enduring strain and stress, regardless of discouragement and opposition, the servant would be seen as worthy.

> In stripes, in imprisonments, in tumults, in labours, in watchings, in fastings (2 Cor. 6:5).

The believer as servant might be beaten, but he would continue to give his testimony. He might be put in jail, but that would not cause him to change his message. There might be riots against him, but he would be found faithful throughout. There might be hard work, but he put himself right into it. He would wait on God and do without things in order to have God's will done. Anyone who saw him would be impressed with his conduct and his testimony.

> By pureness, by knowledge, by longsuffering, by kindness, by the Holy Ghost, by love unfeigned (2 Cor. 6:6).

These are things the believer would do, not thinking of himself. Meekness and steadfastness would mark him; he would not quit nor retaliate when people opposed him. In everything he did he was conscious of the Lord Jesus Christ. He had genuine, sincere concern for the welfare of other people and for the pleasure of God. All these were aspects of the relationship of this believer who really put his faith and trust in the Lord Jesus Christ.

> By the word of truth, by the power of God, by the armour of righteousness on the right hand and on the left, by honour and dishonour, by evil report and good report: as deceivers, and yet true; as unknown, and yet well known; as dying, and, behold, we live; as chastened, and not killed; as sorrowful, yet always rejoicing; as poor, yet making many rich; as having nothing, and yet possessing all things (2 Cor. 6:7-10).

"By the word of truth [teaching the actual truth as it is in the gospel], by the power of God [with effectiveness to be seen in events — when he spoke people listened, and when he prayed things were done], by the armour of righteousness on the right hand and on the left [Paul maintained open conduct that everyone could see for the sake of the gospel], by honour and dishonour [some would praise him, some would blame him; but this did not change him; he remained steadfast in his commitment to God], by evil report and good report [some would accuse him of doing wrong but he was steadfast]: as deceivers, and yet true [sometimes accused of deceiving people, yet always honest in spite of accusations]; as unknown, and yet well known [treated as an obscure nobody yet everyone knew him]; as dying, and behold we live; as chastened, and not killed [he suffered again and again yet he came through with vitality — a marvelous description of the way it is with a person who walks with the Lord]; as sorrowful, yet always rejoicing [there was cause for grieving, yet there was joy in his heart at all times]; as poor, yet making many rich [he was often bereft, yet he brought blessing to everyone]; as having nothing, and yet possessing all things [he was without anything at times, yet he was never lacking]." What a life and what a testimony! This was the case of a person who is an "epistle of Christ," known and read by all men.

Chapter 69

BELIEVERS ARE NOT TO BE YOKED
WITH UNBELIEVERS

Maturity for a believer in Christ is the result of his fully understanding the Word of God. When a person walks in the way of the Lord, he will learn certain patterns of conduct and become skillful in them. However, such development in the way of living the spiritual life is not the result of training inherent powers. It is not passing through a schedule of training activities which result in being inclined to follow the Lord. It is rather an acquired facility, a tendency of doing certain things in response to certain situations.

When a person sees God as his Father and Jesus Christ as his Savior and Lord and understands the Holy Spirit is working in him, certain things happen to him which will result in certain conduct. This will not be because he practices it or preferred it, but because it is a result of his relationship with God. A person does not train himself to reverence God because reverence to God is a desirable thing. A person sees God for who He is and recognizes that reverence is His due, that God in Himself commands and generates reverence. This is the source of reverence in the believing heart.

Paul is concerned that believers should realize the truth of their relationship with God. He knows that in the course of bringing this to their attention he will be speaking directly and personally.

> O ye Corinthians, our mouth is open unto you, our heart is enlarged. Ye are not straitened in us, but ye are straitened in your own bowels (2 Cor. 6:11-12).

When Paul says, "Our mouth is open unto you," he means, "We want to say things that will be helpful to you; we really care about you." The word *straitened* means "narrowed." Believers are not held in and restrained. "In your own bowels" is an expression that reflects the culture of the day. People have found various ways of referring to the emotional aspect of human experience, which has been associated with different parts of what we call the visceral organs — those in the trunk of the body.

For example, it was common among the Hebrews when one was stirred emotionally to refer to the kidneys. Also, the Hebrew would say a dart had hit him in his liver, while we might say today that we have a pang in our heart. Later, in the time of the Greeks (and that is the time when the New Testament was written), there was a tendency to say that the emotional aspect of the human experience was what we would call the psychosomatic reaction — reaction grounded in physical feelings. We talk about the heart, and it sounds very romantic and poetic. So when Paul says, "Ye are straitened in your own bowels," we would say, "You feel constraint in your heart or emotions."

> Now for a recompence in the same, (I speak as unto my children,) be ye also enlarged (2 Cor. 6:13).

"You feel toward us the way we feel toward you. It is in our heart to do you good; you are open in your heart and mind to receive what we have to say. You take it in the spirit in which we give it." This is a plea for close, cordial communication.

Having made this earnest plea, Paul now presses on with an urgent admonition, speaking to these people directly.

> Be ye not unequally yoked together with unbelievers: for what fellowship hath righteousness with unrighteousness? and what communion hath light with darkness? (2 Cor. 6:14).

This is good advice on any level. We often apply it to marriage. When we see a believer considering marriage to an unbeliever, we say, "Be careful about that." But this is true not only in marriage, but in any fellowship, in anything that you do together. There is difficulty and strain when you get two people together who do not have the same ideas. Communion with Christ is far more exclusive than is commonly recognized. If you walk with the Lord, there are other people with whom you cannot walk.

Paul presents a simple line of argument: ". . . for what fellowship hath righteousness with unrighteousness?" The Old Testament asks the question,

Can two walk together, except they be agreed? (Amos 3:3).

Righteousness for Paul in all of his writings means living in believing obedience to the living God. When a person believes in Him and is always conscious of Him, that is righteousness: such conduct will be acceptable. Unrighteousness is living in unbelief, apart from Christ. How can these two be together? ". . . and what communion hath light with darkness?" In light you are in the presence of God; in darkness you are alone.

And what concord hath Christ with Belial? or what part hath he that believeth with an infidel? (2 Cor. 6:15).

The meaning is self-evident. It shows the contrast between a person who lives and walks in the way of Christ Jesus and an infidel, or a person who lives and walks in his own ideas.

And what agreement hath the temple of God with idols? for ye are the temple of the living God (2 Cor. 6:16).

Here we see the temple of God — a place where God is worshiped — in contrast to a place where idols are worshiped and where present pleasures prevail. The temple was sanctified. In fact, the Lord Jesus Christ cleansed the temple when they were buying and selling in it; He drove them out and said, "My house shall be called a house of prayer." Paul is saying if you belong to the Lord you cannot be in fellowship with unbelievers. That is why He gives the call, "Come out from among them and be ye separate" (v. 17).

Chapter 70

BELONGING TO GOD

Belonging to the Lord involves one's entire life and is commonly compared to marriage: we talk about being members of the "bride" and Christ being the "Bridegroom." Marriage is from the time vows are said until death separates. Anyone who wants to walk with the Lord must commit himself to a total arrangement; he must forsake all others to walk with the Lord. Christ Jesus will never be a competitor for our attention or affection. It is He and He alone. When He died for me, He died for all of me. He purchased me with His own blood.

The Bible tells me, "The Lord thy God is a jealous God." I cannot overstate that. People may say they do not think God demands our total surrender, but this only shows their ignorance. And Paul leaves absolutely no room for uncertainty about this. He points out to the Corinthian Christians a basic aspect of what it means to really belong to God.

> Wherefore come out from among them, and be ye separate, saith the Lord, and touch not the unclean thing; and I will receive you (2 Cor. 6:17).

There is a basic condition to be met for blessing, and it involves a definite, selective choice.

> As God hath said, I will dwell in them, and walk in them; and I will be their God, and they shall be my people (2 Cor. 6:16).

I put my hand in His and not in anyone else's. A definite break with the world is necessary for true fellowship with Him.

"Touch not the unclean thing." When is something unclean? Anything that has not been washed in the blood of the Lamb is unclean in the eyes of the Lord. By the blood of the Lamb we mean crucifixion, the denial of self.

And will be a Father unto you, and ye shall be my sons and
daughters, saith the Lord Almighty (2 Cor. 6:18).

Thus a Father-child relationship will be activated.

Today there are earnest people who try to help others draw
nearer to God by giving the impression that God is a kind of
"hail-fellow-well-met" Person. That is not the New Testament
revelation, and it is not wholesome to mankind. God is high
and holy and lifted up, and one must feel in the presence of
God that he is personally a sinner.

Woe is me! for I am undone; because I am a man of unclean
lips . . . (Isa. 6:5).

This is the essence of an acceptable attitude on the part of man.
It lifts him. When a man knows that he is sinful and knows that
God will call him into His presence, he can come with fear and
trembling. This is acceptable to God.

We like to think of God simply as our Father, but Paul
summarizes his admonition:

Having therefore these promises, dearly beloved, let us cleanse
ourselves from all filthiness of the flesh and spirit, perfecting
holiness in the fear of God (2 Cor. 7:1).

The promises were set forth in the final verses of chapter 6:

I will dwell in them, and walk in them; and I will be their God,
and they shall be my people (2 Cor. 6:16).

Believers are brought into the family of God, not because they
are good enough, but because He is gracious and merciful. And
since they have been called into His presence, Paul says, "Let
us cleanse ourselves from all filthiness of the flesh and spirit."

How does a believer cleanse himself? By confessing and
forsaking his sins and by having a repentant heart before God
so that he might be able to say with the apostle Paul:

For I know that in me (that is, in my flesh,) dwelleth no good
thing (Rom. 7:18).

The believer can do this by confessing and forsaking his sins.

If we confess our sins, he is faithful and just to forgive us our sins,
and to cleanse us from all unrighteousness (1 John 1:9).

By filthiness we do not mean just immorality or crude vulgar-
ity; we mean anything that is sinful or unclean. Remember,

Paul is using the words *cleanse* and *unclean*. Filthiness is sin: sin of the flesh. The characteristic of the sin of the flesh is self-indulgence. The outstanding characteristic of the sin of the spirit is pride, failure to humble oneself.

"Perfecting holiness in the fear of God" is bringing it through to its fruit. We speak of a peach tree being perfect when it has peaches on it; an apple tree is perfect when it bears apples; and a believer is perfect when there are spiritual fruits in his life — when he puts the principles of faith into actual practice and conduct. Holiness is being 100 percent sincere in one's commitment to the Lord. This is the mark of maturity. Here in a real sense is the crux of the whole matter of being a mature Christian: It means total commitment to the living Lord.

Chapter 71

THE JOY OF A PASTOR

In these studies we want to see how a true Christian acts, and Paul's life as a believer illustrates what is true for all believers.

> Receive us; we have wronged no man, we have corrupted no man, we have defrauded no man. I speak not this to condemn you: for I have said before, that ye are in our hearts to die and live with you. Great is my boldness of speech toward you, great is my glorying of you: I am filled with comfort, I am exceeding joyful in all our tribulation. For, when we were come into Macedonia, our flesh had no rest, but we were troubled on every side; without were fightings, within were fears. Nevertheless God, that comforteth those that are cast down, comforted us by the coming of Titus; and not by his coming only, but by the consolation wherewith he was comforted in you, when he told us your earnest desire, your mourning, your fervent mind toward me; so that I rejoiced the more (2 Cor. 7:2-7).

These words represent the very personal testimony of this man who had been a pastor in the church at Corinth and who was concerned about the way they felt toward him. He wanted them to remember the blessed fellowship they had together, and he was asking them to keep these things in mind and stay close to him. In another translation of this passage Paul writes:

> Make room for us in your hearts. We have done wrong to no one, have ruined no one, nor tried to take advantage of anyone. I do not say this to condemn you; for, as I have said before, you are so dear to us that we are together always, whether we live or die. I am so sure of you, I take such pride in you! In all our troubles I am still full of courage, I am running over with joy. Even after we arrived in Macedonia we did not have any rest. There were troubles everywhere, quarrels with others, fears in our hearts. But God, who encourages the downhearted, encouraged us with the coming of Titus. It was not only his coming, but also his report of how you encouraged him. He told us how much you

want to see me, how sorry you are, how ready you are to defend me; and so I am even happier now (2 Cor. 7:2-7).

We can feel in this the warm heart of this servant of God; the intimate attitude of Paul toward his former congregation. Note that when Paul claims their good will and wants them to receive him, he does not stress what he has done for them: he emphasizes rather that he has done them no harm and they have no reason to reject him. How often the servant of God must defend himself, even with friends.

Apparently Paul counted on the Lord to prompt believers to share in his testimony, and he was concerned that they should be confident in Christ. His own conscience was clear, and he wanted them to be clear in their hearts as they supported him. In speaking about this he also commented on the fact that God encourages the down-hearted. What Titus had told him about these Corinthian believers assured Paul and gave him great joy.

Chapter 72

THE FUNCTION OF GODLY SORROW

For godly sorrow worketh repentance to salvation not to be repented of: but the sorrow of the world worketh death (2 Cor. 7:10).

These words are taken from a passage of Scripture we shall now consider in which the apostle Paul talks to the Corinthians about the way they responded to his former letter. He tells them the great truth that godly sorrow worketh repentance. Trouble — suffering sorrow — comes easily to man. Some have more, some have less, but it is everywhere. It is common for people to say that trouble will work out for good, but that is not always true. Paul says in Romans:

And we know that all things work together for good to them that love God, to them who are the called according to his purpose (Rom. 8:28).

In some cases suffering can turn out for good, but in other cases for evil. Some people believe in Christ and some do not. What this amounts to is: some people have the help of God in Christ Jesus, and some do not. The person who is standing in Christ has all the benefits of the help of Christ, but the person who is standing alone has no such benefits.

The promise that all things work together for good to them that love God is made for Christians only. Anyone may have this because the Bible tells us, "Whosoever will may come"; but there is a truth here we need to soberly realize. Only those who meet the conditions will receive this promise. The realization of blessing comes only to those who heed the Word of God.

Paul teaches this truth on the basis of what happened in Corinth. Second Corinthians 7:8-16 seems to refer to the member of the church who persisted in living in open sin. Paul wrote to criticize the congregation for their tolerance. Toleration of evil is no virtue. Paul says a little leaven leavens the whole lump. He told them they were to be blamed because they had not done anything about it. Then he told them that they should put out this offender both for his sake and for the sake of all. Apparently they accepted his admonition in the first letter, and when Titus later visited the congregation he found that they had done what Paul had asked them to do. They were warm in their praise and appreciation of Paul. This is now what Paul acknowledges in the second letter, and he rejoices that he wrote to them the first time as he did.

> For though I made you sorry with a letter, I do not repent, though I did repent: for I perceive that the same epistle hath made you sorry, though it were but for a season. Now I rejoice, not that ye were made sorry, but that ye sorrowed to repentance: for ye were made sorry after a godly manner, that ye might receive damage by us in nothing. For godly sorrow worketh repentance to salvation not to be repented of: but the sorrow of the world worketh death. For behold this selfsame thing, that ye sorrowed after a godly sort, what carefulness it wrought in you, yea, what clearing of yourselves, yea, what indignation, yea, what fear, yea, what vehement desire, yea, what zeal, yea, what revenge! In all things ye have approved yourselves to be clear in this matter (2 Cor. 7:8-11).

Fire will do one thing to gold; it will do something else to stone. You can put gold in fire and the fire will burn away the dross, to make it better gold than before. If you put a stone in fire, all you get is ashes. When a believer in Christ is criticized or chastened, he is humbled to admit that he has done wrong. When an unbeliever is criticized or suffering he is offended and upset. A believer will say, "O Lord, forgive me and cleanse me. I am to blame for what happened"; but the non-believer will say, "Why did this happen to me? I don't deserve this." The unbeliever experiences sorrow when he is exposed as a failure, but it will do him no good. The believer will accept sorrow as from God, who loves him; and it will prove helpful. Godly sorrow produces repentance. If you are suffering, trust yourself into God's hands and follow Him: He will make your suffering work for good.

Chapter 73

THE GRACE OF LIBERALITY

Our interest in this study is in the proper conduct of a believer in Christ. In chapter 8 we see that liberality in giving is a trait that needs to be nurtured if we are to be blessed. One might think every Christian would be generous, but this attitude overlooks what is involved. It is natural to covet, to want for self. Giving to others with no thought of receiving is entirely foreign to nature.

Many popular ideas are basically self-seeking. We encourage young people in their studies so they can make their way in the world, to get everything they can for themselves. In our culture we approve acquisitiveness, so that when someone makes a lot of money, we are inclined to say he is a great man. Do we honor the man who yearns to give in the same way?

In our culture we approve self-interest. In international affairs we talk about how each nation is expected to look out for its own interests. It seems that in this world one cannot advance in any other way. But Paul was not writing about this world: he was writing about heaven and about God. We know what Jesus of Nazareth said, "If any man will come after me, let him deny himself, take up his cross and follow me."

There is no principle of education I know of that can bring human nature into the frame of mind to give. Even those who have learned to give for business reasons give because they expect to receive in return. Here we are brought face to face with the Word of the Lord Jesus Christ. Nicodemus asked Him about this very thing; he wanted to know how anyone could live the way our Lord demonstrated life. And we remember how Jesus of Nazareth told Nicodemus, "You must be born again."

The child of God through Jesus Christ will have little interest in self but will have a desire to please God.

There is an important truth that should be remembered: Believers begin as babies and they must grow. The old man of the flesh came first. He had habits of covetous practices from the time he was a baby lying in the crib; the new man in Christ must establish new habits of giving instead of getting. The disposition to give is from the Lord Jesus Christ, and this will come in the spiritual experience as a result of having Christ in you, the hope of glory.

> Moreover, brethren, we do you to wit of the grace of God bestowed on the churches of Macedonia; how that in a great trial of affliction the abundance of their joy and their deep poverty abounded unto the riches of their liberality (2 Cor. 8:1-2).

"We do you to wit" is an old English way of saying, "We want you to know." This "grace of God bestowed on the churches" is a certain gift that God gave to the churches in Macedonia. He inwardly empowered them to act according to His will. We call that His grace. At a time when they were having much trouble and deep poverty, they had an abundance of joy in Christ Jesus. They were close to the Lord and were rejoicing in their salvation though in poverty. In their great trial of affliction the abundance (the amount) they had to give "abounded unto the riches of their liberality."

Often we find in spiritual experience that individuals who do not make much money are very generous. Some churches are like that. And they are happy about their liberality.

> For to their power, I bear record, yea, and beyond their power they were willing of themselves; praying us with much entreaty that we would receive the gift, and take upon us the fellowship of the ministering to the saints. And this they did, not as we hoped, but first gave their own selves to the Lord, and unto us by the will of God. Insomuch that we desired Titus, that as he had begun, so he would also finish in you the same grace also. Therefore, as ye abound in every thing, in faith, and utterance, and knowledge, and in all diligence, and in your love to us, see that ye abound in this grace also (2 Cor. 8:3-7).

Paul wrote that as well as they could manage it, the Christians in Macedonia volunteered to do everything they could. They were giving money that would be taken to another city to be given to poor brethren, and they urged Paul to act as their representative. They first gave themselves to the Lord and to Paul, then they gave the money. This is a healthy spiritual way of doing it. They were setting an example and Paul was anxious that the believers in Corinth should receive a similar blessing.

Titus, you remember, went to Macedonia and visited with the Christians there. He told Paul in Corinth of the wonderful blessing he had in that country. He ministered to the Macedonians and they gave so liberally Paul wanted Titus to preach to the Corinthians so they, too, would give generously. These people had faith in God and they knew about the gospel. They were faithful in everything, and Paul wrote, ". . . see that ye abound in this grace also."

Chapter 74

GRACE PROMPTS GIVING

"The grace of the Lord Jesus Christ be with you all." How often we read this phrase in the Bible. But are we clear in our own minds as to what this really means? The portion of Scripture we are studying has its own message of encouraging believers in Christ to be liberal in their giving. We have this brought to our attention in various ways. Every now and then someone will point out that giving is living, and someone else will say that living is giving. But there are some people who live and give very little; in fact, there are some people who live and try not to give at all.

> I speak not by commandment, but by occasion of the forwardness of others, and to prove the sincerity of your love (2 Cor. 8:8).

When Paul said, "I speak not by commandment," he implied that he did not want to lay down a set of rules. The forwardness of others was their willingness to go ahead and do something. Because other believers had been willing to do something, he felt that he should talk to the Corinthians to test the sincerity of their love for the Lord.

We learn that many spiritual things are easy to talk about, but they are more difficult to put into action. A person may say that he loves God, but the test is, How does he do it? The Lord Jesus said, "If you love me, keep my commandments." Act the way He wants you to act, walk in the way He leads you, and the walking will be a measure of love.

The great verse we so often quote, "For God so loved the world," will help us to understand this. "For God so loved the world, that he gave" — did you notice? God *so* loved the world, that He *gave*. Paul said he was not setting forth rules, but in view of what others were doing, and because the Corinthians wanted to prove their love, Paul talked about giving. What a believer gives is a good sign of his heart's attitude.

In verse 9 is written the best description in this section of the Bible of the grace of God:

> For ye know the grace of our Lord Jesus Christ, that, though he was rich, yet for your sakes he became poor, that ye through his poverty might be rich (2 Cor. 8:9).

Again we see clearly that Jesus was living in heaven before He came here; "though he was rich" refers to His preexistence. Although He was the Son of God and equal to God, He laid that aside and became man, taking upon Him the form of a servant: "That ye through his poverty [through His emptying Himself and making Himself of no reputation] might become rich."

This is the essence of the gospel. Grace was something Christ did for us. He must have had a willingness in His heart, but the word *grace* in particular refers to what He actually did.

> And herein I give my advice: for this is expedient for you, who have begun before, not only to do, but also to be forward a year ago. Now therefore perform the doing of it; that as there was a readiness to will, so there may be a performance also out of that which ye have (2 Cor. 8:10-11).

Paul reminded the Corinthian Christians that they were among the first who wanted to send this money to the poor believers in Jerusalem. They not only started this service, but they were enthusiastic about it. Now Paul urged them to carry it on out. They were to finish what they started to do and to show that they were ready to do as they had planned.

Paul then stated a principle in giving that we should keep in mind:

> For if there be first a willing mind, it is accepted according to that a man hath, and not according to that he hath not (2 Cor. 8:12).

This is a rather round-about way of saying that we should not let the temporary lack of funds stop us. We should give as we can now. What really matters is the attitude of the heart.

This entire portion of the Bible is extremely practical. In the

English translation we read,

> I am not laying down any rules. But by showing how eager others are to help, I am trying to find out how real your own love is. For you know the grace of our Lord Jesus Christ; rich as he was, he made himself poor for your sake, in order to make you rich by means of his poverty. This is my opinion on the matter: it is better for you to finish now what you began last year. You were the first, not only to act, but also to be willing to act. On with it, then, and finish the job! Be as eager to finish it as you were to plan it, and do it with what you have. For if you are eager to give, God will accept your gift on the basis of what you have to give, not on what you don't have (2 Cor. 8:8-12 TEV).

And still another translation reads:

> This is not meant as an order; by telling you how keen others are I am putting your love to the test. For you know how generous our Lord Jesus Christ has been: he was rich, yet for your sake he became poor, so that through his poverty you might become rich (8:8-9 NEB).

All convey the same idea. The Lord Jesus gave what He had for sinners; and if we want to grow as believers, we should let His Spirit move in us.

Do you know what He will move us to do? He will encourage us to take something of what we have and give it in His will. We will want to do this because it is our desire to please Almighty God.

Chapter 75

THE GRACE OF GIVING

If the Lord works in the heart of the believer, will there ever be need of help or encouragement from other believers? Let us see how Paul handles this question. His discussion centers around normal living as believers.

> For I mean not that other men be eased, and ye burdened: but by an equality, that now at this time your abundance may be a supply for their want, that their abundance also may be a supply for your want: that there may be equality: as it is written, He that had gathered much had nothing over; and he that had gathered little had no lack. But thanks be to God, which put the same earnest care into the heart of Titus for you. For indeed he accepted the exhortation; but being more forward, of his own accord he went unto you. And we have sent with him the brother, whose praise is in the gospel throughout all the churches (2 Cor. 8:13-18).

Giving money in the name of the Lord is to be encouraged and expected of believers in Christ. I am raising this question for consideration: Should not the believer do this for himself? If a person is going to honor the Lord in giving, why should it be done secretly? A pastor can help his parishioners by preaching about the promises of God, reminding them of what Christ Jesus has done for them and showing what the Lord wants them to do in response.

Paul envisioned a reciprocal helpfulness among believing people throughout the world helping each other. He felt this would be based on Scripture. Verse 14 indicates that apparently believers should not be guided in what they do by comparing themselves with others, but in consideration of how the Lord has blessed them. It is good to know what needs to be done in my community so I will be aware of the situation; but most of all, I will know how the Lord has blessed me. If you have special means, give accordingly.

The grace of giving can be nurtured by an individual minister like Titus, who came to promote it in the Corinthian congregation and to see them grow in this grace. And in verse 18 we see that Paul actually got an important man to share in this project of collecting money to take to the poor people in the Jerusalem church. This man is not called by name, but there is an appreciation of who he was and what he was doing, which was very important. Paul urged these people to consider that it was important for them to be liberal in their giving. The person who is generous in giving will find that God is generous in blessing.

Chapter 76

GIVING IS IMPORTANT IN SPIRITUAL LIVING

In 2 Corinthians 8 and 9 the apostle Paul wrote to describe how believers should live. He has just pointed out that it would be normal for believers to give money in the Lord's work. He promised them that the more they gave, the more they would be blessed, for the Lord loves a cheerful giver. The Bible speaks much about money, about its use and abuse, because financial resources are actually an extension of life. Money was never meant only for the person who has it. My life and my strength belong to God, and my opportunities come from Him. I have been bought with a price; and neither the activity I share in nor the money I accumulate are really mine.

The Macedonian churches of whom Paul wrote were on spiritual ground. In a previous study we noticed they first gave themselves; and if we give ourselves to the Lord, we are certain to give Him our pocketbooks. Some time ago one of my church members, who was working with me in the matter of helping the congregation to do its work, made this comment: "He gives twice who gives openly." When you give openly, you give your money, but you are also setting an example, and that affects other people. I know that giving alms to the poor, as Jesus of Nazareth talks about it in the Sermon on the Mount, can be a private affair, and certainly the decision to give is made within your own heart, yet it is not altogether private. For instance, in the matter of missions, not everyone actually goes to South America or Africa, yet you can give money that goes there by giving it to the church.

The same is true in worshiping God. Every now and then people say they do not need to go to church since they can worship alone. On the surface that sounds good, but it is not as true as it sounds. A believer is better off in fellowship with others. In your daily life you can eat by yourself, but could you build your own telephone or water system? And so, spiritually speaking, to say that one can do as well secretly whatever he is doing in the Lord's work can be used as an alibi. Sometimes those who are most zealous to keep giving secret are those who give the least.

By the same token, is it not true that more is accomplished when we study the Bible in fellowship with others and make it a point to attend prayer meetings? Our Lord said, "Where two or three are gathered together, there am I in the midst," and "If two shall agree on earth as touching anything that they shall ask, it shall be done for them." This is also true in giving. While I must respond in my own heart, my response will naturally develop with other people. It is important, because it is a joint enterprise, that care should be taken to keep everything above suspicion. There is an unavoidable peril here. In 8:19-24 we see that Paul was very careful about the way he handled the money entrusted to him; he wanted to be sure that his handling of the funds given should be above suspicion.

Remember that the money you give is part of you, and as you give you will be a partner in the work of the Lord.

Chapter 77

GIVING BY BELIEVERS

Does Christ Jesus really need my money? After all, we have read in the Bible that the cattle on a thousand hills belong to God, and that all the silver and gold are His. If I gave everything I had to the church, it would still need more; and if I give all that I have to the poor, I could never give enough. My money would make no great difference. Why then is it so important that I give?

In these chapters the apostle Paul discusses the matter of Christian giving. Elsewhere in the New Testament we do not find anything more illuminating than when we read about the Lord Jesus watching people cast their gifts into the treasury of the temple. When He saw a widow cast in her two mites, He called His disciples together and pointed out that she gave more than anyone. He noticed that she gave all that she had. You see, it is not the money but the attitude of the heart that counts. *It is not that God needs my money, it is that I need to give it.*

> For as touching the ministering to the saints, it is superfluous for me to write to you: for I know the forwardness of your mind, for which I boast of you to them of Macedonia, that Achaia was ready a year ago; and your zeal hath provoked very many (2 Cor. 9:1-2).

Paul had no misgiving about the attitude of these believers in Corinth. They understood how important it was to minister to the Lord in this way, and they were ready to do it. A year before they had indicated their readiness to share in the plan of giving that was before them.

> Yet have I sent the brethren, lest our boasting of you should be in vain in this behalf; that, as I said, ye may be ready: lest haply if they of Macedonia come with me, and find you unprepared, we (that we say not, ye) should be ashamed in this same confident boasting (2 Cor. 9:3-4).

Paul was in Macedonia as he wrote to the Corinthians in Achaia. He had told the Macedonians that the believers in Corinth were ready a year before to give and had begun then to raise the money. Then it occurred to him that because they were still human beings, even though they were believers, they still might find it easy to procrastinate. Perhaps there is no easier time to delay action than when money is involved. So Paul sent Titus and others to arouse the Corinthians to complete the collection.

> Therefore I thought it necessary to exhort the brethren, that they would go before unto you, and make up beforehand your bounty, whereof ye had notice before, that the same might be ready, as a matter of bounty, and not as of covetousness (2 Cor. 9:5).

Paul wanted their contribution to be given freely.

> But this I say, He which soweth sparingly shall reap also sparingly; and he which soweth bountifully shall reap also bountifully (2 Cor. 9:6).

While it was true that Paul wanted them to look good, he knew also that their future spiritual fortunes were at stake here. He would not presume to tell them what to do, but he could give them advice.

> Every man according as he purposeth in his heart, so let him give; not grudgingly, or of necessity: for God loveth a cheerful giver (2 Cor. 9:7).

One basic principle will always apply: "He which soweth sparingly shall reap also sparingly; and he which soweth bountifully shall reap also bountifully." Decide in your own heart what you will give; then give that cheerfully, not by looking at the results but by looking up and seeing the will of God. May God help every one of us to do this.

> And God is able to make all grace abound toward you; that ye, always having all sufficiency in all things, may abound to every good work (2 Cor. 9:8).

The last thing Paul says in chapter 9 is that the Christian's giving not only helps the poor, but it also brings glory and praise to God. In all this matter of giving Paul ends by saying, "Thanks be unto God for his unspeakable gift" (v. 15).

Chapter 78

A PASTOR URGES STRONGER FAITH

As we begin this study of chapter 10, I want to ask this question: Why should any person become a believer in Christ? It may well be said he will be a better worker, a better husband and father, etc. — if he becomes Christian, he would become a better person overall. But all of that is not good enough. If that person were stricken with paralysis so that he could not move hand or feet or utter a word, or if he became bankrupt, or if he died before tomorrow, there would still be reason for him to become a believer in Christ today.

Each man, created in the image of God, has a soul that must stand before God. He must face his Judge and give an answer to Him for the life he has lived. God sent His Son into the world to offer eternal life in place of the sinful life the sinner has in himself. The question is, Will the sinner receive Christ Jesus as the One who died for his sins in the sight of God, and will he accept Him as his Lord for eternity? Again, why should a believer who believes in God through the Lord Jesus Christ, worship God, contemplating the beauty of His holiness and the wonders of His grace? The answer is: because of who God is. Everything the believer has depends on God, because of who God is, and because the Holy Spirit of God lives within the believer.

For all these reasons the believer should take time to worship God, because the benefits in Christ Jesus are operative in him according to his faith, and faith must be nurtured. Therefore, the believer should worship God so his faith will be strong. Eternal values are greater than temporal values, and this must be kept in mind, even concerning what I do with the Lord's Day, what I do with my money, and where my emphasis will be. There will be conflicts of interest, and tension will arise.

> Now I Paul myself beseech you by the meekness and gentleness of Christ, who in presence am base among you, but being absent am bold toward you: but I beseech you, that I may not be bold when I am present with that confidence, wherewith I think to be bold against some, which think of us as if we walked according to the flesh. For though we walk in the flesh, we do not war after the flesh: (for the weapons of our warfare are not carnal, but mighty through God to the pulling down of strong holds;) casting down imaginations, and every high thing that exalteth itself against the knowledge of God, and bringing into captivity every thought to the obedience of Christ; and having in a readiness to revenge all disobedience, when your obedience is fulfilled (2 Cor. 10:1-6).

These words show that the apostle Paul was anxious to bring them face to face with God. He would resist everything that would turn them away from the things of God to the things of this world.

In another translation we read:

> I, Paul, make a personal appeal to you — I who am said to be meek and mild when I am with you, but bold toward you when I am away from you. I beg of you, by the gentleness and kindness of Christ: Do not force me to be bold with you when I come; for I am sure I can be bold with those who say that we act from worldly motives. It is true that we live in the world; but we do not fight from worldly motives. The weapons we use in our fight are not the world's weapons, but God's powerful weapons, with which to destroy strongholds. We destroy false arguments; we pull down every proud obstacle that is raised against the knowledge of God; we take every thought captive and make it obey Christ. And after you have proved your complete loyalty, we will be ready to punish any act of disloyalty (2 Cor. 10:1-6 TEV).

This was prepared by scholars who understand the Greek. The apostle Paul had no question in his mind of exactly how he would face anyone who emphasized something else in the things of God.

Still another translation reads:

> But I, Paul, appeal to you by the gentleness and magnanimity of Christ — I, so feeble (you say) when I am face to face with you, so brave when I am away. Spare me, I beg you, the necessity of such bravery when I come, for I reckon I could put on as bold a face as you please against those who charge us with moral

weakness. Weak men we may be, but it is not as such that we fight our battles. The weapons we wield are not merely human, but divinely potent to demolish strongholds; we demolish sophistries and all that rears its proud head against the knowledge of God; we compel every human thought to surrender in obedience to Christ; and we are prepared to punish all rebellion when once you have put yourselves in our hands (2 Cor. 10:1-6 NEB).

In this way Paul boldly announced that he would not tolerate anything that fostered other than things of Christ. We need to keep in mind that spiritual procedures, spiritual in encouraging faith, are tremendously important. Paul used them to destroy imaginary or visionary ideas. If all the arguments brought to you are based on this world's situation, Paul would confront you in every way with the things of God and would say that you are to realize that primarily you have dealings with God. And God is eternal and almighty. And this is what really counts.

Chapter 79

PAUL'S SELF-DEFENSE

Although Paul was a humble man who did not hesitate to admit that he was the chief of sinners, he would not allow anyone to cast aspersion upon his witness as a believer. We shall see that by common opinion Paul was not an impressive person. He faced the disposition of others to dismiss him as incompetent. Paul was ready to refute this insinuation at any time, having in mind that God was in him, using him. His physical weakness was not such as would allow him to battle with others for the dubious distinction of being the leader of the believers at this time. In other words, he did not try to overcome them with himself, to show himself better than other people. He put the evidence before the Corinthians and asked them to judge for themselves.

> Do ye look on things after the outward appearance? If any man trust to himself that he is Christ's, let him of himself think this again, that, as he is Christ's, even so are we Christ's (2 Cor. 10:7).

He belonged to Christ as much as anyone else did.

> For though I should boast somewhat more of our authority, which the Lord hath given us for edification, and not for your destruction, I should not be ashamed (2 Cor. 10:8).

Paul had been given authority to help others grow. If he should occasionally exercise this authority and make the claim that it was of God, he was not the least afraid that he would be embarrassed, because God would endorse him.

> That I may not seem as if I would terrify you by letters. For his letters, say they, are weighty and powerful; but his bodily presence is weak, and his speech contemptible. Let such a one think this, that, such as we are in word by letters when we are

absent, such will we be also in deed when we are present (2 Cor. 10:9-11).

He expected to act as positively as he wrote.

When we are trying to understand our own spiritual experience as one believer among others, we can have this in mind: if people want to find fault with us, we should not make a big argument to defend ourselves. But if others question our spiritual relationship with the Lord, we must take issue. Nothing that is said can separate us from the Lord if we trust in Him. There is nothing others can say that can contradict His calling us. Paul did not hesitate to believe that God would work through him.

In verse 10 is the evidence that Paul was not impressive. People said of him, "His bodily presence is weak." We usually consider a big man or a man of strong delivery to be imposing, but Paul was not big, nor did he have a strong delivery. '. . . and his speech contemptible": I suspect in his preaching Paul used the language of the street. To some this is a great handicap for a preacher; they want a preacher who uses the kind of language found in theology books. If he can handle that smoothly, they will say he is a great preacher. But Paul was not limited by any feeling of inferiority. As a matter of fact, he did not appraise himself in comparison with others.

> For we dare not make ourselves of the number, or compare ourselves with some that commend themselves: but they measuring themselves by themselves, and comparing themselves among themselves, are not wise (2 Cor. 10:12).

Paul was not confident in his ministry because he felt he was better than anyone else; he was confident because he felt the Lord had endorsed him. When you and I as believers in Christ have dealings with people who challenge us and even question our right to think that we really belong to the Lord, we reply, "We have trusted in Him."

Paul took notice of his critics even though their criticism actually hindered the influence of his testimony. After all, he was not in the community just to make tents; he was trying to win people to Christ; and it was important how they felt toward him. Therefore, when critics cast aspersions upon Paul's testimony he would, on occasion, stand upright. This is brought out in another translation:

You are looking at things as they are on the outside. Is there someone there who reckons himself to be Christ's man? Well, let him think again about himself, for we are Christ's men just as much as he is. For I am not ashamed, even if I have boasted somewhat too much of the authority that the Lord has given us — authority to build you up, that is, not to tear you down. I do not want it to appear that I am trying to frighten you with my letters. Someone will say, "Paul's letters are severe and strong, but when he is with us in person he is weak, and his words are nothing!" Such a person must understand that there is no difference between what we write in our letters when we are away, and what we will do when we are there with you. Of course we would not dare classify ourselves or compare ourselves with some of those who rate themselves so highly. How stupid they are! They make up their own standards to measure themselves by, and judge themselves by their own standards! (2 Cor. 10:7-12 TEV).

Paul is speaking to contradict and repudiate his critics by pointing out that their procedure is not wise.

Still another translation reads:

Look facts in the face. Someone is convinced, is he, that he belongs to Christ? Let him think again, and reflect that we belong to Christ as much as he does. Indeed, if I am somewhat over-boastful about our authority — an authority given by the Lord to build you up, not pull you down — I shall make my boast good. So you must not think of me as one who scares you by the letters he writes. 'His letters,' so it is said, 'are weighty and powerful; but when he appears he has no presence, and as a speaker he is beneath contempt.' People who talk in that way should reckon with this: when I come, my actions will show the same man as my letters showed in my absence (2 Cor. 10:7-11 NEB).

As humble and meek as Paul was, he was not willing to allow criticism to cloud his testimony. His conscience was clear; his faith and convictions were definite; his authority could be demonstrated. As believers in Christ we can take second place, not caring how people treat us; but when they intimate that we are not serving the Lord faithfully, we should object and there take our stand.

Chapter 80

THE CONFIDENCE OF A SERVANT
OF THE LORD

Paul was known throughout the world as an apostle. He pointed out that the importance of his role could have warranted his asking the people to whom he ministered to contribute to his support; yet Paul was not inclined to seek this support by claiming that it was his due. He was willing that it be the spontaneous response of those who heard him and this would sustain him while he was with them. He also expected that this would equip him to proceed on further deputation work among nonbelievers, and that to do it this way would be glorifying to the Lord.

We can learn something from this. If we are known to be members of a church, we do not ask any special consideration on that account. We are perfectly willing for people to look us over — if we warrant their support, interest, and confidence, then we expect them to give us support. Remember, Paul was a veteran preacher of the gospel and that should have been for them adequate qualification for their confidence. He knew what he was talking about. He expected them to support him inasmuch as he had been used to bringing them blessing.

> But we will not boast of things without our measure, but according to the measure of the rule which God hath distributed to us, a measure to reach even unto you. For we stretch not ourselves beyond our measure, as though we reached not unto you: for we are come as far as to you also in preaching the gospel of Christ: not boasting of things without our measure, that is, of other men's labours; but having hope, when your faith is increased, that we shall be enlarged by you according to our rule abundantly, to preach the gospel in the regions beyond you, and not to boast in another man's line of things made ready to our hand (2 Cor. 10:13-16).

What can we learn in this for ourselves? That it is good for us to be humble in our expectation of help from others. It is never wise for us to assume that we will be given certain benefits because it is customary. A minister may expect that a certain amount of good will and consideration will be given to him. When I go into a community as a visiting preacher, I can expect that people will show a certain deference to me. But Paul would not look for that. He wanted only an opportunity to minister, then he expected his record to speak for him.

> But he that glorieth, let him glory in the Lord. For not he that commendeth himself is approved, but whom the Lord commendeth (2 Cor. 10:17-18).

Paul followed a simple principle. He focused all attention on the Lord. He would refer his hearers to the living Lord, then he was willing that they should judge — if they felt the Lord was honored and pleased by what he was doing, they should act accordingly by supporting him. Have you any idea how this would apply to you? For instance, if you work in an office, you work there as to the Lord. Should this win favor, receive and enjoy it; if it does not win favor, that is all right, for you expect nothing from man.

Suppose you are a teacher: you will teach as if you are serving the Lord. If you are appreciated, thank the Lord. If you are not respected or appreciated, trust the Lord. When you take care of matters in the home, do it as to the Lord. If it brings to you health, comfort, and encouragement, thank the Lord; if it brings you nothing, trust the Lord. The policy will always be the same: work as to the Lord. Your concern is that the Lord carries out His will for you.

Chapter 81

THE PURPOSE OF PLAIN TALK

Often the question is asked: Can one brought up in a godly home by faithful parents later be led away from the Lord when he is an adolescent? I must say there is this danger. A young woman may not fully realize the full meaning of accepting her first proposal of marriage. She may not have had adequate information on what is involved. In the same way a young believer in Christ may not have understood fully what accepting Christ actually meant. He may get the idea that the New Testament is not the only guide. He may be led away from simple faith in the gospel to practices that will involve him in bondage and obedience to rules and programs that are not dedicated to the Lord Jesus Christ; and he may do this in good conscience.

In Paul's experience there were some who through his preaching had come to believe in the Lord. They had accepted Christ and were now perplexed by the preaching of some others whom Paul called "false teachers," who proposed to actually improve Paul's doctrine. These persons said that Paul's teaching was correct but incomplete. Then they would lead souls away from Christ.

The basis of the claim of those teachers in Corinth — that they were able to improve on the teaching of Paul — was grounded in their claim that they were apostles also, whose preaching was supposedly superior to Paul's. Part of this claim was based on the fact that Paul used the language of the common people. He talked in a way that everyone could understand. There were those who implied that because he talked as simply as that, it meant he was simple-minded; if he had more knowledge he would use bigger words.

By affecting an impression of their own sophistication, they would ridicule Paul's simple language and give the impression that he was a rather uneducated person. These persons apparently gained the sympathetic ear of some believers. Paul makes his plea to his former followers for their good common sense. We find that he is now battling for their confidence, as we read here:

> Would to God ye could bear with me a little in my folly: and indeed bear with me. For I am jealous over you with godly jealousy: for I have espoused you to one husband, that I may present you as a chaste virgin to Christ. But I fear, lest by any means, as the serpent beguiled Eve through his subtilty, so your minds should be corrupted from the simplicity that is in Christ. For if he that cometh preacheth another Jesus, whom we have not preached, or if ye receive another spirit, which ye have not received, or another gospel, which ye have not accepted, ye might well bear with him. For I suppose I was not a whit behind the very chiefest apostles. But though I be rude in speech, yet not in knowledge; but we have been thoroughly made manifest among you in all things (2 Cor. 11:1-6).

In appealing to them Paul freely admitted that he was afraid they might be led astray, and he felt he must set forth certain truth about himself. He admitted his jealousy and suspicions of their possible defection. He was afraid they were being turned away from him, and he feared they might have been influenced, giving attention to ideas that were different from what he had taught. If the Corinthians had rejected certain ideas in the beginning that were different from Paul's, he would have known where they stood; but they had listened to others, and Paul knew this was dangerous.

At times I hear people say, as they turn aside to new and different ideas, that now they will finally have honesty in the church. I can personally assure them that while I grew up in life as an agnostic, I was honest. At that time I honestly said I didn't know; now I honestly say I do know. Paul admitted his speech may have been common — he deliberately spoke simply so that people would understand him, but his knowledge was authoritative. The simple language of the gospel is often held in derision, while honor is given to those who present an obscure intellectual sophistication. Words like *repentance, redeemed, lost, heaven, hell, believing in Jesus Christ, resurrection,* and *Holy Spirit* are often dropped from usage and replaced by difficult, hazy words of specialized reference. But when the word *saved* is no longer used, the gospel cannot be fully grasped.

Chapter 82

HUMILITY CAN BE MISUNDERSTOOD

In his letter to the Corinthians Paul tried to help them to understand the gospel. He knew that a man becomes a believer by believing the truth about Jesus Christ. No man naturally knows the gospel. We remember how earlier Paul wrote:

> Eye hath not seen, nor ear heard, neither have entered into the heart of man, the things which God hath prepared for them that love him (1 Cor. 2:9).

Believers must share the gospel and demonstrate by their conduct what their message means. In other words, the gospel must not only be heard, it must be believed. And to be believed it must be understood. The reality of the gospel is revealed by those who believe when their manner of life shows the meaning of it.

Paul realized what a sinner he was, and thus it followed properly that he was unassuming, honest, and humble before God. The unbeliever who does not know the gospel at all and even the babe in Christ may misunderstand this humility and perhaps mistake it for weakness or uncertainty. For example, when Paul preached in Corinth, he did not ask for local support because of local conditions. There were opponents to the true gospel who were preaching another message, and they would preach without pay. So Paul also preached without accepting any salary. This was in itself a weakness. It is not really healthy for the gospel to be preached without compensation. Some people assumed that he was not a real apostle.

Paul pointed out to these Corinthians that he had to have money to live, and he used funds he received from other churches to support himself while preaching in Corinth. He intended to keep up this practice, not because he was in opposition to them, but because of the other teachers in the community who were spreading errors. They preached without pay, and Paul was determined to match them in this so they would have no advantage with the people.

> Have I committed an offence in abasing myself that ye might be exalted, because I have preached to you the gospel of God freely? I robbed other churches, taking wages of them, to do you service. And when I was present with you, and wanted, I was chargeable to no man: for that which was lacking to me the brethren which came from Macedonia supplied: and in all things I have kept myself from being burdensome unto you, and so will I keep myself. As the truth of Christ is in me, no man shall stop me of this boasting in the regions of Achaia. Wherefore? because I love you not? God knoweth. But what I do, that I will do, that I may cut off occasion from them which desire occasion; that wherein they glory, they may be found even as we (2 Cor. 11:7-12).

It is strange that many people will receive benefits from preaching but they never feel that they should contribute to pay the preacher. They are inclined to think that if he is a real preacher, he will not ask for pay. This is not true, because they that minister the gospel should live of the gospel. In supporting the preaching one is supporting the gospel. But many a humble preacher is misjudged as weak and of no account because he does not make claims for himself.

I have a friend who is a veterinarian. He had trouble when he first started his practice because he was honest and open. A farmer would bring a sick horse to him, and he would find that all the horse needed was rest, because he was overworked. Often men thought he did not know what was wrong with the horse, so the doctor learned to have a harmless mixture of colored water to be given to the horse so many times a day. Of course, the horse stayed in the barn, rested, and recovered. The farmers would say my friend was a real doctor.

If something on the market seems too cheap, it will not sell. Human nature is like that. So the real believer has this problem: How can one manage to be humble and yet be impressive enough that people will believe what he says?

Chapter 83

OPPOSITION OF SATAN

The Bible leaves no room to doubt the reality of the devil, sometimes called Satan or the serpent. He was active in the garden of Eden and in the days of the kings of Israel. He was active in testing Job: he appeared in the presence of God and accused Job. He was active in the time of Daniel: when Daniel was waiting for an understanding of a certain revelation from God, Satan withstood the messenger who was to bring Daniel the truth. He was active in tempting Jesus of Nazareth, and he is seen as being active in the churches in Revelation. He is seen as active in the great battle described in Revelation with the Word of God in eternity. In that book it is pointed out that Satan is to be finally destroyed in the lake of fire.

The apostle Peter warned believers in Christ that Satan goes about as a lion, seeking whom he may devour (1 Peter 5:8), and Paul warned the believers to put on the whole armor of God that they might be able to withstand the fiery darts of the wicked one. Does he work in a congregation? Why not? Probably nowhere is this more plainly pointed out than in the passage we now have before us, where Paul is speaking of certain persons who were opposing Paul, and who were teaching and preaching a different gospel.

> For such are false apostles, deceitful workers, transforming themselves into the apostles of Christ. And no marvel; for Satan himself is transformed into an angel of light. Therefore it is no great thing if his ministers also be transformed as the ministers of righteousness; whose end shall be according to their works. I say again, Let no man think me a fool; if otherwise, yet as a fool receive me, that I may boast myself a little. That which I speak, I speak it not after the Lord, but as it were foolishly, in this confidence of boasting. Seeing that many glory after the flesh, I

252

> will glory also. For ye suffer fools gladly, seeing ye yourselves
> are wise. For ye suffer, if a man bring you into bondage, if a man
> devour you, if a man take of you, if a man exalt himself, if a man
> smite you on the face. I speak as concerning reproach, as though
> we had been weak. Howbeit whereinsoever any is bold, (I speak
> foolishly,) I am bold also (2 Cor. 11:13-21).

Here Paul is arguing for the support of these people, doing
everything he can to jolt his hearers into realizing what is
involved. In this passage there is evidence of his tense concern.
He names his opponents "ministers of Satan," servants of the
devil who were working in the congregation against the
preacher. Paul knew he was acting like a fool when he talked
about his own achievements, yet he did it because he wanted to
show by comparison that he could stand up to any of these
other people. Then he used sarcasm to wake them up.

This is a serious situation. People can be misled. You can
begin to understand something of what this was like if you think
of the parents of a teen-ager who has been carefully reared, but
in high school has been misled with wrong ideas. How do you
think those parents would feel about the people who were
giving their son or daughter wrong ideas? What should they do
when the teen-ager persists in associating with those who are
communicating wrong ideas? Another recent translation reads:

> Those men are not true apostles — they are false apostles, who
> lie about their work and change themselves to look like real
> apostles of Christ. Well, no wonder! Even Satan can change
> himself to look like an angel of light! So it is no great thing if his
> servants change themselves to look like servants of right. In the
> end they will get exactly what they deserve for the things they
> do (2 Cor. 11:13-15 TEV).

When Paul says these false leaders will get their just deserts,
we may feel some satisfaction in that, but it hurts to think about
those who have been misled by them. In the course of my
lifetime I have been interested in helping young men prepare
to enter the ministry. As I have worked with them, I have
found that ideas have been presented by many who no longer
accept conversion as necessary. I have asked them to show me
where such ideas win souls and if they can turn some man from
sinfulness into godliness; but they cannot do it. If you saw a
man selling candy that was harmful to children, would you let
the children buy it? This was Paul's problem: Would it be

proper to openly condemn another man for being false?

What would move Paul to do this? Paul was thinking about sheep — he was like a sheep dog smelling a wolf. When these men came around, Paul would go out to do battle on account of his sheep.

In dealing with the witness of the gospel to the whole of society Paul could see only two classes: believers and non-believers. On the one side there was the Lord Jesus Christ, who would save the soul, and on the other side was Satan, who would deceive the soul. And Satan himself masqueraded as an angel of light.

There is probably no doctrine as dangerous to man as saying there is no devil. Paul points out that there are many counterfeits. If he had not been a good shepherd, he could have let things go; but he loved the people, and he struggled to keep them close to the Lord. Young believers who have become humbly honest are often the victims of smooth liars, who pretend to sympathize with them, but who actually are leading them away from the very One who would save the soul. We need the help of God.

Chapter 84

EXPERIENCE QUALIFIES THE WITNESS

When someone tells us how something will turn out, we usually want to know one thing about that speaker: Has he ever seen or done it? Or has it ever happened to him? In the course of living there is no substitute for experience. When someone tries to tell us how to handle children, isn't it customary to ask ourselves how many children that person has raised? And isn't it true that if they do not have any children of their own, we quietly discount what they say because we do not think they know what they are talking about? However, let someone who has had a number of children tell us something, and we listen.

In 2 Corinthians Paul does not hesitate to face what others have said about serving Christ. While they contend that one could be saved by doing good, Paul insisted one could be saved only by believing in the Lord Jesus Christ.

> I speak as concerning reproach, as though we had been weak. Howbeit whereinsoever any is bold, (I speak foolishly,) I am bold also. Are they Hebrews? so am I. Are they Israelites? so am I. Are they the seed of Abraham? so am I. Are they ministers of Christ? (I speak as a fool) I am more; in labours more abundant, in stripes above measure, in prisons more frequent, in deaths oft. Of the Jews five times received I forty stripes save one. Thrice was I beaten with rods, once was I stoned, thrice I suffered shipwreck, a night and a day I have been in the deep; in journeyings often, in perils of waters, in perils of robbers, in perils by mine own countrymen, in perils by the heathen, in perils in the city, in perils in the wilderness, in perils in the sea, in perils among false brethren; in weariness and painfulness, in watchings often, in hunger and thirst, in fastings often, in cold and nakedness. Beside those things that are without, that which cometh upon me daily, the care of all the churches. Who is weak, and I am not weak? who is offended, and I burn not? (2 Cor. 11:21-29).

When Paul recounts his experiences in this way, he realizes that he is exposing himself foolishly; but he was so concerned about how they would place their trust, he risked it. We have here in Paul's argument a summary of his life. He speaks of being in "labours more abundant, in stripes more above measure, in prisons more frequent" than anyone else. Five times he was beaten with thirty-nine stripes. The Jewish law prohibited that a man should be beaten with more than forty stripes, so in order to be safe, they always stopped at thirty-nine. All the time he was suffering this from the outside, there was inwardly the anxiety and the care of the young believers.

Notice that when Paul compared himself to his opponents, he did not undertake to debate them. He was not going to out-argue them, but he could outwork them and outdo them. He brought the one basis for comparison that really counts: What did it cost you? Then Paul would tell them what it cost him. Here is the complete answer to all who say that suffering in the ministry and as a Christian is incidental. Some will say you could be a true witness and not suffer at all, but Paul would question that. And some will wonder why it was necessary. We may not know why, but we do know that the Lord Jesus Christ suffered. Sometimes people will say that if you suffer, you must be doing something unwise or foolish. But Christ Jesus suffered rejection, and we know He was perfect. And the servant is not greater than his Master.

At the same time we might ask, Is this the best evidence of a believer — what he suffers? No, because a man might suffer for his own foolishness. We cannot always tell why a man is suffering. Then again, the suffering may be the result of a wicked person maliciously persecuting the believer. But it is a valid line of evidence if a man will endure suffering patiently. The apostle Paul would say to everyone, "A real believer can speak from his personal experience when he gives advice because he knows what it is. He has been through it."

Chapter 85

PAUL'S PERSONAL WEAKNESS

It is a matter of common observation that men estimate other men by their performance. When anyone is honored, it is because of something he has done or experienced. This is impressive to natural man, and it is also impressive to the young Christian who still has much of the natural mind in himself. Babes in Christ readily tell of their own experiences and what happened to them. Often they become enthusiastic and older believers may become impatient with them. Their testimony carries much weight, yet the mature Christian shrinks from doing this.

A rancher I once knew in Idaho had amazing experiences in coming to faith in Christ which he once related to me. He added that it was just the fifth time he had ever told the story, since people might think that if such sensational things did not happen to them, their relationship to the Lord might not be real. They might feel the need for the same sort of experiences such as he told about.

After the Resurrection, when our Lord Jesus Christ appeared to His disciples in the upper room, Thomas was not with them. When told that they had seen the Lord, he refused to believe it, saying he would not believe it unless he could put his fingers in the nail prints and thrust his hands into His side. Later, when Jesus appeared, He told Thomas, "Put your fingers in these nail prints; thrust your hand into this side." And we read that Thomas fell to his feet saying, "My Lord and My God." Then Jesus said to him, "Thou hast seen and thou hast believed; blessed are they that have not seen and yet have believed." The actual physical event is not the most important thing. The public record of the experiences of a believer can be quite impressive, but the mature believer is less disposed to talk about those experiences or focus attention at that level, because those things are hard to understand. God does some things openly to be seen, but the real issue is inward. If a person accepts Christ Jesus as his Lord and Savior yet does not have some physical manifestation, it will still be just as real.

Some people will be profoundly impressed if there are some physical manifestations. There have been instances where, in public worship, people would shake all over. These people were called Shakers, or Quakers. There have been other people who have taken note of the fact that under certain circumstances some persons have been so profoundly moved they began to speak with other tongues. And many have been impressed by that. I do not say that such manifestations are never good; I believe some sincere people have been profoundly affected by such experiences; but that is by no means the best line of evidence. Speaking with tongues, in the New Testament, is considered one of the lesser gifts. The real issue is an inward one: accepting the Lord Jesus Christ.

When telling of experiences it is natural to choose the spectacular ones, because they are the best to listen to and they convey so much. When Paul did this in 2 Corinthians 11, he disliked doing it. He pointed out that if he needed to tell of overt events, he would also tell of certain events which showed his weakness.

> If I must needs glory, I will glory of the things which concern mine infirmities. The God and Father of our Lord Jesus Christ, which is blessed for evermore, knoweth that I lie not. In Damascus the governor under Aretas the king kept the city of the Damascenes with a garrison, desirous to apprehend me: and through a window in a basket was I let down by the wall, and escaped his hands (2 Cor. 11:30-33).

How different it would have been if Paul had straightened himself up, thrown out his chest, spoken a word, and all the soldiers dropped dead. What we actually have here is that Paul sneaked out of sight, crawled through a window, got into a basket, and was let down that way. The real believer will often be made to look like a fool in a discussion, while the one arguing against him will look strong. The opponent of the gospel can flaunt his views with freedom in public, when the believer may be stricken almost dumb.

In our next study Paul will turn to the line of testimony that is more suited to his witness. We shall see that the power of the witness is not in its outward appearance but in its spiritual message.

Chapter 86

EVIDENCE OF A REAL BELIEVER IN CHRIST

We are all aware that generally Christians believe in heaven, which is considered their destination — that is where they will be after the end of everything. This concept can be useful and meaningful. A person can live in this world with strength because he anticipates that one day he will go home, and he can rejoice in the expectation that by the grace of God heaven is waiting for him. Then again, heaven can be used as a term to refer to a future blessedness, when the believer can live in freedom and peace forever.

Seldom is the word *heaven* used to refer to a present sphere of being, but it actually is, a plane of life in the presence of God, where God is now, as Jesus of Nazareth taught when He said, "Our Father, which art in heaven." Perhaps as a child you learned the words "Thou God seest me." That is true. And right now God is ruling and overruling and bringing His will to pass. And I can refer my present, immediate problems to Him now. Am I having trouble in my family? God is right there. Am I uncertain what will happen when I go to my office? God will be there, and I can refer everything to Him now.

This is how it can be with any true believer in any given situation. The believer in Christ can rely on the helping hand of God. Paul could think about this as he lived in glorious confidence based on the power of God. He had had so many things happen, he could have fallen into the snare of feeling that he did not have to think about anything, that God would see to it that everything would be all right. But Paul was disciplined to think of himself in his weakness, and this kept him humble; thus he was more useful unto God. Paul could have boasted of unusual spiritual experiences, but he did not.

> I knew a man in Christ above fourteen years ago, (whether in the
> body, I cannot tell; or whether out of the body, I cannot tell: God
> knoweth;) such a one caught up to the third heaven. And I knew
> such a man, (whether in the body, or out of the body, I cannot
> tell: God knoweth;) how that he was caught up into paradise, and
> heard unspeakable words, which it is not lawful for a man to
> utter (2 Cor. 12:2-4).

This is a highly significant passage. You may feel that this whole
section is beyond you. It is like looking up into the sky: you can
see the blue, but it goes far beyond you. This is the classic
passage which reports a man looking up into the presence of
God. Students usually think that the "man in Christ" was Paul,
and that he is speaking of himself in the third person, telling a
personal experience. The language leaves it open so that it
could be someone else but that would pose other great problems. You need not worry about the phrase "the third heaven."
Another translation of this passage reads like this:

> I know a certain Christian man who fourteen years ago was
> snatched up to the highest heaven (I do not know whether this
> actually happened, or whether he had a vision — only God
> knows). I repeat, I know that this man was snatched to Paradise
> (again, I do not know whether this actually happened, or
> whether it was a vision — only God knows), and there he heard
> things which cannot be put into words, things that human lips
> may not speak (2 Cor. 12:2-4 TEV).

The expression "the highest heaven" and the idiom "the
third heaven" refer to the presence of God. Notice the cautious
tone Paul uses in this reporting. He says, "I don't know for sure
whether this actually happened or if it was just a vision." But he
did know that this man was actually experiencing, in the highest heaven, the presence of God in "paradise."

The word *paradise* refers to a plane of living beyond this
world. But we can catch this right away: this man heard things
that were not lawful to utter. That sounds as though there was
some prohibition; but actually that is not necessarily the case.
Remember the passage "things which cannot be put into
words," things that human lips may not speak. This is probably
a better explanation of what this really means. It implies not so
much prohibition, but inability to repeat what was heard.
When trying to talk about heaven, where time and space are
not used, you and I cannot understand that kind of language. In

other words, Paul says this man saw things that were inexpressible, and we can just leave it that way. Another version of this passage reads like this:

> I know a Christian man who fourteen years ago (whether in the body or out of it, I do not know — God knows) was caught up as far as the third heaven. And I know that this same man (whether in the body or out of it, I do not know — God knows) was caught up into paradise, and heard words so secret that human lips may not repeat them (2 Cor. 12:2-4 NEB).

Paul is saying that if he were going to boast, he would not recount his own record of deeds, but would rather boast about the privilege of being in the very presence of God. Then he goes on to say that if he were going to boast on his own account, he would dwell on his weaknesses, not on his achievements. He could boast on his own behalf, if he so desired — he had valid evidence of great things God had done through him — but he would not do that lest they rate him too highly.

> Of such a one will I glory: yet of myself I will not glory, but in mine infirmities. For though I would desire to glory, I shall not be a fool; for I will say the truth: but now I forbear, lest any man should think of me above that which he seeth me to be, or that he heareth of me (2 Cor. 12:5-6).

He did not want anyone to have an estimate of him that was beyond the evidence of his own eyes and ears.

We have here a wonderful model of a true believer in Christ. Paul was thinking about living, not reveling in great things that had happened through him and to him, or what he has done, but reveling in the great things of who God is and what He had done. Paul kept foremost in mind his own weaknesses and infirmities.

People tend to overestimate a person because God has used him. Paul points out that it is never good to dwell on events in which God has done things through an individual or in which I have shared by the power of God. It is better to dwell on the wonder of God and to be conscious of the weakness of the flesh which was in me, but which did not prevent God from doing His great work.

Chapter 87

PAUL'S THORN IN THE FLESH

In the next few verses of chapter 12 we come to a profound truth. We shall see that in His wisdom and grace God may let a man suffer in order to keep him humble, so that he can be useful to Him. The whole truth of spiritual living is in the phrase "Christ in you, the hope of glory."

Here a serious consideration must be faced: personal pride can hinder the operation of the Holy Spirit. One basic truth we should always keep in mind is that no flesh shall glory in His presence. Nothing that is done by virtue of human wisdom or strength or wit or even human faithfulness or goodness amounts to anything in the sight of God. If I insist on being proud of what I can do and the results of my doing it, God cannot work through me. As a matter of fact, God will not work through me.

If God is to work through me, I must be humble. Even here God intervenes — He does not leave it up to me to humble myself. If He left it up to us to humble ourselves, some of us would become proud about our humility. When great things happen in my life, when I am patient under extreme discouragement, I feel triumph; and if I am not careful, I tend to feel I am doing quite well, and that could be fatal to my spiritual life. Paul's experience is classic — God gave him a thorn in the flesh to keep him humble.

> And lest I should be exalted above measure through the abundance of the revelations, there was given to me a thorn in the flesh, the messenger of Satan to buffet me, lest I should be exalted above measure. For this thing I besought the Lord thrice, that it might depart from me. And he said unto me, My grace is sufficient for thee: for my strength is made perfect in weakness. Most gladly therefore will I rather glory in my

infirmities, that the power of Christ may rest upon me (2 Cor. 12:7-9).

Paul spoke of "the messenger of Satan to buffet me." Does that mean God lets the devil trouble a believer in Christ? Apparently so. Perhaps, as in the case of Job, God allowed Satan to tempt Paul. And He may allow Satan to tempt you. Do you remember what Jesus said to Peter? "Satan hath desired to have you that he may sift you as wheat."

No one knows for sure what Paul's thorn in the flesh was. The language places it "in the flesh," in the human being, including a physical body, mental ideas, and psychological feelings. All of those things belong in the flesh. Another translation expressed it this way, "I was given a painful physical ailment, which acts as Satan's messenger to beat me and keep me from being proud" (TEV). Still another one says, "A sharp physical pain which came as Satan's messenger to bruise me" (NEB), and another, "A physical handicap — one of Satan's angels — to harass me" *(Phillips)*. Each of these translations mentions the devil.

Some people say this thorn in the flesh was Paul's eyesight, and we do know from various things he mentioned that apparently he did have eye trouble. Some say it was a sickness of some sort; while others theorize that it was an inner tendency on Paul's part to a certain sinful action that kept humiliating him over and over again. Some say that these were bitter opponents, human beings, who were jealous of him and who ridiculed and resisted him at every turn. And a few people think that this may have been a disagreeable wife. Although it is reported that Paul did not "lead a wife" (1 Cor. 9:5), in no place are we told that he was a widower, so this view is possible. It would not be surprising that he was married, since it was the custom for a young Jew to be married. In that case he may have had a wife who was not sympathetic with him. I think it is providential that it was never divulged just what Paul's "thorn in flesh" was.

This trouble, whatever it was, buffeted him. Paul understood that this happened to him because God let it happen, as a defensive maneuver, "Lest I should be exalted above measure." If a believer has blessings from God, he can be thankful, but there is a tendency to get overexcited about it. Buffeting can come to "keep me from being proud." That is the reason I may have trouble: to save me from being unduly elated. For a believer to be somewhat elated is acceptable, but to be unduly elated is dangerous. "To effectually stop any conceit" means to keep him from being excessively exalted.

Here is another profound truth: Paul's prayer for deliverance was not granted, for his own good. Three times he prayed to the Lord about this, asking Him to take away this "thorn in the flesh"; but God did not do it. He left it there, but told Paul, "My grace is sufficient for thee."

If you are a believer and have trouble, keep in mind that God is watching over you. He knows exactly what is happening, and He allows it so that you will stay fruitful, to the glory of God.

Chapter 88

THE BLESSING OF INFIRMITIES

The works of God as they are experienced in the believer's life are often marvelous and wonderful. Great things may not happen to him every day; yet when we see how the Lord had led him, we are amazed at what God has done. And the usual testimony of anyone whenever something remarkable is done is to praise someone. Our tendency to praise the person in whom great things are being done becomes a snare to the person involved. There will be a strong temptation for him to accept our praise, at least part of it. When praise is extended to us and we keep some of it for ourselves, we are actually embezzling praise. People do not naturally praise and thank God for remarkable things, but the praise and thanks belong to Him.

We have before us the case of the apostle Paul. When Paul was told why he had the thorn in his flesh, he rejoiced in it and in every hardship. This is the secret of Paul's saying, "We glory in tribulation." This does not mean that Paul liked trouble, but he knew that every tribulation he had "worketh experience and experience patience and patience hope," and everything would redound to the glory of God. Do you find that strange? Would not you and I want that blessing for ourselves? The more suffering, the more power! God does not let us suffer for nothing; He has a purpose, and through it He will glorify Himself. For this reason Paul rejoiced in his infirmities and distresses.

Here may be an authentic clue to the kind of trouble Paul had. He says,

> Most gladly therefore will I rather glory in my infirmities, that the power of Christ may rest upon me. Therefore I take pleasure

in infirmities, in reproaches, in necessities, in persecutions, in distresses for Christ's sake: for when I am weak, then am I strong (2 Cor. 12:9-10).

That is quite a catalog. "In infirmities" may be sickness or physical weakness; "in reproaches" refers to false accusations; and "in necessities" means one is hard up; "in persecution" indicates that there may be people who will hold things against you because they do not like what you are doing; "in distresses" covers everything else. That is what Paul had in mind when he said he would glory in those things that the power of Christ might rest on him.

Regardless of what is happening to you, Almighty God knows about it, and He has allowed it to happen. Furthermore, He can make it turn out for good. Here is wonderful comfort for the believer. Such troubles are no real hindrance to blessing; they can be used by the Lord for His glory. I am not saying they will be easy. They may be hard, but we can remember this: "for when I am weak, then am I strong." When I was studying the New Testament, a fellow student was a specialist in the language. He dug out the inner meanings of Greek words. One day he quoted this verse as, "When I am helpless, then I am dynamite"; that is exactly what the Greek conveys.

Recently it was my privilege to become acquainted with a remarkable young woman who had been addicted to alcohol and drugs and had attempted suicide before she turned to Christ and was saved. She was asked to assume a difficult leadership with other people who were in trouble, and in prayer this woman told the Lord, "I will take this work if You want me to, but You will have to do it." She received assurance from Him that He would. She took the assignment, and those she has helped have said that she was an angel sent from heaven. But this woman knows very well it is the Lord.

As you face tasks and temptations, are you sure that you have no strength and you cannot do it? Thank the Lord! This is the secret of true strength in Him.

Chapter 89

THE MARKS OF A TRUE BELIEVER

In 1 Corinthians Paul wrote about problems of conduct and faith which beset this young group, and he showed in spiritual terms the solution for each problem that was raised. Now in 2 Corinthians he sets forth a description of a mature, fruit-bearing believer in Christ. He does this by describing himself in various situations — not because he is proud of himself, but because he knows himself and he can tell others how a true believer lives. When Paul's record was challenged so that his message became questionable, he takes time in this epistle to remind his readers that if anyone would know about being a true believer in Christ, it would be himself, because of what he had been through.

Those who opposed Paul said that he was inadequate as a teacher since he spoke in humble language while they spoke in intellectual terms. They intimated this made it obvious that they were more advanced than he. They claimed they were also far superior to Paul in that he was too timid and hesitant.

When Paul heard about this he felt obliged to respond in his own defense. He told them he was just as much an apostle as these others, and his ministry was marked by far more impressive results. He claimed that no one could show such a record of achievement as he, he argued that he had suffered far more than they had suffered. He had had spiritual experiences that were more remarkable. Actually they should have been praising him instead of letting him tell about himself. His record would compare favorably with the "chiefest" of apostles, because he had certainly demonstrated what an apostle was like.

I am become a fool in glorying; ye have compelled me: for I ought to have been commended of you: for in nothing am I behind the very chiefest apostles, though I be nothing. Truly the signs of an apostle were wrought among you in all patience, in signs, and wonders, and mighty deeds (2 Cor. 12:11-12).

When Paul used the word *patience,* he was not particularly referring to long-suffering. He meant that he kept at it. Here we have the identification mark of a true believer. We might at this point remember again the case of Nicodemus, who came to the Lord Jesus by night. He said, "We know that thou art a teacher come from God: for no man can do these miracles that thou doest, except God be with him" (John 3:2). Nicodemus was one of the rulers of the Jews, and he admitted that Jesus of Nazareth must have a working relationship with God because He was producing results such as no man alone could ever have achieved. As a Pharisee, Nicodemus would have been impressed with His conformity to the rules as to how He said and did things; but as a man he would recognize a simple principle, "By their fruits you shall know them." If any man's testimony in the gospel is genuine, there will be consequences: they may be in him, they may be in others, but there will be results.

In the case of Paul there were signs and wonders and mighty deeds. He spoke for the Lord and produced works that only the Lord could do. He produced the same kind of works Jesus produced while He was here on earth. We are not apostles, but as believers what should others expect to see in us? Love, joy, peace, long-suffering, gentleness, goodness, faith, meekness, and temperance: the fruit of the Spirit should be manifest. When these signs and wonders and mighty deeds are manifested, then there is authentic example of living in Christ.

How would you know if a person is a true believer in Christ? Not by what he says, but by love, joy, peace, long-suffering, gentleness, goodness, faith, meekness, and temperance. This kind of fruit shows up when the heart and mind are committed to God and depending on Him. Love is not only how you feel about people, it is what you want to do for them. Love is action, helping people live and rejoice. If I really try to help someone, I am, in the biblical sense of the word, loving him. There is no specific behavior that characterizes the love of God, but the normal actions that the believer exercises in ordinary affairs can be exercised with the intention of helping someone, showing that he wants to please God.

Neither is there a particular form of joy. It is the feeling a person has when a person, object, experience, or thought delights him. There is no particular work of peace: it is a state of mind that a person has when things are as they should be, when there is no contention or warfare in his own being. Long-suffering is not standing in the cold for a certain length of time. It will show up in anything that is done for Christ's sake. While patiently going about her housework, a woman can be serving with long-suffering. These qualities can be seen in any deed that is performed, and they will be present if the person truly does believe in the Lord. The evidence of a true believer is to be seen if the fruit of the Spirit shows up in his life.

Chapter 90

THE SUFFERING OF A TRUE SERVANT

When a pastor is faithful, he is like a father to his children. He will seek in every possible way to help his congregation, to encourage and support all of those who "belong" to him. So Paul has sought to bring blessing to his people in Corinth. All the suffering and privation he underwent, he willingly endured because he wanted them to grow and to have all possible blessings. He warned them against all the dangers they might meet; he opposed and exposed all who would mislead them. This took a great deal of time; but for all the extra hours of personal attention, all the grief he bore, the burdens he carried, and the distress he felt, he asked no recompense. He was doing for them what the Lord Jesus had done for him.

Now the Corinthians had been reared in a pagan culture. Their ideas did not fit those of the gospel. Paul faithfully taught them in compassion and love. But at the time he wrote this second epistle, he was facing the peril of losing these people to the influence of strangers who would not promote what Paul had given his life to secure, and what he had desired for his people. Regardless of how he was personally treated, Paul continued to seek their benefits and well-being. These are the virtues of patience and steadfastness as seen in a true servant of the Lord.

But sometimes the very people you want to help will turn away to someone else.

> For what is it wherein ye were inferior to other churches, except it be that I myself was not burdensome to you? forgive me this wrong. Behold, the third time I am ready to come to you; and I will not be burdensome to you: for I seek not yours, but you: for the children ought not to lay up for the parents, but the parents

for the children. And I will gladly spend and be spent for you; though the more abundantly I love you, the less I be loved (2 Cor. 12:13-15).

Here Paul again makes reference to the fact that in working with the Corinthians he had not taken a salary. It would seem strange to one who is not a believer that Paul would count this a possible blemish in his ministry. He did not expect any kind of response from them in appreciation of or in relation to what he was giving them, and he knew that was not as it should be. In Paul's case I do not think it was a blemish: he had to do this to get through to them. As previously brought out, there were other people working there who claimed that the fact they were working for nothing qualified them, and Paul had to match that. The people saw these others preaching without pay, so naturally they would be skeptical if Paul took pay. Thus he went without compensation.

In verse 14 he stated he did not intend to change his ways, giving all he could even though he would get nothing in return. This suggest to us that if we face a similar situation, we will do as servants even though we are not appreciated. Such lack of appreciation shows up in different ways. Church members can fall into a habit of being critical of their pastor, even while they are charitable to those on the outside. A man may be faithful to his home and provide everything he can for them, but his family will often take him for granted. But he keeps right on doing it just as he is doing it for the Lord. It may also be felt keenly in the case of a woman who is married to an ungrateful man. She tries to be helpful to him at all times, but she may receive no credit. She may actually be treated as if she were an irritant; but she will keep right on doing what she knows to be right because the Lord leads her to do it.

This is what Paul did, and this is what you will do as you grow in Christian faith and maturity.

Chapter 91

A PASTOR'S CONCERN FOR HIS PEOPLE

When a person becomes a believer, he is interested in other people. He cannot help but be. The Son of God cared about other people. When God made His promise to Abraham, He said, "I will bless thee and make thee a blessing. In thy seed shall all nations be blessed." It is the purpose of God through His people to bring blessing to others.

Now there is a rather difficult aspect of living by faith. When the believer yields in the will of God, he should be careful that others understand that this was done in obedience to God and not because of the fear of men. Paul had just stated to the Corinthians that he was aware he was largely unrecognized among them and often discredited, and this was a real burden to him. To humbly serve and then to be blamed for what goes wrong is not easy to take. But it is not unusual. It may strike him as being unreasonable, and it is, but it is normal. It is part of the sufferings of Christ. That does not lessen the pain, but the believer should not feel that there is anything unusual about him. It may strengthen the believer's spirit to know that it is happening to him just the way it happens to all who walk in the ways of the Lord. He can learn from Paul about this. When Paul was being falsely accused and discredited, he did not remain silent.

> But be it so, I did not burden you: nevertheless, being crafty, I caught you with guile (2 Cor. 12:16).

Paul is saying, "I didn't take it out on you." He did not let the situation hinder his obedience to his Lord; he did not let that stop him from doing what he was supposed to do. "I conducted myself in such a way that I was able to gain your confidence even without your realizing it."

Now this particular passage can be translated differently; it can be made into a question: "Did I do it this way?" But in any case the picture seems to be clear that Paul tried in every way to win these people to him, and at this point the believer can take heart. Even if he is unrecognized and unappreciated in what he is doing, he may yet be able to accomplish his aim if he continues in it.

> Did I make a gain of you by any of them whom I sent unto you? I desired Titus, and with him I sent a brother. Did Titus make a gain of you? walked we not in the same spirit? walked we not in the same steps? (2 Cor. 12:17-18).

Paul had a clear conscience. He had not profited personally from these believers; and when he sent Titus in his place, Titus did not ask anything for himself either. And here we learn it is important for a believer to keep a clear conscience about his conduct, that he does not do anything for his own advantage.

> Again, think ye that we excuse ourselves unto you? we speak before God in Christ: but we do all things, dearly beloved, for your edifying (2 Cor. 12:19).

Paul had no interest in defending himself. He was not interested in apologizing for what he had done. He wanted only to promote their welfare. It was important that they retain confidence in him and in his message, so therefore he argued. But that was done only for their welfare, not for his own.

When a believer knows that he is not seeking personal advantage, he can proceed with confidence in what he is doing. Paul was anxious that they should live in the blessedness of spiritual unity, and he was doing everything he could to lead them into the fullness of blessing in Christ Jesus. This would be possible, of course, only as they were yielded in the Holy Spirit; and this Paul brings out.

However if the believers seek to make something of themselves, then their fellowship will be distrubed, and there will be the evidence of self-centeredness.

> For I fear, lest, when I come, I shall not find you such as I would, and that I shall be found unto you such as ye would not: lest there be debates, envyings, wraths, strifes, backbitings, whisperings, swellings, tumults (2 Cor. 12:20).

Is not that a list of what could go on among the members today in any church?

Here is another translation:

> I am afraid that when I get there I will find you different from what I would like you to be and you will find me different from what you would like me to be. I am afraid that I will find quarreling and jealousy, hot tempers and selfishness, insults and gossip, pride and disorder (2 Cor. 12:20 TEV).

All this is inspired by people who think only of themselves. Becoming a believer in Christ does not mean that a man's nature is immediately transformed so that he becomes an angel. When he receives the Lord Jesus Christ, he receives Him into himself; the old man is still with him, but the new man, the born-again man, starts to grow in him.

For a length of time a believer can have Christ and also the old man working in him; and if he is not controlled by the spiritual things, then the old man will take over. This is how another translator expresses it:

> I fear I may find quarrelling and jealousy, angry tempers and personal rivalries, backbiting and gossip, arrogance and general disorder (NEB).

That is terrible, but it can be found among believing people if the Holy Spirit does not have control in the hearts of the people. Phillips reads:

> I am afraid of finding arguments, jealousy, ill-feeling, divided loyalties, slander, whispering, pride and disharmony.

Such a list! And all of this happens in a person when self is in charge. It happens when people are thinking about themselves and their own: "I, and my wife, my son John, his wife; us four and no more." This is the kind of feeling that causes quarreling, temper, selfishness, whispering, gossip, arrogance, and disorder.

> And lest, when I come again, my God will humble me among you, and that I shall bewail many which have sinned already, and have not repented of the uncleanness and fornication and lasciviousness which they have committed (2 Cor. 12:21).

In his concern for these people Paul was looking at them realistically and anxiously.

All of these things can be overcome in the Lord, and this is what Paul wanted for his people.

Chapter 92

SIN SHOULD BE JUDGED

If I have faith in Christ Jesus, I cannot be selfish; I will think about others. Because I believe in Christ I wonder about the man next door, the woman in my office, and others I meet. I care about these people because the Spirit of the Lord Jesus Christ, who came to seek and to save the lost, is in me. Why is it necessary to save them and why would Christ Jesus have to die for them? What is the big problem even after they turn to Christ? And the answer in every case is sin. If we believe in Christ, another person's spiritual condition is our concern.

If you are a teacher, should you care whether or not the students are healthy? I think you should. Or, if you are a parent, should you be concerned about your children's conduct? And if their Sunday school teacher tells them that the Bible stories are not true, should you not inform the officers of the church to be more careful about what the children are hearing? Believers are involved with other people, and if they see someone doing something wrong, they should try to stop it because it could infect others.

Paul knew that in Corinth there were some people in the church who had not ceased from sinning. There was in that church a dangerous kind of tolerance. We cannot afford to be tolerant about sin. We may love the sinner, but we must hate the sin. If one is doing wrong and refuses to quit, then he cannot be with us.

In our country there are two mental disciplines that are quite successful. One is engineering, in which we have produced outstanding results. When engineers work, they do not allow anything but exact measurements. They speak of how much "tolerance" there will be: a fraction of an inch that they will allow for any particular measurement to be short or long. The other is medicine, where we are definitely intolerant about anything that is infectious. If you have been present when preparations were being made for surgery, you know how careful they are about infections. Believers in Christ must be like that.

> This is the third time I am coming to you. In the mouth of two or three witnesses shall every word be established. I told you before, and foretell you, as if I were present, the second time; and being absent now I write to them which heretofore have sinned, and to all other, that, if I come again, I will not spare: since ye seek a proof of Christ speaking in me, which to you-ward is not weak, but is mighty in you (2 Cor. 13:1-3).

Paul considered that Christ in him would personally judge the unrepentant sinner. A true believer will not condone sin anywhere, but will expose and repudiate it for the good of all and for the glory of the Lord.

Paul would hoe any weeds he found in his garden; none would be left. May God help us to be as faithful.

Chapter 93

THE POWER OF GOD IN THE RESURRECTION

The resurrection of the body of Jesus of Nazareth is the supreme example of the power of God. Many miracles are recorded in the Bible and many works of wonder shown. We see many works of creation around us, and God has done many marvelous works; but the greatest of all these to show the power of God is the resurrection of the crucified body of Jesus of Nazareth.

What do we mean by the power of God? When we think about power, we often think of a great mechanical crane with which a locomotive can be lifted out of a ditch onto a railway, or perhaps a great bulldozer putting a shovel into the side of a hill and moving tons of earth at one time. Or we may think of a tornado that sweeps through an area and tears houses apart, or a tidal wave moving in from the ocean and overflowing towns by the beach. The opening of a flower blossom demands power. An acorn falls to the ground and starts growing to become a giant oak tree. It has power.

Power is a word used to describe the doing of something. It is natural to feel that if something needs to be done, man will do it. But the truth is: God is my salvation — by exercising His power on my behalf. Something happens in me and to me that is not exactly like a crane or a tornado, but more like the opening of a flower. The great thing is that "once I was blind but now I see"; once I was in death and now I am in life. At one time my heart and mind were filled with thoughts of self and selfishness; now I think of God and of Christ and of righteousness. This great change is the work of grace, and we call it the beginning of salvation. It is by the power of God. Whatever is being done in and by the gospel, God will do it. He will do it in man after death. The gospel points out what God will do in man after that man reckons himself dead.

To have created the angels would have been an act of power; to make beings like His Son and to create them that way would have been an act of power; but God has seen fit in the Scriptures to show that it is His intention to create His own children out of men who were dead in sin, and this is glorious. To demonstrate this work of regeneration, God raised up Jesus of Nazareth. This formula — this combination of events — is found throughout Revelation. First there is weakness — the weakness of man; and then there is power — the power of God. Just as first there is sin — the sin of man; and then there is righteousness — the righteousness of God. First there is death — death in the man in the human nature; then there is life — life in God; just as first there is night and then there is day. Scripture says, "Weeping may endure for a night but joy cometh in the morning."

Here in this world things go wrong; but in the world to come they are wonderful. This arrangement is set forth in Scripture:

> For though he was crucified through weakness, yet he liveth by the power of God. For we also are weak in him, but we shall live with him by the power of God toward you (2 Cor. 13:4).

This is something that God can and will do. The believer should have faith to follow this route, so that out of his weakness he may be made strong.

Have you had the experience of being conscious of your own weakness and then seeing God's power? For instance, you yielded in the will of God; you reckoned yourself dead and did not strive. Have you then been conscious of the fact that when you can count yourself a dead man, God is able to work in you? The life of God will show up in you, and you will win for eternity; but it required you to yield in this world that you might live forever there. This world is not perfect, but if you yield yourself to the will of God, you will die to self and immediately you will begin to live the life in God of rich fulfillment. Crucifying the flesh, the self, always hurts, but the living that comes afterward is always glorious.

Paul has said, "For we also are weak in him [we have no power to save ourselves], but we shall live with him by the power of God toward you." The plan of God is to be seen in new beings replacing old ones. The resurrection of Jesus Christ is the believer's assurance of his own resurrection; just as Jesus of Nazareth was set free from death, so shall it be with the believer.

Victory over death is possible for the believer in Christ.

Chapter 94

WHERE DO I STAND?

Every man or woman is either for the Lord Jesus Christ or against Him. Years ago I was asked by an old farmer if I was a believer in Christ. I began to hem and haw and tried to think what to say, when he said to me, "That's all right. Thank you; I know now." I resented him at the time. I could not understand how he could know when I had not told him; but he knew. If I get to the place where I am not sure whether I am for or against Christ, I need to take time to get that settled.

Sometimes a person can be so confused he does not even know whether he should or should not count himself a believer. The Scriptures say, "Whosoever received him, to them gave he power to become the children of God"; but right away some will say they do not know whether they have received Him or not. So we can appreciate this word of Paul:

> Examine yourselves, whether ye be in the faith; prove your own selves. Know ye not your own selves, how that Jesus Christ is in you, except ye be reprobates? But I trust that ye shall know that we are not reprobates (2 Cor. 13:5-6).

Paul let them know he was not a reprobate — they would know that Christ was in him by the way his talk would reach them.

How do we test ourselves? We should ask, Do I believe in God? Do I believe that He is the Creator of the heavens and the earth, the Keeper of all things on the face of the earth, the Judge of all the earth? Do I believe Christ is the Savior of those who put their trust in Him? This is essential for "without faith it is impossible to please him." Do I believe I am responsible to God, that He can and does control my life, that I have to answer to Him for everything I do? Do I believe in the law of God, that the Ten Commandments show me what God requires of me?

Do I admit that I have sinned, that I have not kept the Ten Commandments?

Do I understand that if I have sinned, I am doomed to die? For Scripture says, "The soul that sinneth it shall die." If I am not doomed to die, then I do not need salvation nor do I need the Lord. Many people would stop right there; but if I feel that because I have done wrong I am not acceptable to God and am doomed to destruction, do I believe the gospel? Do I believe that Jesus Christ died for sinners, that He died for me, and that He bore my sins in His own body? The next thing I should ask myself is: Have I received Jesus Christ as my Savior, and do I believe that the Holy Spirit is in me, teaching and leading me in the way I should go? If I can follow through in these things, I belong among the believers.

Is it clear to me that if I lie, I lie in the presence of Jesus Christ? If I am irritated, do I realize that in my irritation He is standing by me? Do I realize that this presence of the Lord is the source of every joy I will ever have? And I could ask myself one more question: Do I ever have joy? What I am doing here is examining myself. Paul wrote, "Examine yourselves, whether ye be in the faith."

It is not only what I say about these things, nor what I believe to be true about these things, but it is what I *do* about these things. For example, do I look upon God as my Father? When I think of Almighty God, the Creator of the heavens and the earth, do I accept Him and recognize Him as my Father? That would be evidence that the Holy Spirit is in me, because the Holy Spirit moving in me will cry out, "Abba, Father." Can I come to Him, bedraggled and dirty as I am, and expect Him to receive me and to care for me? This would be evidence that the Holy Spirit is working in me.

Do I believe that Jesus Christ is at the throne of God, praying for me? Do I think I can have God with me at all times? Yes, because that is what He promised. How can the Holy God work and live and walk with one who is not holy? It is because Christ Jesus is praying for me.

> Wherefore he is able also to save them to the uttermost that come unto God by him, seeing he ever liveth to make intercession for them (Heb. 7:25).

Do I think He is coming back, and do I think that I am going to meet Him? Do I really believe that when I breathe my last, I will go to meet the Lord?

All of this is a matter of examining myself. Now what would be the one condition that would make me what Paul calls a reprobate or a failure? It is this: if Christ is not in me. I would not have to change myself to be a failure, that is what I am. And if Christ is in me, then He is the One who is strong. If He is not in me, I will just stay like I was, and that is a failure in the sight of God.

These are the thoughts that come to our minds when we try to understand what Paul meant when he asked us to "examine yourselves, whether ye be in the faith." Think on these things and prove yourselves. If you can humbly and sincerely admit that you trust in Him, be thankful because it is a gift from God.